With a ferocious-yet-fragile heroine, resonant themes, and a sweepingly gorgeous backdrop, Amaskan's Blood *delivers food for thought and frank enjoyment."*

MAIA CHANCE, AUTHOR OF THE *FAIRY TALE FATAL SERIES*

[In Class-M Exile] *Oak hurls you thousands of years into the future and hits you at the core of your being. It's a fresh look at science fiction in a charming "hillbilly" fashion... The plot has as much intrigue, suspense and action befitting a much larger work...*

OPEN BOOK SOCIETY

[Dragon Springs & Other Things]...a mesmerizing debut collection...showcasing Oak's versatility and mastery of various genres.

MIDWEST BOOK REVIEW

"Weightless"...explores generosity and community in the wake of disaster...Fans of space opera, fairy tales, and postapocalyptic stories will revel in the reinvention of beloved tropes and the wealth of eye-opening creativity—and disabled readers will be especially moved.

PUBLISHER'S WEEKLY

OTHER TITLES BY RAVEN OAK

The Boahim Trilogy
Amaskan's Blood
Amaskan's War
Amaskan's Honor*

Ear to Ear: A Boahim Collection*

The Xersian Struggle Universe
The Eldest Silence*
Class-M Exile

Stand Alone Works
The Bell Ringer & Other Holiday Tales
Dragon Springs & Other Things
Space Ships & Other Trips
From the Worlds of Raven Oak: A Coloring Book
The Ringers
Ol' St. Nick
Inocen Lost*

* Forthcoming

VOICES CARRY

A STORY OF TEACHING, TRANSITIONS, & TRUTHS

RAVEN OAK

GREY SUN
— PRESS —

BOTHELL, WA

VOICES CARRY

A STORY OF TEACHING, TRANSITIONS, & TRUTHS

Raven Oak

Grey Sun Press
PO Box 1635
Bothell, WA 98041

Cover art by DL Designs

Absolutely no A.I. was used in the creation of these stories or cover art.

ISBN: 978-1-947712-22-5
Library of Congress Control Number: *pending*

For all those who formed the village that raised me, and for my chosen family now. I wouldn't be me without you.

FOREWORD

Voices Carry is a memoir that carved out a place in my mind mid-January of 2024. As an author, I live by a variety of time-lines, but in this case, the muses wouldn't shut up. Perhaps that's for the best considering the contents inside—my thoughts about my life as both a former educator in the southern United States and a disabled queer. While all names, locations, etc. have been changed, these are my experiences as I lived them.

From childhood onward, I've been invisible to many around me. Society excels at pretending certain people don't exist, and why not? It's easier to ignore what makes us feel some sense of guilt about our own lives and choices. As I type this, some states are passing laws making it difficult, and in some cases illegal, for certain members of society to exist. Why should I be surprised to find myself invisible?

I've knitted stories together my entire life, first as a wanna-be child writer and then as a published author, but it wasn't until my forties that I discovered the power in story-telling. Even younger me grasped the power of words as I've always stood out for creating new worlds and characters. But for me to recognize the power in my voice, let alone my lived experiences?

That took time, not to mention several therapists.

From the moment I set foot in the classroom, I swore to be the teacher who fought for my students' rights, even when it risked my job. That's what I thought I was doing, but looking back, I allowed societal pressures to dictate my actions too many times. I allowed society to diminish me. To silence me.

During the moments when I spoke out, people accused me of "airing dirty laundry." People who made waves were problems to be disappeared because no one wanted to hear what people like me had to say.

Worse, I believed them.

Too many snapshots of my past show me silencing myself to please others, but the past few years have changed this for me as I've become a member of the disabled community. I've always been an autistic queer who's watched as society deemed me expendable, but seeing how the world treats its weakest citizens has been eye opening. I'll be damned if I'm going to remain invisible and silent.

So who am I and why should you care about what I need to say?

I'm a former Texas public school teacher turned full-time author and artist living in the Seattle area. Besides being opinionated, I swear. A lot. I've been disabled for longer than I wanted to admit, I'm neurodiverse, and I'm a nonbinary liberal married to a transwoman. For those in the back, that means I believe that equality and equity are *human rights* and that love is love is love. I also suffer from long COVID or post-COVID syndrome in addition to several autoimmune disorders. Oh, I *love* footnotes! You'll see quite a few of them in this book, either as snarky commentary or as sources for anything I say that needs citing[1].

This memoir is full of politics, religion, and all those topics that people say you shouldn't discuss with family at Thanks-

---

1. See? I couldn't resist placing one in the foreword. I mean, who does that? Besides me?

giving dinner, and I'm going to swear a lot while doing it. In fact, I'll probably drop an f-bomb or three. Besides teaching, topics may include prejudice in medicine, science fiction & fantasy fandom, child and adult abuse, eating disorders, and COVID. I will do my best to warn before diving into sensitive topics in order to help readers who may need to skip sections.

If any of this sounds horrifically offensive, perhaps this isn't the book for you.

It's okay. You can go back to re-reading *50 Shades of Whatever* and pretending it's high literature. Seriously—I won't judge[2].

In the past ten years as a full-time author, I've learned there are many of us who feel alone in our struggles: teachers, disabled people, those suffering from long COVID, creators, queer members of society, or something else entirely. Many of us feel invisible. Silenced. Whatever muse beat me over the head with this memoir made one idea very clear: **you're not alone**.

I see you. I *hear* you.

And I hope you hear me too.

---

2. Not much anyway. 😉

CHAPTER
ONE
IT TAKES A VILLAGE

*Let the villages of the future live in our imagination,
so that we might one day come to live in them!"*

MAHATMA GANDHI

I HAVE AN AMAZING MEMORY, or so I've been told
by others who can't remember what they ate for breakfast
yesterday[1]. As I'm now entering my late forties, some of my
earliest memories are fuzzier than they used to be, but I can
still recall the layout of my grandmother's house from when I
was three, right down to the black, upright piano that rested
against the dining room wall.

This was my maternal grandmother, Elle, a woman who
won numerous awards as a public school teacher in California and taught me to read and write when I was a toddler.
There's a bookshelf in my home library with children's books
she bought for me—everything from Dr. Seuss to ancient
books that had been hers when she was a child[2].

---

1. For me, it was a serving of Honey Bunches of Oats cereal and a Dr. Pepper
Zero. How about you?
2. I have a thing for old books. Something about the smell of old paper sparks
memories in me like nothing else.

My memories of Grandma Elle revolve around her love of language and teaching others. As a full-time author, one of my greatest joys comes from educating others on writing fiction. Considering how neither of my parents enjoy reading or writing, this devotion to the written word must have come from her and my earliest years living in her apartment.

Since the age of five, I've had three life goals: to be a writer, a musician, and a teacher like my grandma. Other topics of interest pulled me sideways as I grew up, but those core wants never changed. I managed to be all three, but in doing so, I lost myself as I allowed others to dictate what it meant to be each.

Most people don't remember what their child-self wanted. I'm lucky that I do, thanks to my grandma. She bought me one of those scrapbooks that's supposed to travel with a kid throughout their entire K-12 career so that they can one day look back and see what their childhood education was like. The book was divided into twelve sections, one for each grade level, and there was room for photos as well as notes about teachers, classes, hobbies, grades, friends, and what-ever else one wished to write about. There were even envelopes for holding awards or various items from each school year. At forty-six, I'm still in possession of that book and consider it my first scrapbook. When I skim through it, these goals were the remaining constant in my life, especially after my grandma died.

Many have called me a virtuoso and a child prodigy. Since the age of five, I've been able to play music from memory *(aka by ear[3])*, and I have gifts in both writing and art as well. If I'd been born into money, it's probable you wouldn't be reading

---

3. Most musicians play music by reading sheet music. Some people, like myself, can do more. "Playing by ear" is a phrase that means we can hear a song, sit down, and play it just by having heard it. Sometimes we get it in one go, but sometimes it may take a few listens. I like to think of it like a photo-graphic memory but of sound. I hear something once and I can hear the entire piece in my head—each layer of the instrumentation, the vocals—all of it.

this as I'd likely have been afforded an education at some musical conservatory or art school. I didn't have the chance at music lessons, so everything my child self knew about creativity was self-taught.

My father was a single parent in his early twenties when custody shifted from my Grandma Elle to him. We were poor enough that sometimes he skipped meals so I could eat, which was often bologna and cheesy mac or fast food dollar menu items. Like many men of his time, he was too proud to accept the government assistance he was owed as a military vet and college student, so we lacked food stamps and free health care[4]. Some of the health complications I have today come from that lack of early health and dental care, which is a sticking point for me. My father tried, but his pride certainly made a mess of life. His evangelical beliefs added to this as they taught him to accept help from no one.

Out of everything he did wrong, he tried to do right by my creativity. Rather than ignore my talents, he used credit cards to fill my bedroom with used books, art supplies, and a tiny electronic keyboard[5]. Being sent to my room as punishment was a vacation for me as I don't think he realized what an escape it was to dive into those worlds.

While I tried to teach myself to read music, my ear was more reliable. When I wasn't outside swimming or exploring the native wildlife of North Florida, I was writing songs, spinning tall tales about my epic adventures, and tutoring neighborhood kids, whether they needed it or not. Nothing would stop me from my dreams. I had a promise to keep to Grandma Elle and to myself.

I spent the summer after sixth grade writing an entire 350+ page fantasy novel, which I still have pieces of. It's utter

---

4. Though he had no trouble accepting public education grants to help pay for college. Funny how that pride works.

5. The musical kind, not a QWERTY. I'm a techie, but we didn't have a home computer yet.

drivel, but that summer proved to me I could finish what I started.

By fifteen, I was invited to join a local critique group of professional genre fiction authors, who made money from their craft. While my writing lacked the nuance of an adult, the foundation was solid enough to be the only minor in the group. I found it odd to be a teenager surrounded by people who had lived experiences[6] I'd only read about, but it helped me develop my voice and better understand what writing as a career was all about. I attended my first professional writing conference at sixteen[7]. While attendees were surprised at a teenager taking copious notes and hanging onto every word spoken by editors and published authors, they never questioned my right to be there.

It was during this year that I also learned my first harsh lesson in the writing world. A local author had spotted my online posts about a book idea I had and suggested we "meet up for coffee" to potentially cowrite the novel together. Feeling quite grown up, I was elated by this idea. My father worried—as he should have—and suggested *he* talk to the man first. When the local author realized I was a teen, he wasn't sure about cowriting but after seeing a sample of my work, he agreed to come to a supervised meeting at our apartment to talk further.

We spent an entire Saturday afternoon discussing plot and character arcs. I showed off the character sketches and maps I'd made, and the local author was very excited to work with me. I think we met four or five more times as we worked to flesh out my ideas. Then he ghosted[8] me.

---

6. It also taught me what real adult relationships and families looked like as my views of both were twisted by growing up in a religious, abusive household.

7. Thank you ArmadilloCon's writing track for your support and advice.

8. If you're not up on the lingo, being ghosted is when someone suddenly stops communicating with you without explanation. They just disappear.

Many, many years later, I see he tried to publish[9] "our" work through a vanity press with little success, which doesn't surprise me as the ideas we had weren't novel or unique. Most of what I dreamed up at sixteen was rather juvenile, but I guess he lacked his own ideas and thought this to be the way forward. Thirty years later and he's still trying to find a publishing deal without any luck. Maybe if he wrote his own words, that might change. For all that I was a teenager, I grew up before my years. I wasn't stupid. It was obvious to me what he'd done, and for a good stretch of time, I didn't trust anyone with my creative endeavors.

As a person on the spectrum, I clicked better with adults than with others my age as they were less inclined to dismiss my ideas and thoughts as easily as my father and other kids did. As a pre-teen and later teen living on the bloom of home computing and the Internet, I'm amazed I never fell afoul of online predators[10]. While smart, I was still a vulnerable child who was confused about my own role in the world.

Being neurodiverse means that I don't always see the forest for the trees. While my father did the best he could to provide for me and encourage my talents, juggling college and several jobs meant he wasn't always around, and when he was, exhaustion and irritability fueled his decisions. And of course, religion—evangelical style.

My family follows their own flavor of religion—a mix between Southern Baptist and Pentecostal. They aren't quite Quiverful[11], but they come close in their fervor. While many of my friends are Christian, Jewish, Hindu, Buddhist, Pagan, and so on, I am not. At least, not anymore. I'm a live-and-let-

---

9. Vanity presses are scams. They prey on gullible writers who haven't had success with traditional publishing. They charge thousands of dollars and claim publication, when it's little more than going down to your local photocopier and having them print out your book. These kinds of places still exist, but few use them for obvious reasons. Good rule of thumb: money goes *to* the author, not the other way around.

10. Aside from writing thieves.

11. Though I wonder about one of my aunts…

live person until those ideas and beliefs harm others. Growing up as I did, I do carry some religious baggage as religion was frequently used to silence me and hide the fact that I was being abused. When my father was a young man in his twenties, he exuded a charisma similar to the type used by many a pastor, which challenged any suspicions of abuse.

Being a military brat and a poor one, we moved often before settling in Florida during my elementary school years, followed by Texas for the rest of my K-12 education. When they say it takes a village, they're telling the truth. During elementary school, we lived in student housing[12] for students with families and children, and it was there where I found many parents willing to dote on me in the absence of a mother.

I was expected to wake and dress myself, eat breakfast alone, and walk myself to the bus stop because my father was catching the only sleep he'd get that day. While there were plenty of single parents living in student housing, most of our neighbors were married couples with children. I found myself "adopted" by many mothers who made sure my hair and teeth were brushed. Feeling such love from people who weren't blood relatives gave me my first lessons in chosen family.

In second grade, my teacher worried about how my shoes were too small and my clothing too big,[13] but my mind was curious to a fault. She stressed over my calling her "Mom," especially when I tried to persuade her to marry my father. Meet the Teacher Night was embarrassing for them both as I played match-maker. Grandma Elle had taught me that

---

12. Since the writing of this, I've learned that the university demolished this student housing village in June of 2023, leaving many student families without housing. This makes my heart ache as I have so many memories of my village. You can read more about the closure here: https://www.alligator.org/article/2023/06/trees-over-profit-gau-holds-peaceful-protest-for-graduate-housing
13. The issue with hand-me-downs is that you can't guarantee the clothes fit.

teachers were our heroes, so I was sure this superhero had been tasked to save me from a motherless life.

When she announced she was pregnant, I danced at the idea of a sibling. Looking back, I can't imagine how she handled it with the grace she did. Each day in class was a new adventure and in her room, I was encouraged to express myself and be me. At the end of the year, our district fired her for having a child out of wedlock because that's how we roll in this country. Having spoken to her since, she never returned to teaching. Society missed out on an amazing and kind teacher with the patience of a saint because she had a child.

While teachers like her were chased away from the field with pitchforks, others were branded as model teachers, like Mrs. Blane. She taught one of my AP classes and believed that rote memorization of people and facts was the best way to learn. Having the life I'd had, her class bored the snot out of me. It didn't challenge me and my way of doodling my notes distressed her nearly to the point of apoplexy. It's been thirty years since her class, but I can recall this event clearly. Like a sunburn, my skin crawls at its memory.

Halfway through the second semester, Mrs. Blane sat down with every student individually to encourage them to take the AP exam for her course and gain college credit. Being the 10th grade faculty advisor, she also discussed students' futures and career goals with them. When my turn came, she frowned.

"I see you've already signed up to take the AP Exam," she said, and when I nodded, her frown deepened. "I don't think that's a good idea. I'm not sure you'll pass it as you often struggle to pay attention in my class[14]."

"Your class is the only AP class I have trouble with. If I could just—"

---

14. Like many of my generation, I had undiagnosed ADHD and autism. Between that and boredom, I'm not surprised I "struggled" in her class.

I'd been about to suggest she allow me to take notes *my* way rather than hers, as I'd comprehend the material better that way, but being a stickler for her way or the highway, she didn't allow me to finish my sentence.

"Look, I know you have your heart set on college, but I don't think college is going to work on you. You aren't college material."

Every teacher I've ever had disagreed with her, but for some reason, her words burned me.

"Some students have it—that gift of thought and the drive to accomplish their goals, but not you. I don't see you amounting to much of anything, if I'm honest. Perhaps you should look at a trade school or stick with your grocery store job."

For a mostly A+ student like me, she couldn't have insulted me more if she tried. "But I want to be a teacher—"

She laughed at me. Outright laughed.

"I don't think that's in the cards for you."

That day, when I got home, I swore I would be a teacher. I promised myself and my now deceased Grandma Elle that not only would I be a teacher, I'd never be a teacher like Mrs. Blane. She was *not* part of a tribe that raised me, but in many ways, she became a living example of what not to be.

I met my wife in 10th grade computer class, and yes, we were high school sweethearts. Mrs. Blane told my wife similar things, completely ignoring that she'd just lost her mother to cancer and had reason to suddenly struggle in school. Other high school teachers saw our talents and our struggles and worked to encourage us to be whatever we wished, lessons we took with us out into the world together. Many of these educators suspected the abuse I suffered at home but helped me figure out how to escape it and succeed in spite of it.

Both my wife and I graduated in the top 10% of our class, and I graduated with honors. We remained in the Lone Star

State for both of my college degrees[15] at a school known for its teachers and musicians[16]—University of North Texas, formerly North Texas State Teachers College. What began as a music composition degree, shifted to one in education as I sought to keep my promise. After college, I spent thirteen years as a public school teacher across Texas, which was…an adventure.

Seeing as I'm a disabled, neurodiverse queer, it shouldn't be surprising that I'm very liberal. Teaching in a conservative hellhole while being me was like threading a needle the size of an atom while blindfolded. I survived it by the skin of my teeth, and when I had the opportunity to jump-ship to Washington State, I seized it.

If you know any teachers, you're probably familiar with the idea of "love the students, hate the politics," which is exactly why I'm no longer a K-12 educator. Most of the time, my students were amazing. Even when they had rough home lives and inevitably brought it to school with them, we found ways to understand and learn from each other. What drove me from education was twofold: bully administrators and helicopter parents, both of which I'll be sharing in more detail in the following chapters.

I've spent the past eleven years as a full-time author and artist, which has given me the freedom not only to find myself but to be myself. In Texas, much of my identity was nailed firmly inside the closet, though not by choice and not by me.

When my teaching career began, I wasn't yet fully disabled, though it didn't take long to join that group as teaching is a physically and mentally demanding job. I was born with an undetected birth defect in my spine that causes my nerves to fuse together. It's thought to be related to teth-

---

15. Bachelor of Science in Education with minors in English, Music Composition, and CECS. Master of Science in CECS.

16. Famous alumni include Norah Jones and Don Henley. (Yes, *that* Don Henley.)

ered spinal cord syndrome[17] and spina bifida[18]. With my major nerves fusing, I'm slowly losing my ability to feel in my legs. Throughout my twenties, I suffered increasingly horrific lower back pain that impacted my ability to function and work. After a decade of failed surgical procedures and physical therapy, both of which worsened my symptoms, I discovered a doctor willing to diagnose me correctly.

Our move to Seattle was about me taking a chance to write for a living, but it was also an opportunity to have a profession that wasn't as brutal on my spine. I hadn't realized it yet, but I was well on my way to understanding that I'd never hold a normal 9-5 job again.

One of our first adventures in the Pacific Northwest was to drive up Mt. Tahoma[19] to one of the ski lodge restaurants as well as adventure onto some of the shorter trails. During this trip, I discovered that the lack of sensation in my legs left walking on uneven surfaces challenging. I couldn't tell when I'd stepped on a rock or if my footing was solid. This led me back to physical therapy and another doctor in hopes of finding treatment.

Other symptoms began to occur and soon after, I was also diagnosed with several autoimmune diseases, one of which destroys nerves, meaning there was no reversal or cure for my symptoms. Walking on level carpet led to several falls and broken ankles, followed by doctors labeling me a "trip

---

17. This is a neurological disorder caused by the melding of tissues that can limit the spinal cord's movement. ("Tethered Spinal Cord Syndrome – Causes, Diagnosis and Treatments." www.aans.org, American Association of Neurological Surgeons, www.aans.org/en/Patients/Neurosurgical-Conditions-and-Treatments/Tethered-Spinal-Cord-Syndrome. Accessed 18 Mar. 2024.)

18. Spina bifida occurs during fetal development when the neural tube in the spine doesn't close all the way. This results in damage to the spinal cord and nerves. (*What is Spina Bifida? | CDC*. (2023, October 4). Centers for Disease Control and Prevention. https://www.cdc.gov/ncbddd/spinabifida/facts.html)

19. Tahoma is what this super volcano was named by the Native peoples of Washington. Americans named it Mount Rainier after Rear Admiral Peter Rainier in 1792.

hazard." I was instructed to walk carefully at home, but when out and about, use a wheelchair or scooter to ensure I didn't continue to harm myself. In 2016, I gained the official label of disability, complete with parking placard.

Several bouts of COVID worsened both my autoimmune diseases and my spinal damage, leaving my body irreparably damaged. Even if I wanted to return to teaching, my body wouldn't allow me to do so. Writing tends to be something I do in short bursts broken up by long breaks where I rest and stretch carefully. Through the brain fog, I've fought to return to writing and in doing so, I've found the pieces of my broken self as less jagged than I remember.

Like a kaleidoscope, I've handled each piece and memory with care, but with a critical eye as well. For much too long, I've hidden fragments of myself and with this book and the help of so many villages, I say, no more.

MY CHILDHOOD WAS...DIFFERENT to put it mildly. Besides growing up in a religious, abusive household, my mother hopped in and out of my life—though only when she needed money[20]—leaving me confused about what it meant to be a young woman. All the questions one normally would ask their mother, remained silent on my tongue. Even if I'd had the courage to ask my father, doing so meant potential consequences.

Middle school is a time already fraught with chaos and angst as kids suffer through puberty and bullying. It's challenging enough to face with a normal childhood and two parents, but for me, it was hell. Actually, it was worse than hell. I personally don't believe in Satan, let alone heaven or

---

20. A shitty habit she's passed on to my half-sisters.

hell, but if Satan existed, I think he would have taken one look at my teenage years and noped the fuck right out.

I suspect that's why I chose to teach middle school. Deeply rooted in my being was the need to help students survive what was the second worst time of my life. Trying to convince your single father that puberty is an actual event occurring to you is rough, or at least it was for me. Despite teachers and nurses explaining to him that I needed to wear a bra as my overly large breasts were a distraction for everyone, he couldn't admit that my body was changing, and I was no longer his little girl.

This began well before sixth grade, but when I began my period, he couldn't avoid the topic any longer. It's embarrassing enough for most teens to ask their mothers for period supplies or advice on cramps but asking your avoidance-loving father is an exercise in cruelty and shame. For a time, other friends' mothers would take me bra shopping. I'd change into my bra on the school bus[21], attend school, and then take my bra off again during the bus ride home. On Fridays, my bras went home with a friend where they would be laundered and returned to me come Monday's bus ride.

One day, I forgot to take off my bra.

When I walked into our apartment, I'd expected my father to be attending class. Instead, he sat on our ratty couch, surrounded by textbooks. His gaze shot to my chest.

"What are you wearing?"

He was off the couch in an instant, and he slid aside my t-shirt's collar.

I remained silent. He didn't want an answer. He already knew it was a bra and answering would be seen as 'talking back.' What he wanted was for the moment to be undone.

"Go take it off. Don't let me see you wearing it again."

---

21. I used my shirt to cover myself as I pulled the arms into my sleeves to put on and remove the bra. It was challenging at best and embarrassing at worst. I was the subject of many bullies who wondered why I'd be changing clothes on a school bus surrounded by other kids.

Ladies, gentlemen, and everyone else, I was twelve. I was wearing a C cup by necessity as I had inherited my mother's ample chest. I'd been needing a bra since I was ten, but goodness forbid I be comfortable in my own skin.

That was a sin.

Goodness forbid I not be the butt of yet another joke. It would've been nice to not be grabbed and rubbed by pubescent boys who thought I was the best thing since sugar.

I'm sure that would've been a sin too, but to my father, it was my fault. Somehow, I was "encouraging" it and needed to pray harder.

Needless to say, puberty was a rough ride for me, full of secrets and hiding and wishing with every ounce of my being that I had a mother.

What further complicated these years was the experience of figuring out who I was as a person in terms of attraction, crushes, and gender. My upbringing meant that I never knowingly encountered someone of the LGBTQ+ community until high school. I've learned since that several people I knew then were queer, but back then, no teen was openly out if they could help it—especially not in middle school or in Texas, land of the Deere not Queer. Because of this, I didn't have the terminology to identify as much of anything.

Rather than understanding that I was queer and nonbinary, both of which were normal, I figured myself as weird or odd. Broken.

While my friends were boy crazy and hopped from crush to crush and boyfriend to boyfriend, I didn't. At least not at first. Looking at a magazine photo of a topless teen heartthrob did nothing for me. My friends flushed pink and fanned themselves while I stared at the photos, emotionless. These heartthrobs were strangers to me. Without knowing them or having any connection to them, they could have been completely nude and I'd have only shrugged.

Why didn't I want to kiss these boys like my friends did?

Why didn't I feel anything?

I wasn't a stranger to kissing as I saw my father do it often enough with the coeds he dated. In fact, I had my first kiss at age ten though it meant about as much as tying my shoes. I couldn't figure what all the fuss was about. Most boys weren't 'hot' or 'cute'. They were just boys.

The word for how I feel attraction or the lack-thereof is demisexual, which falls in the asexual or ace umbrella. For me to have a sexual attraction to someone, there has to be a deep connection to them first. I need to know them, to be friends with them, and have a form of emotional intimacy first before feeling anything else. This is a term I didn't discover until my thirties and once I found it, I found that portion of me wasn't broken, just different. Everything about me and who I'd been clicked into place.

"It's a-me[22]!"

For a time, rumors floated around my middle school that I was a 'lesbo' or a 'dyke' because of my lack of kissing partners. On the rare occasion that I found myself a boyfriend, folks called me a prude because the relationship never progressed further than kissing. I mean, I wasn't stupid. Not with my mother being who she was. My father's only advice with boys was "don't," but I'd had sex education in school[23]. Become a teenaged mother like my mom? No way. I'd seen how *that* turned out for her. It helped that none of these boys were anything more than friends, and some, barely that. Certainly not a strong enough connection for me to consider anything more than a kiss.

The pressure to give a boy a hand-job sent a fair number of my friends into places they didn't want to visit. You could tell who gave it up based on the speed with which they cycled through boyfriends. As a former teacher, I taught my

---

22. Inside joke for the video game lovers out there.
23. Useless as 'abstinence only' education is, science classes and medical textbooks teach a lot more than folks think. Lucky me that I loved the library and was well read.

share of pregnant middle schoolers, which makes me both cringe and cry[24].

Because I was seen as uptight and potentially gay, my middle school years included nasty notes, cold shoulders, and a few dead animals stuffed in my locker. Where we lived, even the Catholics pretended to be Protestant because this was the Bible Belt. If you weren't Southern Baptist or Evangelical Christian, you were run out of town. Or at least they'd try. So I kept my head down and muddled through.

But then seventh grade happened and with it, Shelly.

Part savior and part hellion, she changed my life by setting me more firmly on the path to finding myself. When I say this, I'm well aware of how cliche it sounds, but honestly, I might be a different person without having met her.[25]

Shelly was an enigma.

She lived with her single mother who was a die-hard feminist and liberal. In fact, Shelly was probably my first exposure to someone who truly believed in a woman's right to choose, not to mention the idea that the patriarchy needed to die in a fire. Shelly took after her mother and showed up for the first day of school wearing a t-shirt that read, "A woman without a man is like a fish without a bicycle" and khaki cargo pants. Her sandals were something out of Burning Man, which didn't exist yet, and her long, blonde hair sported a single side braid woven with colored thread. She carried her books in a bohemian-style messenger bag instead of the traditional backpack, and the bag was covered in patches with all manner of liberal expressions. Around her neck, she wore a

---

24. Looking back, I think we had it easier than students these days. With easier and broader access to porn, the pressures and expectations these days are intense.

25. If you've ever read my sci-fi novella, *Class-M Exile*, you may recognize some of this story as I turned it upside down and reinvented the ideas behind it for that story.

massive silver pentacle[26], and in her hands was a pack of Robin Wood[27] tarot cards.

The only knowledge I had of tarot cards was from my father and the Bible. They were evil. They were a tool of witches and only evil people used them because no one knew what the future held but God. But Shelly didn't look evil to me, so I was genuinely curious about her. She lacked moles and green skin, so I figured I was safe enough.

When Shelly stepped out of an old, beat-up hatchback, a herd of dogs tried to follow her. The barking gained the student body's attention as we awaited school to open, but her—her appearance and confidence—scared the hell out of everyone. It was almost comical the way people fled towards the school doors, which were still firmly locked.

I kept my distance at first and observed.

Besides sharing my English class, I discovered we also shared band. During the passing period, I found her sitting on the carpeted floor, her tarot cards spread before her as she did a self-reading. People gave her wide birth, though they were brave enough to throw a few nasty words her way. Rather than be like them, I sat down next to her and introduced myself.

She smiled, then gestured to the cards. "Ever played with tarot cards before?"

I shook my head and she grinned as she gave me a quick reading. I was destined to try too hard, but in the end, I'd succeed. Or something like that. I remember being impressed at the time and wondered if it was true.

Over the next few days, I spent more time with Shelly,

---

26. Dating back to the 1500s, pentacles are five pointed stars used as magical talismans in a variety of spiritual and religious practices, including Wicca and forms of Paganism.

27. American artist specializing in game art and fantasy, most known for portraits of characters from Anne McCaffrey's *Dragonriders of Pern* series, the Robin Wood Tarot Deck and the cover art for several of Scott Cunningham's books on neo-Paganism.

who taught me about the huge world of science fiction and fantasy books. While my father enjoyed a good spec-fic[28] flick, he hated reading, whereas I loved it. He'd never told me that some of the movies I'd seen were books. Shelly made me a lengthy list of "must reads" and I devoured every book I could get my hands on. Lucky for me, my father never looked too closely at what I was reading.

From Shelly, I found the worlds of Anne McCaffrey, Raymond Feist, Mercedes Lackey, and many other speculative fiction giants. I ran through the books in our school library in a week as it didn't have much genre fiction, so Shelly's mother took me on a trip to Half-Price Books. This was back when they still had their half-off half sales. I rushed home yammering about it to my tired father, who took me back in order to get me to "shut up about it already."

Because my father wanted to encourage my love of books, he began taking me to their sales semi-regularly. I'd have $10 in spending money and figured out the older the book, the cheaper the price. There were a few exceptions to this but since those special editions were behind locked glass, I never gave them a second glance. Instead of paying $2.99 for a $5.99 paperback, the old copies had a retail price on the cover of $1.99, so half off would be 99 cents! Take into account the half-off half, I could get a book for 49 cents. That meant walking out of Half-Price with twenty new books[29] to read.

I budgeted wisely in those days, and in reading these books, I encountered unique characters—people and alien civilizations full of neurodivergent folks, queer relationships, and societal concepts I'd never encountered before.

My father never made the connection between these books and my sudden interest in liberal ideals, nor did he understand that the *Star Trek* show he watched was incredibly

---

28. Short for speculative fiction, the overarching genre encompassing science fiction, fantasy, and horror
29. Or at least new to me.

liberal for its time. The original series made waves for having a white man kiss a woman of color, not to mention the Next Generation, which hosted universal healthcare, a lack of capitalism, and a desire to represent all people as equal. It was during this exploration of fandom that Shelly and I became best friends, but there was more to it than that.

I loved her.

I held a platonic love for all of my friends, don't get me wrong, but there was something more to my relationship with Shelly. I think that had I been raised in a family supportive of being yourself, even if yourself was queer, I could have had a nice romantic relationship with my friend as I absolutely had a crush on her—probably my first *real* crush. Even though she later came out as gay, she never knew my feelings for her. It wasn't something I could admit to myself at the time, let alone anyone else.

Being demi means that friendships are a must. I could never have a one-night-stand as strangers are empty for me. Because relationships are the most important piece for me, a person's gender has never mattered. Does that make me gay? Yes. Does it make me straight? That too.

Be it a man, woman, nonbinary, or transgender person, it's all about the relationship; the wrapper or physical body around the person doesn't matter much at all. It's easier to tell people I'm bisexual, but the actual term for what I am is pansexual[30].

In many ways, my crush on Shelly set me up for the people I would encounter in high school—an amazing group of geeky, queer folks who broadened my world in so many ways. It was here that I realized that not every household was like mine, and that abuse wasn't limited to the physical.

---

30. Pansexuality is the romantic, emotional, and/or sexual attraction to people regardless of their gender. Like everyone else, pansexual people may be attracted to some people and not others, but the gender of the person does not matter.

Verbal and emotional abuse were real problems, and ones I was intimately familiar with.

I also learned that love is love is love. That queer people are people too and deserving of equality, as are people of color. Rather than remaining rooted in an ideology that wished me to be racist, homophobic, and misogynistic, I grew into a person who saw people for who and what they are and encouraged others to live their lives as their true selves.

Looking at those words now, it feels silly to say that queer people are people too. My brain automatically wants to respond with, "No shit, Sherlock!" but for a stretch of my childhood, I was taught otherwise. Anyone who wasn't white and wasn't Christian was evil and lesser. They weren't people in God's eyes and thus, I should avoid them at all costs.

Imagine growing up in a world that small and bigoted. The fact that I escaped and became the person I am today is nothing short of amazing, and I have to attribute it to people like Shelly. People who led by example and demonstrated real love for others.

My experiences are part of what made me a great teacher, one that students sought out when they needed help, and it's what made me an even better writer.

As I'm typing this, my partner is beginning her transition from male to female, to become who she has always been internally. I have transgender friends whose relationships fell apart when they decided to live their truths. It doesn't always happen that way, but it can. For me, the exterior wrapper changing means nothing as she's still the person I married and the woman I love.

I don't think I would have been ready for a relationship like this without all the people before her. My ability to love and be loved comes from the understanding that everyone is worthy of love and that no one is deserving of hate[31].

---

31. Except Nazis.

CHAPTER
TWO
HOLDING ON FOR LIFE

> *Stay afraid, but do it anyway. What's important is the action. You don't have to wait to be confident. Just do it and eventually the confidence will follow."*
>
> CARRIE FISHER

NO MATTER what anyone might tell you, we all seek the approval of others. Consider it a survival mechanism held over from when we were crawling on all fours from the primordial ooze. Being different, being *other*, can be dangerous. It means you stand out. You're either a threat to others or an abnormality that threatens the species' continuation. Of course, this is all from an anthropological and biological perspective as we humans are no longer mere animals fighting for survival. If anything, we're more like a plague on this planet as we pillage its resources and endanger its other inhabitants. The fact that many people see being different as a danger is, to some degree, understandable.

But after thousands of years, you'd think we'd have evolved beyond this instinct. Most people don't walk down the street, see someone with different colored skin, and flee screaming to the hills. Yet racism and bigotry run rampant as people like me fight for our existence.

Currently in the United States, it's a daily fight for my right to live as myself, and sadly, I'm not alone. These days, being different leads to ostracization and hate crimes. Laws are passed to make your life difficult[1] or impossible. In some countries, my existence would mean death[2].

We've seen this behavior before and while many don't realize it, we're seeing it again. As I write this, there are currently 479 anti-LGBTQ+ bills being tracked by the ACLU —everything from defining gender as binary and denying healthcare to LGBTQ+ people to curriculum censorship and forcing students out of the closet[i].

These laws may not be as extreme as an event like the Holocaust, but ask yourself how did society become a part of that event in the first place? Our ancestors didn't wake up one morning to Hitler in power. Evil takes its time. It plans. It corrupts and manipulates. It waits for people to look the other way.

"I can't watch the news these days. So depressing."
"Not my circus. Not my monkeys.[3]"
"*I've* never seen that happen before. Must be fake news."

We make it easy for hatred to thrive. The idea of "See

---

1. It is currently legal in the state of Florida for CPS to take children from LGBTQ+ parents because being gay is legally seen as supporting pedophilia.

You can read more details about Florida's Don't Say Gay Bill here:

The dangerous consequences of Florida's "Don't Say Gay" bill on LGBTQ+ youth in Florida. (n.d.). Georgetown Journal of Gender and the Law | Georgetown Law. https://www.law.georgetown.edu/gender-journal/online/volume-xxiii-online/the-dangerous-consequences-of-floridas-dont-say-gay-bill-on-lgbtq-youth-in-florida/

2. There are countries where it is illegal to be LGBTQ+ and the punishment is death.

3. I hate this phrase. It's one of the most dismissive, selfish phrases I've ever heard as we're all in this together. Genocide is everyone's concern.

something, say something" is nice but following through on it takes guts. It places us at risk.

"What if the hateful person comes after me? What if they're armed?"

This isn't a question for teachers alone. While school shootings are a real threat in the classroom, mass shootings have occurred in places of worship, movie theaters, parades, music venues, clubs, court houses, government buildings, and restaurants.

While the bravery needed to fight hatred could fill the sun, advocating for others is how we remain human. We've seen it throughout history—Rosa Parks, Martin Luther King, Jr., the Stonewall Riots, those who sheltered Jews during World War II—all folks who understood the risks to themselves and their families, yet they stood up for what was right.

Members of marginalized communities such as BIPOC[4], queer, deaf, blind, neurodivergent, or disabled, could fill your mind with story after story, each one an example of when hate ruled and the response was silence. No one stepped forward to stop it from happening, no one uttered a word of protest, and no one called for help.

It's one of the reasons why when you're attacked, self-defense classes teach you to shout, "Fire!" People will respond to *that* threat, whereas shouting for help tends to make people close their curtains, eyes, and ears. People don't want to know what's happening because they're afraid. They don't want to assume the risk that comes with *knowing*.

But change only comes when we're aware.

Woke is a term that's tossed around these days as a pejorative by folks who will never understand what it's like to live in a state of constant fight or flight. It's exhausting.

The term "woke" isn't a modern word. It dates back to the 1930's.[ii] In those days, the term referred to being aware of

---

4. Pronounced "bye-pock," this term stands for Black, Indigenous, and People of Color.

social and political issues affecting people of color. A paramilitary youth organization called the "Wide Awakes" was formed in Connecticut back in 1860 to support Abraham Lincoln in his run for presidency, meaning the term has roots older than the 1900s. Each time, the word was used as a metaphor for activism, much like it is now.[iii]

It's been used by musicians throughout the 20th century, by protestors and activists, and by people of marginalized communities who understand that being awake or *aware* of hatred around you is not a terrible thing.

Knowledge is power.[5]

Knowing about hate and how it operates is how we stay safe. It's how we stand up against it.

Educating others is how we instigate change.

It's why I became a teacher. It's why I write.

Being othered is painful and scarring. No one chooses to be othered. No one comes out as gay or trans because they want to be harassed. These brave people choose to live life as their authentic selves in spite of the hate they face.

COMING FROM AN ABUSIVE CHILDHOOD, I ran away from home with every intention of hiding from my father. High school was more challenging for me than middle school as my father suffered a major medical scare that convinced him he was going to die and soon[6].

Spring break of my sophomore year had begun. I stepped inside our apartment to find my father home rather than at work. There was no greeting or excitement about a week off

---

5. Most often attributed to English philosopher Francis Bacon, the phrase was also used by Thomas Jefferson and spread by many teachers throughout the world. It's up there with "Shoot for the moon because even if you miss, you'll land among the stars," which is to say engraved in most US classrooms.
6. Spoilers: He didn't.

of school, just three words that ripped through any plans I might have had.

"I have cancer."

His doctor said he *might* have it, but with my father's severe thanatophobia[7], he heard that it was the big C and death was imminent. Before I could process this information, we were in the car, along with a fat stack of credit cards.

I've stated before how poor we were, but to put things in perspective, my father sucked at budgeting. He'd refuse government assistance but take out dozens of credit cards to pay for "extras" like medical bills, car repairs, and clothing.

Meant to store business cards, his dual-sided holder had nearly split its seams after holding fifteen credit cards and a few more for department stores back when those still existed. This wasn't my father's daily wallet, but the fat-pack he pulled out when shit got real.

"I need to hit a few ATMs, but I need you to keep watch," he whispered as he placed the extra wallet in my lap. "While I'm maxing out the card, you shout if you see anyone nearby."

He was concerned about being robbed, a valid concern in our neighborhood, but at fifteen, something about his word choice scared me. Maxing out a credit card was a bad idea according to my economics teacher. I worried we were doing something illegal. His erratic mannerisms frightened me.

I'd seen my father angry, but I'd never seen him scared.

With ATM withdrawals being limited, we hopped from ATM to ATM for the next hour. All over town and then the next town over. By the time we arrived home, I held over $100,000 cash in my lap.

He tucked the money into a massive envelope. "I have surgery in two days. If something happens to me, if it's cancer, you're to call Grandma Ruth. She'll buy a plane ticket for you. Take a cab to the airport and take this money with

---

7. The fear of death or dying.

you. Don't tell anyone you have it except Grandma. She'll use it to take care of you. Now I need a nap."

And with that, he stretched out across his beat-up recliner and fell asleep.

I was fifteen years old, and in the space of two hours, my life had gone from spring break to my father's dying, here's a stack of money we're hiding, and maybe go live with Grandma Ruth.

Upstairs in my room, I tried calling various friends but no one answered. They were off to destinations unknown and adventures that didn't involve frightening runs for cash. I spent the next two days alone with my fears as I waited for the bomb to go off.

My father survived the biopsy, but that spring break changed my life.

It wasn't cancer but likely an autoimmune disease that could be deadly, though not as quickly. Despite the news, my father's mood flit between terror and exhaustion. One day post-op, he drove us to the store. We needed groceries and the plan was I'd shop while he remained in the car. One mile from the store, our beat-up car died.

"Just steer the car into that parking lot while I push."

I shouldn't have glanced in the rearview but I did. His skin was gray and slick with sweat. He had no business pushing a car in his condition, so I panicked.

Rather than steer the car properly, I lost control and we hit the curb. It didn't help that I didn't know how to drive yet, but none of that mattered when he swore.

According to him, I did everything wrong as he continued to swear. Between the stress, pain, and anger, my father raised his fist with every intention of punching me in the face.

While I had been abused growing up, most of the physical abuse had been subtle: squeezing my fingers too tight until stress fractures occurred or slapping me across the face, but never a fist.

"I'm gonna kill y—" My father never finished the sentence.

A stranger saw what was happening and intervened. "Hey, man, no need for that," he said as he pulled my father's arm away from me. "What's going on and how can I help?"

"Our car died. My dad just got out of the hospital..."

My father gave a brief shake of his head, and I stopped talking.

"Let me give you both a ride home, okay?" said the stranger.

My father had hitchhiked a few times when I wasn't around as we'd never had reliable transportation, but we'd never accepted a ride from a stranger together. He saw it as too dangerous, so when he accepted the offer, my stomach dropped out of me.

Either he was really sick or he was really angry. I wasn't sure which frightened me more.

Our entire drive home, the stranger glanced at me in the rearview. Whatever he saw, it wasn't a man post-op running ragged. His eyes met mine too many times and he opened his mouth to speak, then closed it as he thought better of it.

My father was weak, but a fire burned in him.

I hopped out of the car first and ran to unlock the front door.

The stranger tapped me on the shoulder. "You don't look okay. Do you need help?"

In all my years of abuse, this was the first time someone had ever asked me this question. My tongue hovered on the word yes, but as I watched my father struggling out of the car, I couldn't tell the truth.

"I'm fine. Thanks."

The stranger hesitated, but when my father reached us, he gave a half-smile to me and left us to our business. When I closed the front door, my father grabbed my arm.

"I wanted to kill you," he said, and then he released me to collapse in his recliner.

27

I'm not sure how long I stood at the front door. Everything in me demanded I flee. Just open the door and run.

But where would I go? He was sick. How would he function without me to take care of him[8]?

I stumbled up the stairs as my father snored, and inside my room, my memories raced as I dug through a box of old diaries. As I flipped through the pages, the pieces fell together.

My father was abusive, and today wasn't the first time.

I knew the Bible said we were to obey our parents and that they could punish their children with the rod so to speak, but this felt different. Off. What sort of God would bless a man for punching his child to death?

I couldn't think of one. More pages and more memories, each evidence that this wasn't normal. I needed to escape.

Whatever I planned, it wouldn't be sudden. Not if I wanted to succeed. When I returned to school, I sought out the school counselor. I dropped my art class the next semester and signed up for driver's ed. On my walk home from school that day, I stopped into the nearby grocery store and applied for my first job. The pay didn't matter as long as it was money[9]. Every dollar I earned I'd use to leave.

I thought I'd learned to be sneaky. Despite hiding my tracks, my father's suspicious nature meant he'd been reading my diaries and emails for years. It wasn't long before he discovered my plans.

He pinned my arm to my bed as he spoke in a firm, level voice. "You will go to college wherever I'm teaching as it will save you money. You'll live with me until you get married to a nice Christian boy. There's no need to worry about bad roommates and rent. You'll stay with me and it'll be great."

---

8. Emotional abuse is manipulative, and it teaches the abused not only to rely on their abuser but to make excuses for their behavior. While I know he was struggling, adult me looks back on this and shudders.

9. Once it was clear my father wasn't dying, he paid off all his credit cards with the cash he'd removed.

My father wasn't in his right mind.

I'm not a psychiatrist, so I can't say for certain, but it felt like a psychotic break. Things he would never have done or said, were done and said that day, all of it with an eerie calm. He thought he was doing me a favor. He thought this was what fathers did.

Instead of trusting him, I agreed to stay while I continued my plans to escape. He taught me to hide and lie with ease.

I suspect that's why I hid who I am for so long. Once you go into hiding, you tend to stay there. It's easier. It's safer.

At seventeen, I left home to live on my own. I changed my name to help me hide but also because the prior name was never me. All it held was pain and hatred. No, I'm not going to dead name[10] myself and yes, I consider it a dead name[11]. The courts granted my name change to keep me protected as name changes are common with abuse victims. I've been Raven Oak since 1996—a long time.

While my father and I did end up repairing our relationship to some degree, it was many years before I felt comfortable occupying the same space as him. Even now, I tend to avoid certain topics of conversation, because I know where it will lead and what arguments will result. Despite being back in my life for almost thirty years, my father is the one person who continues to dead name me.

He refuses to call me by my name.

His attachment to my dead name makes little sense to me as he didn't name me. My mother did—after a friend of hers. I can't help but wonder if his refusal is a way for him to feel he has control over me. Almost a form of ownership.

I am the black sheep who ran away from home, changed

10. A dead name is the birth name of a transgender and/or nonbinary person who has changed their name as part of their gender transition.

11. I hadn't realized I was nonbinary at the time, but as I am and nonbinary people fall under the transgender umbrella, the term fits.

my full name[12], and became a liberal and an atheist. In his mind, I left and became everything he'd warned me against.

In refusing to properly name me, he doesn't see or know the *real* me.

He doesn't see the person fighting for equality for everyone, the person who supports everyone in being themselves. He doesn't see the queer, nonbinary person who loves and supports her wife through her transitioning. He doesn't see the writer and artist who is changing the world, one fight at a time.

He doesn't get to experience who I truly am at all.

While it's his loss, it remains a chasm between us. Our relationship can never heal as long as it remains.

He'll never understand why I fight, but I don't need him to. I have a right to be me—the *real* me—no matter what he may think.

Part of finding your voice and identity is the realization that you don't need anyone's approval and never did.

WHILE GRANDMA ELLE LIVED, she did everything in her power to make me the complete opposite of my mother— intelligent, curious, and kind. Before you knock me for insulting my mother, please note that she spent the majority of my life addicted to hard-core drugs and sleeping with whatever men would get her high. Nothing against people empowered by choosing sex work as their occupation—after all, it's one of the oldest professions out there—but that's not what my mother chose. She picked drugs over me, more times than I can count. When I say that she's a narcissist,

---

12. But I didn't follow the Bible and change my last name when I married my wife, which automatically was seen as an embarrassment to the rest of my family.

believe me. No one wanted me to end up like her, least of all me.

While I am happy to be an author, the portion of me that wanted to be a teacher grew out of the change my grandmother instilled in so many. Sure, I can change the world through the written word, but teachers change the world too. They shape and mold young minds and help people find themselves. At least some of them do.

I taught for a total of thirteen years because I wanted to be the change I wanted to see in the world, to reshape our world into a better place, and help young adults understand that we are *all* worthy of love. That equality is proof of that love. In thirteen years, I'm not sure I made a chip in the chaos that is growing up in America, especially in the south.

The experiences in these pages are common. Too many teachers burn out too fast while being underpaid and unappreciated[13]. When my wife and I settled in Seattle, WA, a place many consider a liberal paradise, I discovered that most people are unaware of what occurs in the typical classroom. I would tell stories about teaching in Texas, and people uttered the wildest statements.

"Things like that just don't happen up here!"
"Where was your union[14]?"
"There's no way that happened. Really?"
"How did you survive?"

That last question is a doozy. I survived because that's

---

13. If someone tells me one more time that at least teachers have paid summers off, I might blow a gasket. Contrary to popular belief, teachers are only paid for nine months of work. The paycheck is split across 12 months, making it seem like we're paid for 12 months. Also, many states require teachers to use their summer for professional development hours like continuing education classes at a university. Most of the time, I had 3-4 weeks of true vacation time which I needed to gain back my sanity.
14. Nonexistent since you can't have a teaching union in Texas. Instead, there are teaching organizations with exactly ZERO bargaining power.

what I've always done, though I earned dozens of gray hairs by the time I was twenty-eight. Job stress shaved years off of my life. At the time, I wondered if I were alone in my experiences, but if you ever hop into teaching groups on social media, you'll see that what happened to me is fairly normal.

The education system in this country is absolutely broken.

Sadly, I've heard stories online that make my experiences look easy. There are some amazing superheroes out there in the classroom and not just teachers. These villages are held together by the thinnest of threads and that was before the pandemic.

My commutes to and from work were an hour long each way, and I used the time to call my paternal grandmother, Grandma Ruth. We'd talk about my day and every day, she thanked God that I was still alive, that no one had shot up my classroom. She prayed that I would reach the kids and while I'm not religious, I appreciated the thought.

With all the obstacles teachers face, why stay? Why'd I wait thirteen years before leaving?

It's the answer all of us give: the kids.

Poverty causes more than hungry stomachs. It causes stress, heart break, and grief too. Students come to school lacking so much, and for thirteen years, I was able to help combat that. In microscopic ways, I was able to change the world.

Despite administrators and politicians.

Despite rotten and absent parents.

Despite society's obsession with tests.

For thirteen years, I kept my promise.

Teaching didn't end with me educating my students. Many times, they taught me as I grew up through my twenties. The classroom environment helped me discover who I was and what type of adult I wanted to be.

Every time we encounter someone different from ourselves, we gain an opportunity to learn and grow as people. For this reason, diversity is not only important to our well-being but to our very lives. People don't enter teaching because of the hours or the pay. They do it because without them, society would crumble to dust.

While I taught my share of challenging students, my kids were amazing people who were in the middle of figuring out who they were as citizens of this world. Yes, I taught them English and various computer classes, but inside the classroom, I was also a model of what a good person looks like. For some of them, I was a teacher and a mother figure. For others, I was often an ear to chat to when no one else was there.

For many, I was but one member of their village.

CHAPTER
THREE
DREAMS

> *Hold fast to dreams, for if dreams die, life is a broken-winged bird that cannot fly."*

LANGSTON HUGHES

WHENEVER I'M the most stressed, my dreams and nightmares involve teaching, I suspect because those years involved high levels of stress for me. Sometimes, those dreams feature the classroom from hell where the students won't listen to me or they hate me. Other times they attack me or bully me into leaving the classroom. Most often, the dreams are all about the administration.

If you've never taught, a school's administrators can make or break a school. Without proper support, teachers can't teach and students can't learn. The very pieces that divide society become microcosms in the classroom, especially once administrators and parents are involved.

In college, we're taught that parental involvement is wanted, and for the most part, that's true. Nothing's worse than a student with parents that don't give two shits about them. You can call about their grades, their behavior, anything at all, and if you're lucky, they answer sober[1]. If not, it's statements like, "From 7 to 4, they're your problem" and "I'm busy. Go away."

It may be odd, but I find both of those better than helicopter parents who've decided that their children are God's gift to everyone, their children are perfect angels at all times, and it's a parent's responsibility to dictate everything about your classroom, including for other people's children. Those parents and administration's reactions to them are the ones who dominate my dreams.

I'd love to believe that teachers make it a ways into their careers before experiencing an event like this, but the fact that this happened during my first year of service means it can happen to anyone at any time. My first teaching job was at East Valley Middle School in Texas where I taught seventh grade English and reading classes. Some class periods served your average kiddos while others focused on students with above-average intelligence. These were labeled as Pre-AP and functioned as preparatory for high school AP classes.

It was in one of those Pre-AP English classes that I had the stereotypical thirteen-year-old boy: a bright adolescent but not as bright as his parents believed him to be, incredibly chatty at all times, and for this particular student, a compulsive liar. For the purpose of this tale, we'll call him *Josh*, and I'll apologize in advance to any of the Joshes out there for borrowing your name.

No matter what I tried to redirect his extra energy and chatter, nothing worked. He talked through me and over me every chance he got. When I called Josh on it, he lied.

It wasn't him. It was someone else talking.

It wasn't his fault. He needed to borrow a marker in the middle of a lesson.

I was hearing things. Must be my ears.

To be honest, he was a constant pain in my ass.

---

1. If they answer at all.

36

Three detentions and two phone calls later, his behavior hadn't changed one bit. At this point, I met with his other teachers. Surprise, surprise—his poor choices occurred in every class with every teacher.

Two days later, I caught him talking during an exam. He claimed he was asking for a pencil—never mind that there were free ones in a container at the front of the room—and five minutes later, he was talking again.

I asked him why he was cheating.

His face flushed beet red as he tried not to cry. "I wasn't! Honest."

"Then why were you talking...again? You already have a pencil."

"I needed an eraser."

I pointed at his pencil. "It's right there."

Unable to come up with an answer, he handed me his test. Josh had answered none of the questions correctly. Most of the answers were sarcastic commentary on my teaching style.

This time, I wrote an office referral. This meant another call home, both from me and the principal.

I will admit that my first year of teaching, I had the best principal ever. This was the one rare time I had administration who supported me and genuinely cared about kids. Despite this, what happened next has stayed with me decades later.

The morning after the previously mentioned referral, I sat in my classroom prepping for the day as my first period was my conference period. My principal knocked on my open door, and I waved her inside as I smiled in greeting.

Dr. Web didn't make it down to my end of the building very often. She was retiring at year's end and her body didn't move like it used to, but in that moment, she reminded me of a crocheting grandma who'd stab someone with a needle if they even said boo to her grand-babies.

Something was very wrong and as I stood, she motioned for me to return to my chair.

"You're going to want to be seated for this," she said as she dragged a chair towards my desk.

Being told to sit by your boss is never a good sign. My first thought was that I was being fired, but for that, she would've made me visit her office and not the other way around. Then I wondered if I was being sued for some unknown reason. The actual reason was nothing I would have ever considered in a million years.

"You remember the referral on Josh that you wrote yesterday?"

I nodded. Constant disruption in class, failure to pay attention, talking back, lack of respect, and refusal to serve detention[2].

"I'm going to tell you something that happened this morning, and I want you to know that I have your back. When we're done talking, go to the gym or go home and beat up a punching bag because you're going to want to. I've already hired a sub. It won't come out of your PTO."

My stomach tried to battle its way out through my intestines. What the hell had happened?

Dr. Web had eyes the color of flint and when they focused on you, you knew shit was about to hit the fan, but this time, they melted as she studied me.

"Josh's parents were in my office at the opening of school this morning because they wanted me to fire you on the basis that you are a 'Satan worshipper.'"

I opened my mouth, but she held up a hand to stop me.

"It gets worse. Apparently, they found out that you're a musician. I guess they found your website?"

Mentally, I raced through the entirety of my music site. I had programmed and designed it myself so I could crawl through every inch of it. There was nothing offensive on there, let alone anything screaming Satanic. We were well out of the 80's and the Satanic-panic that drove parents to idiotic

---

2. I can still picture that referral perfectly to this day.

decisions, so what in the world had these parents thought they'd found?

"They told me that you wrote piano music, correct?"

I nodded.

"They stated that your music was 'in a minor key' and thus, proof that you were in league with the devil. Apparently, when Josh got home yesterday and his parents confronted him about his behavior, he told quite a tale about you. He said that you wear black clothing to class every day, and that as you teach, you constantly try to convince and… brainwash was the term…the kids into worshiping Satan with you."

At this point, I couldn't help it. I burst out laughing. "Black is slimming. I do wear colors but most plus-size women I know wear some black. As to writing music in a minor key… have they ever listened to any classical composers?"

She gave a forced chuckle. "Josh claimed that last week, you brought one of your cats into the classroom and killed it in front of them. That you sacrificed it to Satan."

The laughter died on my tongue.

See, I love animals. While my autism is not profound, it is present enough that I feel events as if they are my weight to carry. Reading about children in a war zone can lay me flat. I cry at any sappy commercial you play. Even the idea of one of my cats dying, let alone me killing it…

Bile rose in my throat, and I grabbed my trash can.

Once my dry heaves stopped, Dr. Web continued. "Obviously, this is complete and utter bullshit, which is what I told them. Even if you were a Satanist, that's a protected religion under the First Amendment, but I know you've never done any of those things. When I told them that it was likely Josh was lying and I wouldn't be firing one of my best teachers, they left my office in a huff. And Raven, I truly thought that was the end of it."

"You mean there's more?"

She nodded. "Apparently, Josh's father is church buddies with Dr. Dence, our district's superintendent. Both parents went straight to his office with the same accusations. Now it wasn't just you, Raven. Josh was written up by another teacher yesterday, one who's been in the district for 25 years. He told his parents she was senile and talked to the 'cockroaches in the ceiling lights' during class. That she asked their opinions on how to give grades and referrals. Sadly, these parents believed these lies as well."

Dr. Web reached out and patted my hand. "Remember, I have your back, okay? This will be all right."

Her need to remind me of this, terrified me.

"Dr. Dence believed them, Raven. He went to your website and when he saw you in a photoshoot wearing what I would assume are raven wings, he claimed they were demon wings. He believes you are a Satanist and a true danger to students. He immediately called and ordered me to fire you. For the children[3]."

Never had more ironic words been spoken by a shriveled up man-child who was gullible enough to believe oblivious parents. I honestly wish I were making this up because it would be easier than living with these memories and the knowledge that in Texas, where it's not legal for teachers to organize[4], he could do it. It's a right-to-work state where teacher contracts have morals clauses[5] written into them. While they don't actively say you must attend church, reading between the lines made it very clear that this was the Bible Belt.

If you fucked around, you found out.

"Now, I have no intention of firing you. In fact, I called Dr. Dence an idiot. I told him that if he actually believed any of

---

3. Anyone using this phrase isn't doing anything *for the children*.
4. Meaning we have no teacher unions
5. They are vague and basically state that as a teacher, you can be fired for any reason seen as "immoral." Who gets to decide what's moral and what isn't? The top dogs, who are almost always white Christian men.

this, I had some ocean front property in Colorado to sell him and then I hung up," she said.

"But he's your boss!"

Dr. Web nodded. "I'm going to tell you something that's not public knowledge yet, but I plan to retire at the end of this year. My husband is Dr. Dence's right-hand-man and when I called my husband, he already knew as he'd been at the meeting where they discussed your future in the district. He said he couldn't keep a straight face and had to excuse himself to go have a laugh in the hallway. The thing is, this is the hill I will die on. They can't do much to me at this point and I'll be damned if I'm going to let them ruin a promising career over such nonsense, so don't you worry. You're not going anywhere.

"Since I knew this would upset you, I've got a sub here. Go somewhere and let all this out. When you come back tomorrow, we'll figure out a plan. I can't tell you whether or not to obtain legal representation, but you might want to consider that."

At first, I'd been afraid of losing my job or worse—but as I sat there, I realized that I held the upper-hand. Dr. Dence may have ordered me fired but if he followed through, I'd be walking away with a lot of money when I finished my lawsuit. Bible Belt or not, I knew my rights.

I shook my head. "Dr. Web, while I appreciate the sub, I don't think I need it. If Dr. Dence wants a fight, bring it. I'm no Satanist and even if I was, as you said, that's a protected class. The worst he can do is strip me of my teacher's license, but the worst *I* can do is drain this district of millions and millions of dollars. I'd be sitting on an island, sipping fruity drinks and making art. I love teaching, but I'll be damned if I'm going down without a fight."

A huge grin brightened her face. "Good girl," was all she said before she left my classroom.

The first thing I did was call my wife who was as pissed off as me. She wanted to find these parents and beat them with the belt they clung to, and if I'm honest, so did I. Instead, I smiled as students streamed into my classroom, completely unaware of the chaos in my world.

Seventh graders are more aware than most people think. In my thirteen years teaching middle school students, there was rarely a time they didn't pick up on something bothering me. Being autistic, I realize that I tend to wear my emotions on my face, but I know how to mask being normal when I need to.[6]

My first class was unusually well-behaved and upon leaving, one of my usually rambunctious students gave me an unsolicited hug and hoped "everything was okay."

Oof.

Josh's class was split across lunch. If you know anything about teaching, you know these split classes always end up having the worst behavior. Something about coming back from lunch to the same classroom and picking up where you left off is beyond teenagers, especially 7th graders.

As expected, when he walked towards my class, he had a chip on his shoulder a mile high. I truly believe he thought I'd be gone because when he saw me in the doorway, he froze. The smirk fell off his face and he stood in the middle of the hallway like a kid who's been told "No" for the first time.

One of his friends bumped his shoulder, then gave him a brief shove in my direction. "You're blocking traffic, man! Move."

Josh stumbled into my room and took his seat in unusual silence.

I had to bite my tongue as I really wanted to ask if he was surprised to see me. My day went from furious to slightly less furious with a touch of *schadenfreude*[7]. For that entire class

---

6. If you're not familiar with masking in autism, look it up. Most of us do it because society tells us we have to get along to go along, but it's a form of silencing people different from ourselves. It's not something we should be encouraging.

7. German word meaning to derive pleasure from someone else's misfortune.

period, he remained silent. A miracle if I've ever seen one. *Subdued* would be the word for it.

Two days later, I was called into a meeting between Dr. Web and Josh's parents. While I believed I legally had power, this was Texas. The district could find other ways to destroy my career. Being a first year teacher, they could non-renew my contract claiming budget cuts. The phrase *last in, first out* is muttered constantly in schools across the country. They could keep me as a teacher, but assign me to the worst performing school with the toughest, most challenging and violent students or assign me to teach classes no one wanted. They could have me teaching one class and spending the rest of my day babysitting students in the I.S.S. Room (*in-school suspension*). Or they could just fire me altogether and not give a reason at all.

Welcome to at-will employment.

Despite all my bravado, I'd packed an extra pair of clothes that morning.

Dr. Web winked at me before she introduced me to two adults already seated. Neither parent accepted my offered hand. I'd intentionally worn a bright blue dress with green and teal teardrops on it, and as I said, I spied the mother studying the pattern.

"It's paisley," I said and waited for her to fire off something about it being *foreign*[8].

Instead, she flinched at my words as if I'd struck her. This woman was terrified of me.

Something of note—I'm 5'2" on a good day, and I'm fat. While all of my family is tall, I inherited my great-grandmother's short and wide genes. Someone being afraid of me is like being afraid of a kitten, though on second thought, kittens have razor sharp claws…

Dr. Web summarized the events prior to our meeting and

---

8. The paisley design or pattern is based on a teardrop shape of Persian origin called the boteh or buta.

asked me to follow up with Josh's behavior in class. I brought up dates and specific behaviors, which I'd noted in my lesson plan book, and nowhere in these notes was any sort of sacrifice or hailing of Satan. I didn't say that, but I surely wanted to. My principal then asked what Josh's parents wanted to see as a result of the meeting.

The first words out of Josh's father's mouth was a tirade about me being a Satanist and wanting me fired. Dr. Web held up her hand and tutted the way teachers often do to silence a young child. "Mrs. Oak's employment isn't up for debate. She's done nothing wrong here, while your son has. He's been a constant disruption in all of his classes, so unless you'd like to fire all seven of his teachers, that's not a reasonable solution. What can we do to help Josh better succeed?"

Way. To. Principal!

I mean, wow! Every time Josh's father opened his mouth to discuss my alleged sins, she refocused the meeting on Josh. It was a serious lesson in how to deal with helicopter parents, though it was sad to have to learn it so early in my career.

By hour's end, we still lacked a plan on how to help Josh succeed. Dr. Web dismissed me to go teach my next class, and as I left, Josh's father was already ranting and railing against me, Dr. Web, and the district.

For two weeks, radio silence.

Josh stayed relatively well behaved, though he wouldn't meet my gaze or talk to me unless he absolutely had no choice. In fact, when he needed help, he'd ask every single classmate before coming to me, and when he sat beside me for help, he sputtered and winced like my words were verbally whipping him.

Discipline through fear was something I knew too well. I didn't want it for him or for any of my students, so one day, I called Josh up at the end of class. "You and I both know I'm not evil incarnate. I'm not a Satanist, and I've never sacrificed anything in my life. The first day of class, I told you all that I've been a vegetarian since I was a teen. You got in trouble,

44

and your way of getting out of it was to make up lies about me, right?"

He stared at me but said nothing.

"Look, you're stuck in my class. I'm the only Pre-AP English teacher for the entire 7th grade so unless you're wanting to mess up your high school plans, you're stuck with me. I appreciate that you're behaving now, but you have to stop acting like I'm going to flay you alive. If you need help with something or have questions, ask them. I'm not going to bite."

He remained silent but gave the briefest nod of his head before the bell rang and he fled my classroom.

It was a week after this that I had my first opportunity to meet my superintendent. Because Dr. Web was retiring at the end of the school year, the district had decided to throw her a retirement party. Dr. Web warned me in advance that Dr. Dence would be there. "You can skip it. No reason for you to be there."

"I'm not missing your retirement party. Also, there's no way he's chasing me from my own school."

"Good girl," she said in a short email response.

When I arrived in our school's library for the party, he stood near the door amongst a group of 6th grade teachers. I didn't know them very well, being new to the school and district, but I enjoy meeting other teachers. I'm an extro-verted-introvert meaning that when I'm with others who I see as like-minded people, I'm in my element and love talking. Sometimes nonstop.

Dr. Dence was almost as short as me and carried himself delicately, which surprised me. I'd pictured someone who held himself like a leader, someone tall and maybe imposing, especially for a man threatening my job. He was soft-spoken but his warm laugh held more force than necessary.

He spotted me when I was a few steps away. His eyes widened as he stiffened. Whatever he'd been saying, he stopped and excused himself before striding away from the group and me. After that, he spent the majority of the party either fleeing me or staring at me.

When I mentioned this to Dr. Web, she gave a hearty laugh before leading me towards the corner where he talked with Dr. Web's husband. For all that Dr. Dence could run from me, he couldn't run from the guest of honor.

"Dr. Dence, I'd like to introduce you to one of my best teachers here, Mrs. Raven Oak."

I held out my hand and honestly thought he'd die before he shook it. When he did, he touched me as little as possible. If there'd been a decontamination room in that library, he'd have run straight to it. Instead, he said, "Um, well..." and stood there in silence.

"It's nice to meet you, Dr. Dence, but I do have a meeting I need to get to. One with my attorney."

Did I really have a meeting with my attorney? Of course not, but watching that little man squirm was worth the white lie.

Despite Josh and his parents, I made it through my first year teaching. No matter what his parents said to Dr. Dence, no more effort was made to fire me that year. I held the power, and he knew it.

Throughout my career in his district, we ran into each other a few more times. Each time, he fled like his tail was on fire. Perhaps seeing me was a special kind of hell for him.

The kind where liars and judgmental folks go.

FOUR YEARS AFTER JOSH, his brother ended up enrolled in my class, which terrified me. It shouldn't have, but I worried I'd be dancing in front of a noose again and this time, Dr. Web wasn't there to save me as by then, she'd retired.

My new principal, Dr. Ridgeway, was not a good man. He

was the kind of administrator who played whatever game was necessary to further his own career, no matter who he stepped on to get there. There would be no support found with this man. If he thought it would gain favor with Dr. Dence, he'd have me locked out of my classroom in seconds.

Would the parents lie in an attempt to have me fired? Would brother John show up the first day or class or would this be a nonstarter before the school year began?

The first week of school was met with crickets from both parents and admin, though John entered my classroom with hesitancy and fear. Two days in, he found himself enjoying my class and relaxed into a goofy, easy-going student who tried hard to impress me with his knowledge of facts. By this point, I was teaching one class of Pre-AP English for gifted and talented students. In order to join my class, they were required to be tested and labeled as G/T by the district[9].

The fact that John was nothing like his brother helped me unwind, at least until September's Meet the Teacher night. When I had taught Josh, his parents didn't attend, but after the chaos of being labeled as evil, would they now show up for John?

This particular school ran their Meet the Teacher night as a typical school day. Parents were given their children's schedules, and then they moved classroom to classroom on a bell schedule. Teachers had ten minutes to present themselves, their classrooms, and their subject to parents crammed into student desks. When the bell rang, parents rotated to the next class like their children did during the school day. The trick

---

9. The label for gifted & talented was based on a serious of tests, including an IQ test, which demonstrated both general intelligence and creative intelligence. Districts receive federal funding for classes such as these in order to help these students excel. Often, general ed classrooms move too slowly or don't dive deep enough for these students. They grow bored and often fail.

was to take up the entire ten minutes so that no parents could corner you[10].

Nothing like having to call child protective services on a parent for abuse during week one of the school year and then wonder what they'd do if they got you alone in your classroom. This schedule was originally implemented by Dr. Web, but its success meant the format continued long past her principal career.

If parents wanted to discuss their kids further, they were instructed to use a classroom sign-up sheet to request a private conference. This also protected the students' privacy. With thirty-two students in a class, these evenings usually meant fifty parents crammed in my room, all clamoring for my attention.

Surprisingly, both of John's parents showed up, though older brother Josh was nowhere in sight[11]. They didn't corner me or say anything during the ten minutes in my room, so I thought I'd escaped any drama. By the evening's end, as parents were ushered by administrators towards the exits, John's parents squeaked through the hallway and into my classroom. Lucky for me, a colleague saw them and intervened.

"If you want a meeting with Mrs. Oak, you'll need to schedule one later. All parents are to leave the building," my colleague said as she followed them into my room.

John's mother held up her hand. "One moment please. I need to apologize."

I'll be honest—I almost burst out laughing. Her? Apologize? Four years later? I gave a brief nod to my colleague who remained in the doorway to stand guard.

"Back when you taught Josh, I... I believed a lot of awful

---

10. Trust me, they try. They want to turn a short introduction into an entire night about their special snowflake.

11. I've often had former students come back on these nights to say hello as they tagged along with their younger siblings. Meet the Teacher Night becomes a family event.

things about you, things my son told me, and I'm sincerely sorry. He's in high school now and failing miserably. I— We've discovered that Josh is a compulsive liar. He has mental health issues and is getting help, but we realize now that everything he accused you of doing was a lie. You were just trying to do your job, and we made things difficult for you."

"You tried to have me fired."

She flinched. "We did. I'm really sorry. So is my husband."

He nodded when she elbowed him in his side.

"You don't have to forgive us, but we wanted you to know that you won't have any trouble this year teaching John. He's a good kid and if he isn't, you let us know, and we'll fix it."

With that, they quietly left my room.

I waited a few moments before a 'holy shit' escaped my lips. Every teacher in the building had known there was something wrong with Josh, and now, the parents did too. They'd learned and apologized, something that teachers rarely see happen. I wasn't sure if I wanted to laugh with glee or sob with relief. Maybe a bit of both.

So much of my past is steeped in being silenced and boxed in by others. It's a pattern since childhood and one that needs breaking if I'm to heal. In the case of Josh, I stood up for myself because I had the support to do so. I had a principal who didn't take bullshit lying down and protected her staff, so it had been easy for me to stand up against parents and administrators that year.

Other years, it wasn't always the case. Most of my life, trauma has closed me in and pushed me away from making the choices I would have[12] made. This particular instance ended well, but to this day, it still marks me.

Their choice to believe me capable of killing animals and wishing harm on others is so ridiculous and so against who I am as a person that it's a struggle to laugh about it. How

---

12. Should have.

could anyone think that of me? How could anyone believe that about a stranger?

Is humanity that flawed that when we meet someone new, our first assumptions are the worst?

This moment set the stage for my teaching career, which yo-yoed between being seen as "too strong" and allowing myself to be caged and tempered. It's why I made it thirteen years and then left.

Like many good educators, I couldn't survive the politics and bailed.

Like many good educators, I'm still struggling through the PTSD echoed in my dreams and nightmares.

WHILE NOT EVERYONE has seen the movie *Mean Girls*, we've all been kids. Something about school turns normal children into cliques from hell. For me, it was the preppy kids, often from wealth; the desperate, who circled the in-crowd like a pack of hyenas; the jocks who lived as sports' gods; and the outcasts who held no interest in others outside their geeky or misfit circles. If you spent your middle and high school years in Texas, as I did, there were also the hicks —boot wearin', country-lovin' folks who boot scooted their way across the Commons[13].

Other than the jocks, I've been a member of all of the above while attending high school. In college, I found that very few people gave a shit about such groupings. Most of us were too busy studying while juggling jobs or partying or some mix of both. I guess the frat houses might've cared, but

---

13. At my high school, there was a large square at the center of school located outside the cafeteria. Students hung out there before and after school as well as in-between classes. Some chose to eat there instead of in the cafeteria as they hovered around the vending machines, trying to act cool. Ours was called the Commons, meaning the common area.

the college I went to wasn't known for its fraternities and sororities. In fact, they existed in name only. No college row existed to party hardy your way through the years.

I left college and entered teaching expecting that I'd be surrounded by other professionals seeking to change the world or at least help students learn. Knowing that I was teaching middle school, a special hell that many struggle to survive, I figured this would be especially true.

I was wrong.

For all that we enter the field with the greatest of intentions, education runs similar to police departments. Some educators *(and police officers)* seek the job for power. For control. They never stopped being *that* bully and thus, they form their own cliques amongst their colleagues.

This was especially true in the Bible Belt.

East Valley Middle School was located in a major suburb with a mix of middle class families. While our student body was mostly Caucasian, this was Texas, so we had our share of Hispanic students. A sprinkling of people of color comprised the rest of our demographics. One thing most of these families had in common was church.

They were either Catholic, or they were attendees of the local megachurch. Even those families that were atheist attended church somewhere if for no other reason than to fit in. I can count on one hand the number of Jewish, Mormon, or Jehovah's Witnesses I taught at that school.

My first year teaching provided little time to meet my colleagues, outside of training days or staff development. On those days, I worked other English teachers in the building and discovered that for some people, high school never ended.

The 6th grade teachers—every last one of them—attended the megachurch. One teacher in particular—her husband worked closely for the superintendent, Dr. Dence, so of course they knew *all* about Josh, his parents, and the scandal that almost cost me my job.

At our first time professional development day, we all sat in a 6th grade English classroom to plan what changes we'd make to the curriculums for next year, which included a lot of decisions about what books were read during what grade, what skills needed to shift around where, and so on. When it came time to take a lunch break, all of the 6th grade teachers huddled together in a circle of hens after some good feed.

Discussions of where to eat happened rapid fire and they were off, a small group out to eat lunch. Being the new teacher on the block, I thought perhaps they might invite me to go with them but not a chance. I wasn't a part of their group.

One of the 8th grade teachers saw my confusion and patted my arm. "You don't go to church around here, do you?"

When I shook my head, she patted my arm again before she left the room.

A 7th grade colleague invited me to join her for lunch in her classroom, which while sweet of her, wasn't nearly as cool as going out somewhere as a group and those 6th grade teachers wanted me to know it.

As the year progressed, I discovered several facts about the 6th grade clique:

- If you didn't go to *the megachurch*, you were not welcome to be friends with them.
- If you didn't go to church at all, you were someone to avoid at all costs.
- If you were named Raven Oak, you were evil as they believed everything Josh's parents had accused me of doing and being.

I mean, who has a name like Raven Oak?

It wasn't so much that they believed the lies, I didn't care what they believed, but their ostracization and cliquish rules followed me all six years that I taught at this school. There were a few teachers at this school that I befriended[14], but for the most part, the teachers moved in packs much like high school.

These teachers actively gossiped about me, they spread rumors about me, and when I ended up with their children in my Pre-AP classes, they became the helicopter parents from hell.

"Why does my child need to study science fiction? Why do they need to read Ray Bradbury?"

While I love sci-fi and write it, the topic and author in question were part of our state mandated textbook. It wasn't as if I had chosen it just to ruffle their precious feathers.

"*Fahrenheit 451*?! My kid's not reading that 9/11 conspiracy shit![15]"

"Why are you showing pictures from the Civil Rights Movement in your classroom? My kid doesn't need to see that!"

You mean they don't need to see your white parents screaming and attacking people of color? They don't need to know the level of hatred that still fuels this country?

Every topic I taught was challenged. Every book or story we read was *inappropriate* in their minds because they were convinced that their perfect, angelic children had never seen or heard a single cuss word in their entire lives. They surely didn't know how babies were made and didn't see the pregnant 7th grader walking down our school hallways, so discussing either topic in the context of literature was also deemed inappropriate. These students only needed to read

---

14. I'm still friends with a few of them many years later.
15. Just to note that the books *Fahrenheit 451* by Ray Bradbury and *Fahrenheit 9/11* by Michael Moore are two completely different things. The first is a dystopian novel by a Master of Sci-Fi and the other is a documentary film by a political commentator.

Biblical literature. Being that this was the aughts, this was well before the chaos of teaching now where any school district or library containing books related to anything LGBTQ+ is threatened by pitchfork, or all the books about people of color and slavery being banned[16].

If I were teaching today, I think I'd be in jail.

If you want your kids to encounter nothing other than Christianity and other white Christians, perhaps a private school is a good idea. Or a sledgehammer to the head. In some ways, segregation never went away. It's just sneakier. Students are going to see and hear about topics and people you might not approve of. How they deal with that is all about what you teach them at home.

I did manage to break through with one sixth grade teacher. Her daughter not only loved and excelled in my class, but she was challenged in her thinking. She was given an opportunity to explore and be creative in thought. When the mother saw how much her spoiled daughter was changing for the better, to be a kinder, better person, she changed her mind about me, but it was rare that such moments happened[17].

It was towards the end of my time at this school when I taught my first Pagan student.

She'd survived ostracization by the entire 6th grade class and the teachers, something I had experience with, not just as a child but now as an adult. Being different is challenging enough, but when people actively seek to harm you for it, it makes life that much more difficult. She came to my class with all sorts of labels: oddball, weird, "some sort of psychosis present," problem student, failure, and of course, *evil*[18].

---

16. We wouldn't want them to learn about *history* or anything, right?
17. Sadly, this former student of mine was killed at age twenty by a drunk driver. A drunk teacher no less.
18. I swear these people don't know what evil means. Maybe they should look in a mirror.

54

The first day of class, she walked in proudly wearing a pentacle[19] around her neck. It wasn't flashy or gaudy. In fact, it was no larger than the size of most crosses the other teachers and students wore.

Did anyone *ever* complain about teachers wearing crosses? Not one bit. But the moment this student set foot in school, she became public enemy number one.

"She shouldn't be allowed to wear Satanic symbols."

"What she wears is a distraction to the learning environment."

"The other students are afraid of her. I can't teach with them this afraid."

Any and every excuse in the book was rallied as a rationale for why she shouldn't be allowed at our school at all.

Over the course of the first week, I got to know my Pagan student. Instead of someone suffering from mental health issues or an agent of evil, I found a young woman who wrote beautiful poetry, loved music and anime, and enjoyed my class for the freedom it gave her to be herself. An early parent-teacher conference with her folks and all of her teachers confused everyone but me.

"Why is she failing all of her classes but she's passing yours, with a 93 no less?" the other teachers asked.

"I think she feels safe in my room."

Confused faces stared at me in response.

"She says you don't allow the other kids to bully her," said her mother.

Of course, her other teachers were adamant they didn't allow bullying in their rooms either, but bullying can be subtle. Did you frown when you saw what she was wearing when she entered class? Did you allow other students to edge

---

19. Dating back to the 1500s, pentacles are five pointed stars used as magical talismans in a variety of spiritual and religious practices, including Wicca and forms of Paganism.

their desks away from her? How did group work function in your class? Was she alone?

I rattled off a dozen questions.

While I grew up in a religious household, I am not religious. As one of the only atheist teachers I've ever met during my career in Texas, I knew what it was like to be seen as someone to be avoided at all costs. I knew the ways people othered you, and the micro-aggressions people used to make you feel unwanted.

Because I understood from personal experience, I could prevent it from happening—at least in my classroom. Being atheist also meant that I wasn't afraid of Paganism. What she chose for her religion was between her and her gods. My job was to treat her like a human being and teach her.

Of course, by discussing this in the conference, I outed myself as an atheist.

Smack in the middle of the Bible Belt.

There are a million ways people can cause paper-cuts with their actions, and it didn't take long before I was the center of school gossip yet again. The notorious 6th grade clique made sure to accidentally discuss it with their kids, so it wasn't just my colleagues who wondered if there was any truth to the early rumors spread by Josh and his parents. Students, colleagues, and hell, even the custodians gave me wide berth as they wondered if I were going to suddenly cast a spell on them or curse them.

Folks, atheism is not the same as Satanism, which is not the same as Paganism. While I wish we lived in a world where we could teach children about *all* of the major religions of the world, it's places like Texas that make this a problem. In Texas, any class like this would quickly become, "Christianity 101" or "All these religions are evil." Despite the freedom of religion provided to us in our Constitution, many would rather we have one established religion and to hell with anyone else.

While it sucked to be in the rumor mill hot seat again, it

gave my student a break from the bullying as everyone focused on me.

I never made friends with the cliques in that school, but I'm not sure I wanted to once I realized what the cost would be. While I was outed as an atheist, I was still very much in the closet in terms of my gender identity and queerness. At the time, those weren't battles I wanted to fight.

Not yet.

CHAPTER
FOUR
CRIME & PUNISHMENT

Pain and suffering are always inevitable for a large intelligence and a deep heart."

FYODOR DOSTOYEVSKY

I'VE NOT ALWAYS BEEN KIND to myself. There have been moments when I should have stood up against others and advocated for my protection, but I chose not to do so out of fear. It's punishing to do right by others, let alone yourself. Sometimes choosing right means consequences, which can ripple far beyond your reach.

Dr. Ridgeway, the principal at East Valley Middle School, had eyes on being superintendent after Dr. Dence retired, so this was his last year as my boss. Our school gained a new coach that year, a big man with a history of taking football teams "all the way." I have no idea why a middle school needs a coach like that since no one in the NFL is drafting from 7th graders, but in the south, sports are everything.

I'm going to say that again—sports are *everything*.

If there are budget cuts, sports get cut last. Extra money in the budget? Time for new athletic gear, even if the current gear is lightly used. Teachers are laid off before the athletic budget is touched. It's not like middle school sports brought in the money either, not the way high school football does, but boy howdy, you didn't lay a finger on the sports programs or coaches unless the sky itself was on fire.

For the purposes of this book, I'm calling our new educator Coach Rage.

Any of my former students will tell you that I love humor, including "dad humor" and bad puns. If it makes students groan, I love it all the more. I used it in the classroom whenever I could, but sometimes it came back to bite me in the ass.

I have a sarcastic sense of humor which sometimes borders on wry, so occasionally, students don't get my jokes. One such time was when Coach Rage needed a DVD player[1].

Because I taught reading and writing, the day's lesson involved writing with senses other than sight. I was in the middle of demonstrating this by sticking my hand into a darkened box and describing what I felt but couldn't see when Coach Rage poked his head into my classroom. "My DVD player is broken, and I need one for class today. Do you have one I can borrow?"

This was back before we all had projector screens hooked up to computers for easy streaming or video viewing. We didn't even have DVD players in every classroom. Both the VCR and DVD player in my classroom were my own personal devices that I bought for classroom use—a common thing for most teachers, including Coach Rage. If they stopped working, your plans went straight out the window, so when he asked, I had no problem allowing him to borrow mine.

As I was disconnecting it from the TV mounted in corner, I asked, "What are you watching?"

Besides coaching football, Coach Rage taught two classes of Texas History. He rattled off some movie or another

---

1. This was 2005 and yes, we were using DVD players. Blu-rays weren't a thing yet and many of us still had VCRs too.

dealing with the Alamo, and I said, "Sounds like a great time to be in *your* class! Movie day!"

When I was a kid, movie days were cause for celebration. While some chatted or slept through the movie, I had options. As a visual learner, I connected more with films so I enjoyed movies. Despite the reputation, movies can be a way of learning, so as teachers, we like them too. When I made this comment about movie day being great, I meant it.

He said, "Yep. You know me, I love movies."

"So do I. I'd show them every day if I could." Now this part was said in jest. We both knew the reputation movie day had, and since we joked around quite a bit in the hallway, I thought nothing of my comment.

So I laughed. Coach Rage laughed. The students laughed.

He left my classroom, DVD player in hand.

Two class periods later, it was time for lunch and I set off for the teachers' lounge. Unlike other schools I've taught at, East Valley had an actual lounge for teachers, so I enjoyed chatting and relaxing with my colleagues during lunch. Inside the lounge was a set of three folding tables stretched out to make one long table. There were probably thirteen or fourteen of us inside eating, along with a teacher using the copy machine and another snagging a soda from the vending machine.

We made a point of keeping the door closed to give us privacy from nosey students. While we chatted, the lounge door flew open so hard that the handle left a dent in the wall. Everyone froze. Those facing the door, sat silent, eyes wide, and those with our backs to the door *(like me)*, turned around to see what the commotion was.

Coach Rage stood in the doorway, his face cherry red. He strode around the table until he stood across from me.

When he lunged, it was unexpected.

As a teacher, I could be attacked by a student, sure, but a colleague? Teachers scattered out of his way as he jabbed his meaty finger into my face. "What the fuck is wrong with you?" he shouted.

"I'm sorry?"

"Don't you ever, ever, *ever* tell students that I'm a worthless teacher. How dare you! You ever say anything like that again, and I'll wipe the floor with your fat ass."

At this point, I was very confused, not to mention frightened. I hadn't said anything of the sort. Every time he shouted, teachers, including me, flinched. He stood 6'4" and outweighed me by a good amount. His hands were braced on the table, maybe three inches from my lunch as he continued to shout accusations.

A nearby teacher picked up the lounge phone to call for help.

Another from a nearby classroom poked her head into the lounge, then disappeared from view.

He stopped long enough to notice the witnesses to his rampage, tossed my lunch across the table, and stormed out.

A minute later, one of my colleagues asked, "What just happened?"

"I have no idea."

My answer confused them as they questioned me. Had I said that about him? Had I said anything that could have hinted that I thought he was a bad teacher? How could I not know what this was about?

I burst into tears.

I don't like crying. I was taught it was weakness, and doing that in front of others only makes it worse. When people yell at me, I'm a little kid again. Flashbacks from childhood shoot my anxiety into space. Rather than planets and asteroids, my space is comprised of tears and terror.

"No matter what was or was not said, he had no right to yell and threaten you like that." One colleague patted me on the shoulder and handed me a tissue. "Get cleaned up and go to the office. This needs to be reported."

"I have class in a few minutes," I said as I blotted my eyes.

"We'll cover for you."

Several teachers worked out a plan to watch my students as I set off towards the front office. If I reported this, I wouldn't be able to do so without crying. I *hated* the idea of letting my guard down with Dr. Ridgeway, especially since he was such a stickler for everything sailing smoothly in his school. Nothing was going to get in the way of his dreams to be superintendent.

Especially not verbal assault.

When I arrived, the school secretary rushed me back to the principal's office with a worried glance. "He's waiting for you," she said.

I knocked once before I opened the door, only to find Coach Rage splayed across a chair as he faced Dr. Ridgeway, who indicated that I should take the other.

The last thing I wanted was to discuss what had happened with my assailant beside me.

"Can we talk a moment without…him present?"

Dr. Ridgeway shook his head. "Coach Rage has already informed me of his side of events, and—"

His side? Are you kidding me?

"I'd like to hear what you believe happened."

At this point, my fear flipped over to anger[2]. "First off, there are no sides here. I was eating lunch in the teacher's lounge when Coach Rage barged in, knocked a hole in the wall with the door, lunged across the table, and began threatening me. I have no idea what set him off or why he came at me like that. I have over a dozen witnesses willing and able to back up what I'm saying."

Coach Rage opened his mouth and shouted at me. "You know damn well what you did!"

---

2. This happens a lot with me. Sometimes it works to my benefit by giving me the fuel I need to protect myself or someone else. Sometimes, it doesn't work at all.

I must have had a deer in the headlights look on my face as Dr. Ridgeway motioned for the coach to stop.

"What exactly do you believe I said and when?" I asked.

"You said that I'm a worthless teacher and all I do is show movies all day!"

I frowned. "And when did I say that?"

"In your classroom when I borrowed your DVD player." His face was red again, and he'd stood up as he shouted.

Folks, I couldn't facepalm any harder if I tried. Of course, this is over fifteen years ago now so it's easy for me to see how incredibly stupid this man was but at the time, his words had me grinding my teeth.

"Dr. Ridgeway, earlier today, Coach Rage interrupted my class because his DVD player broke. As I disconnected mine to loan him, we *both* joked about how fun movie days were and how we wished we could *both* show movies all the time. Coach Rage laughed at my comments and made a few of his own that were of a similar vein. At no point did I ever say he was a bad teacher, nor did I ever state that he only showed movies in class. I have no idea where he got his information from, but he certainly had no right to verbally assault and threaten to 'wipe the floor' with my 'fat ass,' which is a physical threat of violence."

My principal paled. The terms I used could result in a police report and lawyers, both of which he wanted to avoid like a bad case of hemorrhoids. "Coach Rage, did the conversation just mentioned occur earlier today?"

"Yes."

"And you were both joking?"

"Well, *I* was."

"What do you mean?" asked Dr. Ridgeway.

"One of my students said he heard Mrs. Oak in the hallway after class saying I was a bad teacher and that she wasn't joking. She was talking to the teacher next door."

Tears burned in my eyes, but this time, they were my angry tears. You know I'm irate when I'm crying and silent.

"Call Mrs. Bors. Ask her. I guarantee that conversation never happened. In fact, I wasn't in the hall after that class period because I had a phone call from the front office about a delivery of books that arrived addressed to me."

Dr. Ridgeway scooted a box of tissues in my direction, and I snatched one as Coach Rage sputtered denial.

"Did it ever occur to you to ask me about this 'conversation' before you decided to rage on me?" I asked the coach.

Before I could ask any more questions, my principal waved a hand at me and asked me to return to my seat. "Which student told you this?" he asked.

The name the coach gave was a known trouble maker in the building. The moment the name popped out, Coach Rage all but melted in his chair. Somewhere beneath his anger, he knew how ridiculous this rumor was.

"What I see here is a miscommunication. A student heard you both joking and decided to take it too far, and you..." Dr. Ridgeway said as he pointed at Coach Rage. "You didn't clarify the rumor and lost your temper on a colleague. Now what can we do to settle this?"

My boss—the guy who was supposed to protect me— gave me this look, this tired, placating look that spoke volumes about how this was going to roll. He didn't look at Coach Rage. He wasn't *the problem*, as far as Dr. Ridgeway was concerned.

I was.

Coach Rage turned in his chair to face me and muttered an apology.

Dr. Ridgeway nodded. "Good. I know you both have classes to get back to so—"

"Wait, that's it? He threatened me physical harm!"

"Which he didn't mean, did you?"

Coach Rage shook his head. "I was just mad."

"But I had no way to know that, nor did anyone else in the lounge. For all we knew, you were going to beat us all up."

"I think that's your background talking," said my boss, and my shoulders fell.

He knew I'd been abused as a kid. I'd had parents threaten me and trigger my anxiety before, and as my boss, he knew that I didn't do well with men shouting at me. But rather than see this star coach as the unstable liability he was, my boss decided it was easier to assume I was *triggered*.

Tears rolled down my face, and I didn't bother to hide them. "I don't care that he's mad. What he did is not acceptable. He threatened me. Witnesses heard it. So he says he's sorry but what's to stop him from doing it again, maybe next time with a child?"

"Coach, you can go. And close the door please." My principal waited until the door clicked shut before he continued. "Look, you and I both know you could turn this into a whole ordeal. You could call the police. They'd make a report. You could press charges. But we both know it wouldn't go anywhere since he didn't mean anything by it. You could even hire an attorney, but the truth is that no one likes a teacher who makes waves."

That's me—wave maker.

Or at least, I'd had that reputation since squaring off against Dr. Dence.

"If you don't drop this, the district will find a way to non-renew your contract. You'll get labeled as a problem. You'll have trouble finding a teaching job anywhere else in the area. Maybe even in the state. We both know how rumors travel in education."

The bastard was not only victim blaming me, but he was using his position to keep me silent. To keep this event from getting out and causing a tsunami.

Being earlier in my career, he had me backed into a corner. This man knew powerful people—people in higher places than a measly superintendent. As he stared at me, his face a rocky cliff, I knew there would be no help from him. It wouldn't be the district who non-renewed me. It would be Dr. Ridgeway.

I choked back my tears and asked, "What can I do?"

"You can pretend this never happened. Accept Coach Rage's apology and move on."

So that's what I did.

I should have fought it. I should have made the biggest stink in the history of Texas education, but I didn't. I was afraid of losing my career and the paycheck we depended on, and I put that before the safety of me and my students.

As that school year progressed, rumors reached me about Coach Rage.

"He cusses at the kids."
"He shouts until the kids cry. No one wants to play football anymore."
"He throws the football at students, and not in a good way."
"Once, he slapped a kid upside the head."

Every rumor was a reminder that I should have fought for them and for me.

Both of us had our contracts renewed but towards the beginning of the year, his rage was witnessed by the wrong parent. Coach Rage was quietly 'let go' from the district without anyone having any idea as to the details.

It never made the news either.

I truly hope they yanked his teaching certificate. Or better yet, locked him in a padded room with a DVD player.

DESPITE HAVING some parents abhor me, most of the parents I encountered loved me as their child's teacher. I had parents who looked forward to my teaching all of their children. Tales were told by parents and students to younger ones about how much fun I made learning, and when I moved away from East Valley Middle School, many expressed their sadness that one kid or another wouldn't know the joys and challenges of my class.

It's what every teacher hopes for—students who are forever changed by their classes and appreciation for what we do. As an English teacher, I did my damnedest to ensure that every topic we covered tied into world history and culture, that topics tied into art, music, and even math when possible. I believe everything we learn is interconnected so I made a point of demonstrating that to my students on a daily basis.

My classroom was a safe space for all backgrounds and beliefs, but I also made it a place where students could be themselves. I spent one summer painting video game characters on my walls, characters who made a running commentary on whatever we were learning about. When we studied about Greek and Norse mythology, I made connections between those heroes and gods to everything from the shoes they wore to the games they played. When we read *The Watsons Go to Birmingham—1963*, a historical fiction novel based on the real life 16th Street Baptist Church bombing in Birmingham during the Civil Rights Movement—I made sure we did more than talk about Rosa Parks and Martin Luther King, Jr. We dug into prejudice and racism, both then and now, and watched videos about Jane Elliot's blue-eyed, brown-eyed experiment[3], where the educator taught her first graders about the realities of prejudice.

Many would now argue that what I taught was too "woke," but in reality, what I taught was real life. The words we read and say don't exist in isolation. Every book written comes from a kernel of reality, even fantastical stories, and great books change society in ways we don't immediately see.

---

3. You can find out more about educator Jane Elliot and her experiments regarding prejudice here: https://www.pbs.org/wgbh/frontline/article/introduction-2/

Not to talk about the existence of hate, including where we've been and where we're going, would have been a great disservice to every child I taught.

Photos from the Civil Rights Movement showing white men and women harming people of color, blocking them from entering places, and tearing off their skin with fire hoses? Those were some of my students' grandparents and great-grandparents. Lynching didn't disappear with the passing of the Civil Rights Act of 1964. Hatred may have hidden for a while, but current day politics show it's always been here.

We studied dystopias through books like *The Giver* by Lois Lowry and *Fahrenheit 451* by Ray Bradbury in order to understand how writers use words to warn as well as imagine. Yes, we learned grammar, spelling, and mechanics, as well as how to write essays, but I did my best to demonstrate and model how important words are.

Words can change the world.

It was during this time that I taught Georgia, a 7th grade student with her own ankle monitor and parole officer. While in 5th grade, she'd stabbed a teacher in the chest[4]. After spending 6th grade in juvie, she'd returned to our school district...with strings, or in this case, ankle monitor attached. Because students who often struggled behaviorally succeeded in my classroom, she was placed in my general English class with the hopes that she could stay out trouble.

Her first day in my room, she refused to take notes and when asked, told me to fuck off. Georgia held herself in a fighting stance. There was no flight in this young woman who was ready to throw down rather than to be seen as weak.

I pulled her aside and asked her what she wanted. At first, she said, "To get outta this fucking place." When she realized I was serious, she added, "For you to leave me alone."

When I explained that she was in my class to learn and

---

4. The teacher lived and fully recovered.

would have to do *something*, she scowled. "You're just like the rest of them. You don't give a shit either."

For that first day, I let her be. When it came time for lunch, I asked permission for her to eat lunch with me in my room.

"Alone?" came the response from our school's police officer.

"I will leave the door open."

"I think that's a bad idea. What if she decides to stab you?" the woman asked.

I shrugged. "I'll give her a chance before deciding she's still homicidal."

If I'd thought she would stab me, I wouldn't have made the invitation. I believed in second chances, but I wasn't stupid. No one had bothered to ask her what she wanted. She was tired of being ordered around, and I thought having a moment to just exist in peace might give us a moment to bond. With approval, I asked Georgia to eat with me.

Since it meant not sitting with the school's police officer, she jumped at the chance in hopes she could get what she wanted from me. Instead, I asked her about herself.

"What are your interests?"

"Sex. Drugs. Typical shit."

"What do you do for fun on the weekends?"

"Fuck around. You?"

Most of her answers were sardonic bullshit intended to shock me or get under my skin. I ignored those and kept talking until she gave a few honest answers.

She enjoyed finding rocks with unique patterns. "They make good weapons too." Georgia enjoyed art. Drawing gave her time to think, something I was familiar with myself.

So I struck a deal with her—if she listened while I taught, she could draw or write in her notebook all she wanted. I wouldn't give her homework as long as she could convince me she was listening and learning. Obviously this would have to change at some point because grades were a part of school, but for now, I wanted her to trust me. I needed her to

70

understand that my room was safe. That she didn't have to fight me to exist.

Over time, she opened up to me. Not completely, but enough that she was writing for me and reading the stories and books in my class. She wouldn't do anything at home, and from what she told me *(and what I learned from school counselors)*, her home life wouldn't have allowed for that anyway. Her father was absent, and her mother, an alcoholic. After school, Georgia spent her time "elsewhere" until dark when she'd sneak into her house via her bedroom window to hide from her mother.

On a good day, she'd listen to music on her headphones to drown out her mother's drunk arguing with the latest boyfriend. Bad days...she didn't talk with me about those. Whatever happened was horrible enough that she remained mute on the topic.

When it came time for report cards, Georgia earned her first B—in my class. She failed all her other courses, including gym. A team meeting was held where my boss, Dr. Ridgeway, wanted to know how she'd "earned" a passing grade in my class, a class known to be challenging.

"I'm assuming she cheated, but I'd like to know if you suspected it or just missed it?" he asked.

When I glanced around at the rest of her teachers, every one of them wore the same expression he did.

Incredulous.

The idea that she could be successful was so far removed from their thoughts that they could only believe her to be a cheat, which meant they thought me inadequate as a teacher.

How else could a known juvenile delinquent pass?

When I explained to them how I'd earned *some* of her trust —let's be honest, I knew she didn't wholly trust me—and how I'd worked her interests into what I taught to encourage her to engage, it was like I'd slapped them. Utter shock and surprise.

"But she's not going to be here very long. Why spend so

much time on her when you have thirty other students?" This from a colleague whom I'd previously looked up to.

I understand that some people are too ingrained in their ways to change—some people will fight you with their last breath when faced with even the hint of doing something different—but we were teaching minors. Yes, Georgia was fourteen, but she was still a young woman in our care. Our job was to give her every opportunity to learn. If she chose not to, that was her decision, but how could she make that choice or any other if we assumed she was incapable of that from the get go?

"Georgia may have come to us from juvie, but we're not that place. I treat her like any other student I have and expect her to work. She didn't cheat. She chose to work in my class."

Because they couldn't believe me, Dr. Ridgeway decided to randomly drop into my classes with Georgia. The moment he walked in, she froze. Then her old self roared up.

When she refused to do the warm up, I asked her to try.

"Fuck you, bitch," she said.

I asked to speak to her in the hallway, where she explained that she didn't like Dr. Ridgeway. "He's a creepy asshole. Probably touches children."

"While I doubt that, I personally don't like him either," I answered, and we both laughed. "But I didn't invite him here, Georgia. I certainly didn't invite him into my classroom to get you into trouble. As teachers, we're often observed as part of our job, so try not to think of this as being about you. For all we know, he's here for me."

"Whatcha do? Stab someone?"

I gave her a half-hearted smile. "No, but you'd think I did the way some folks look at me. Let's just say I understand your distrust. My room is a safe space, okay? Remember that and try to get a little work done for me."

Georgia rolled her eyes, but upon returning to my room, she worked. Dr. Ridgeway noted that she doodled a lot while listening, but when it was time to read or write, she followed instructions as asked.

He popped into class a few more times in the coming weeks, each time leaving with a confused look on his face. I was doing something different, something that was working, and he couldn't place his finger on *why*.

In reality, I believe it was honesty. I didn't lie to her about my feelings regarding my boss or colleagues. I'd suffered enough in my early teaching years that had little to do with me and more to do with other people's fears. While I'd never resort to stabbing someone, I understood her rage. Being able to connect with her and show her she could be herself in my classroom meant she was more inclined to work. Did I have to make accommodations for her? Big time. But they were worth doing in an attempt to save her from becoming a statistic.

Dr. Ridgeway met with the other teachers to share what he'd seen in my room. A few refused outright to try and connect with her.

"How do I know she won't connect with me by way of a blade?"

"She's a lost cause and should be back in juvie. They're the only ones able to keep her in line."

"If I hear the f-word one more time outta that child, I'm done and she's gone."

My boss suggested they try, but the results weren't good. Georgia could read between the lines, and my colleagues' attempts to connect read as the falsities they were. This only served to piss her off.

They were lying to her and if there was one thing Georgia couldn't stand, it was liars.

Liars like her mother.

Two weeks into the next quarter, she'd had it. She stood up in Texas History class and said, "Ain't no one give two fucks about all these old, dead people at the Alamo. All they

73

did was steal this state from brown people like me. Ain't stealing wrong?"

When her teacher asked her to sit down, she picked up her desk and tossed it across the room, narrowly missing the teacher. Our student desks were the kind with a swiveling desk top attached to a chair. They were large enough, and Georgia's teacher slow enough, that if she'd wanted to hit the teacher, Georgia could have. When asked, she admitted she'd missed on purpose. Her emotions got the better of her and unable to do anything with them, she'd lashed out.

Considering what she'd done to go to juvie, it was improvement. She'd tried to rein in her anger but had failed. None of this mattered to the parole officer and the judge. Her passing grade and behavior for me were moot considering her behavior outside my room. Back to juvie she went, where feeling betrayed, she stabbed a guard.

Last I heard, she was serving time in adult prison for a felony.

Part of my rationale for teaching and writing is to help people like Georgia. When we give up on them early in life, we set them up for the prison pipeline. We have to show people that there is another way to live and that the horrors of childhood don't have to continue into adulthood.

In finding my voice again, maybe I can show others that you don't need violence to change the view. With words, you can determine your future. You can break the cycle of violence and change the world, one word at a time.

MY SECOND YEAR at East Valley, I had a student named May. She was your typical ADHD-fueled 7th grader with a wicked sense of humor. As someone who loves sarcasm, she was my kind of kid as we exchanged jokes on the daily. But behind her smile was a seriousness that I recognized, a hint that something serious was bothering her that she didn't feel comfortable giving voice to.

I'd met May's father at Meet the Teacher Night—a fairly large, blue collar worker who was polite enough to me, which is to say that nothing struck me as a potential threat when I met him. Nothing that could have warned me of what was coming that year between the three of us.

A few days before Thanksgiving break, May walked into my classroom one day after school. She pulled up a chair in front of my desk with a heavy sigh. "Do you have a minute to talk?"

"Sure."

At first, she remained silent as she pondered her words. Something deep hung in the air between us, and I put down my grading pen to give her my full attention.

"If I tell you something, do you have to tell anyone else?"

It's the question that teachers dread, because it means whatever we're about to hear is absolutely going to have to be told to someone else—at a minimum a counselor or principal, but at worst, Child Protective Services.

As teachers, we're considered mandated reporters of any suspected child abuse, which means that if we don't report any suspicions, no matter how minor, the state will revoke our teaching license. We'll also serve jail time for failure to report. It doesn't matter if there's actual abuse or not. Any suspicion must be reported and left for the authorities to deal with.

"If what you tell me means that you or someone else is in danger, I have to tell someone. By law. If I don't, I can go to jail. Do you still want to talk to me?"

No answer.

I nodded. "I understand. If you want, I can call one of the counselors. Maybe you'd feel better talking with them?"

May shook her head. "No, I want to tell you. Just give me a minute."

My stomach dropped to the floor. When victims come forward, there's always a reason, and this one felt monstrous.

"If I go home today, my dad's gonna beat me."

As a teacher, it was my job to notice any bruises or broken bones a child had because they could have been indicators of abuse[5]. It doesn't mean we reported every bruise, but we were supposed to keep records to see if any patterns develop. With May, I'd never observed any signs of abuse, but it's always possible a parent is being careful. Some are very talented at hiding their work.

"Why do you think that?" I asked.

"I'm failing two classes."

"Has your father hit you before for failing?"

May nodded. "It's not just spanking—I mean, everyone gets spanked[6]—but my dad likes to use a belt or a tree branch. He...he keeps it to places under my jeans, but I don't wanna get hit, miss. I'll walk in the door, and he'll be drunk, and he'll beat me. He always drinks but after he gets a call from the school, he *really* drinks. Sometimes I can hide but with the break coming up, there's nowhere to go. Can I come home with you? You're so nice, and you have cats. I like cats—"

Her rationale rattled on as my head spun. This wasn't just an outcry, but a child who wanted to run away and live with me, which was never going to happen. Telling a victim no is crushing in a moment of vulnerability, so I needed to choose my words carefully.

"You've told me that your father abuses you, which I have to report, but as your teacher, I can't encourage you to run away. I can only say that you should do whatever you can to

---

5. Not that anyone ever noticed with me, at least not until high school.

6. No, everyone doesn't! Nor should they. We teach kids not to hit each other. In fact, if I hit another adult, it's called assault and I can go to jail for it. So if we teach them it's wrong, why do some folks use it as discipline? How is assault on a child going to teach anything?

keep yourself safe. Is there a friend you can stay with tonight?"

For all that May was funny, she caused too much drama for most others. Like many geeky or odd neurodivergent kids, she didn't fit in well, so when she shook her head no, I wasn't surprised. I'd never seen her sit with anyone at lunch, let alone talk with a friend in class.

"What about other family? Anyone like an aunt or something you could call?"

Another head shake.

"I'm sorry, May, but you'll have to go home today. But I'm going to call someone and get some help to you as quickly as possible, maybe even today—"

"You're just like the rest. No one believes me."

Had she reported this before? To whom? "Who else—"

Before I could finish, she bolted out of her chair towards the door. She halted, one hand on the doorframe. Tears streaked her face as she faced me. "I'm gonna kill myself. I know where he keeps his gun. Was nice knowing you, Mrs. Oak."

With that promise, she was out the door. By the time I reached the hallway, she'd already exited the building amongst a sea of students.

She was in imminent danger and CPS would be too slow. The first thing I did was call the front office and tell them I had an emergency and needed an administrator immediately. When I hung up, I called 9-1-1, which at the time, automatically dispatched police to the school if the call came from a school phone number.

I gave the dispatcher a quick summary, along with May's name and home address, as well as her father's name, and warned them that there was potentially a gun in the house. The school counselor, my principal, and the police all strode into my classroom soon after where I updated them what May had disclosed and promised.

The police set off to update any officers responding at the

scene and my principal followed them out. The counselor stayed with me as I made my first call to Child Protective Services.

There's nothing like making that report. You wonder if you're doing the right thing. What if the child's lying? I could be destroying someone's family or life over nothing. You question whether you reported everything correctly as it was said to you or if you missed any information. When the call is done, you wrack your mind through the past months in some desperate attempt to recall any warning signs you might've missed, anything that could have warned you that this child was being harmed.

I've taught at schools that tried to prevent teachers from reporting suspicions of abuse, but I can gladly state that East Valley Middle School supported their teachers in moments like this.

When the police arrived at May's home, they found chaos. I can only piece together what happened from what the school counselor told me, as no teacher is privy to police reports and such, but the officers found May and her father engaged in a screaming match. There was a gun in the home, unsecured, but no one had reached for it yet.

The father claimed that May was mentally unstable, that while she'd had an initial diagnosis of ADHD, her psychiatrist believed her to be bipolar, a mental disorder that's challenging to diagnose in children. As puberty can trigger a variety of mental illnesses in teens, it was believable. May's father said he'd been struggling to force May to behave because she'd often "fly off the handle." He stated she was known to throw things at him and grew "more violent each day."

I know it was only my second year teaching, but I'd never seen this side of May. Not once. In fact, none of her teachers had. She'd never so much as tossed a pencil at the ceiling. A further investigation showed no signs of bruising on May, and every bone break was documented with reasonable rationales. In other words, if he were abusing May, he covered his tracks well.

May didn't come to school the next day…but her father did. After school, he managed to sneak in through a side door that students used to exit the building. He didn't have a visitor badge, yet no one stopped him in the hallway.

One moment I was jotting notes down in my lesson plan book and the next, a shadow crossed my desk. I glanced up to see May's father, his face a living rage.

"The next time you have questions about whether or not I'm beating my kid, you call ME. Not the cops, not CPS. ME. You get it?"

He kept his voice quiet enough that no one outside my room would hear, and I glanced at my desk phone.

"Don't bother. I'd be gone before anyone got down the hall." He placed both hands on my desk as he leaned forward. "If you ever call the cops on me again, you'll wish you hadn't."

When he released his grip, my desk slid a few inches towards me and I flinched. May's father had been right—he was through the doorway before I could pick up the phone.

My coworker from across the hall rushed in. "That was a short meeting…" She stopped when she saw my face.

"This is Mrs. Oak. I need the principal. Now," I said into the phone and then hung up.

"What happened? Are you okay?"

I shook my head but said nothing until my boss arrived. A quick review of hallway cameras showed how easily he moved through the school. Several colleagues at the end of the hall could be seen waving to him as he passed by[7]. When I explained his threats, I reminded my boss that the man owned a licensed handgun.

"I don't want him in this building. I don't care if May's a

---

7. Needless to say there were policy changes made as a result of this.

student or not, he gets a phone call and nothing more. He's dangerous," I said.

My boss shook his head. "He arrived home to police and CPS. I don't think he's going to do anything. He's just angry and blowing off steam, but we'll keep an eye on things."

After I'd had enough time for the adrenaline to fade, my first thought was of May. While the police and CPS weren't sure of any abuse, this parent had sneaked into our building and threatened me for doing my job. No one wants child protective services called, but most parents understand that we are *required by law* to do so.

Even if a child's lying.

Nothing came of the threats against me. May's father had her committed to a mental hospital. The investigation into the abuse allegations was dropped and the school year continued as if May had never existed.

With five weeks left in the school year, the school counselor showed up at my door. "I didn't want you to hear this from anyone else, but May's coming back tomorrow."

"Really?" I hadn't heard a word about her since November. "How is she now?"

The counselor sighed. "You might not know but most no or low cost mental health facilities aren't the best. The staff's usually overworked and underpaid, so most of the time, they drug the patients into oblivion, which is what they did to May. She's like a zombie now. I didn't want you to see her in the halls and not know what was going on."

"Will she not be returning to my class?"

She shook her head. "Because of the medication she's on, she'll be in SPED[8] classes. I don't think she even knows where she is."

Surely she was exaggerating.

That was my thought until the next day. May trailed along in a line of students being led towards the bathrooms. She

8. Short for special education

dragged her feet as her blank eyes stared down the hallway. She didn't look at anyone or anything in particular, nor did she respond to my hello. The counselor had been right— whatever made May "May," was gone.

No one was home.

May lasted another two weeks at the school before she threw a chair at a teacher. None of the details of that incident made it to me. Only the result, which was expulsion.

I still think about May and wonder if I missed something. Was she really bipolar or had she been forcibly medicated to keep her in line?

This story sits uneasy in my stomach to this day because parts of it align closely with my own background. Charismatic parents can hide all manner of abuses and do so in ways no one suspects. It's possible that May was lying and genuinely needed a mental health assessment, but it's also possible that she'd been truthful with me in hopes that someone would see what harm had been done to her and save her.

If that's what happened, then society failed her. I failed her.

Many will say that I followed procedure and did everything I could to help her, and that's true, but sometimes, I feel like I must have missed something. Or maybe it's my own glaring past with all those teachers and adults who "missed something" with me.

Perhaps May's tale haunts me because society failed me too.

CHAPTER
FIVE
IT GETS BETTER

When we're growing up, there are all sorts of people telling us what to do when really what we need is space to work out who to be."

ELLIOT PAGE

Content Warning: *I will be referencing suicide in the following bit. I won't give details, only mentioning its existence, but if this is a topic that harms or hurts you, feel free to skip these next few pages. You can pick back up at the note saying it's safe. Please remember, if you need help, help is available 24/7 at the 988 Suicide & Crisis Lifeline. Just dial 988 from any phone.*

FOR ALL THAT Texas has some bigoted ideas as to what should and shouldn't be taught, they pulled no punches in making the D.A.R.E. Program[1] a part of every classroom curriculum. Since I grew up in the 1980's, I remember when police officers visited elementary school classrooms to talk about drug use and its harmful effects. They talked about

---

1. D.A.R.E. or Drug Abuse Resistance Education is an education program intended to prevent drug use by K-12 students.

how to resist peer pressure as the program was created as part of the "War on Drugs" in the United States.

Even though it reached its peak in the 80's and 90's, Texas teachers are required to do one lesson from the program per semester. Topics to cover include everything from drug use and abuse, to violence and suicide. Most teachers resented the interruption to their regularly scheduled programs, but as a teacher who grew up with knowledge and experience in all four, I didn't mind taking the time to discuss complex issues with middle school students.

At this point in my career, I was teaching 6-8th grade computer classes at Rogers Middle School. Most of my classes were for high school credit, with the exception being my 6th grade Introduction to Computers class. This particular school was a Title I school, meaning that the majority of our students lived in high poverty, so most of our students were also familiar with abuse and violence.

During the 00s, there was a public service announcement called "It Gets Better," that focused on suicide prevention, particularly for members of the LGBTQ+ community. The idea behind it was that no matter what was going on in life, it was a moment that would pass and life would get better.

The PSA's were videos featuring a variety of celebrities speaking about their experiences with bullying or drugs, their thoughts of suicide, and how their lives changed as they became adults. Since this was an approved topic for the D.A.R.E. Program, I decided to show one of these videos to all of my classes and discuss how suicide is a very permanent solution to a temporary problem.

In my 7th and 8th grade classes, the lesson was a success. Students cried as they discussed their experiences, and our school counselors helped out if anyone needed a moment to talk to a professional. Suicide is a heady topic for any age, but our students were growing up with drug dealers, gang leader parents, and so much worse[2].

When it came time for my 6th graders, we adjusted the lesson a bit because the students were only eleven. While students at that age need to talk about intense topics too, you tend to approach it in a more age appropriate manner.

Despite this, one student, Becky, went home and told her mother that she was confused by the video we watched in my class. What confused her was that the video stated it was okay to be yourself, that being straight, gay, etc. was acceptable and living your true life wasn't wrong.

The video did say this—but it did so because it was expressing that being gay was no reason to kill oneself. LGBTQ+ youths are at much higher risk for suicide[i]—not because they're queer but because of how they are mistreated and stigmatized by society. In fact, LGBTQ+ youths are "more than four times as likely" to attempt suicide than their peers.

Because of the topic, I'd emailed home a link to the video beforehand so that any parent could watch it and either choose to talk with their child about it before or after, or they could opt out of watching it altogether if they felt it was too much. Rather than viewing, Becky's mom assumed the video wasn't about suicide but instead was teaching kids how to be gay. She immediately ran to my principal, Dr. Thomas, to complain about me indoctrinating students.

Dr. Thomas has a long history of homophobia and bigotry, which I'll get into more in other chapters, but let's just say that she agreed with the mom. Dr. Thomas called in both the counselor I worked with to develop the plan and me to a private meeting before we would meet with the parent. In this meeting, she watched the video and then asked the counselor why I was showing it to 6th graders.

---

2. One student I taught had a father high up in the Mexican Cartel. He only returned to the US when he learned his son had been misbehaving. In his words, you treat your teachers like you treat your abuela *(grandmother)*, with utmost respect. Nice man, but a scary man.

Her thoughts were that suicide was too complex a topic for middle school and should be left for high school students. If we were going to cover this topic, we should have found a video with a "less gay" celebrity to deliver the message[3]. Dr. Thomas chided the counselor and sent her on her way before inviting the parent into the meeting room.

"Please explain your concerns," Dr. Thomas asked Becky's mother.

"In my house, we believe in the one, true God, Christ Almighty, who says that lifestyles like homosexuality are a sin. Becky believed the word of God until she saw this video. It made her question God because it said it was 'okay to be gay.' My daughter wanted to know why Christ wanted gay people to kill themselves."

"That wasn't what the video was about." I tried to argue my point, but like many, this parent wouldn't hear it. We watched the video together in that meeting, and the mother's face grew redder with each word.

"How dare you show this to children! Aren't you a computer teacher? What does this have to do with computers?"

Rather than explain that all teachers were required once a semester to teach a D.A.R.E. lesson, Dr. Thomas left me to explain the purpose and requirement. "If you have an issue with this requirement, I would suggest you contact your state representatives as this is a state-wide requirement for all grades and all classes, elective or otherwise."

"I want a survey done."

I frowned at Becky's mom. "A survey? Of what?"

"I guarantee Becky wasn't the only confused kid. I bet many kids went home questioning their religious beliefs and

3. The video I showed featured Adam Lambert, who was very relevant at the time from his days on American Idol. Now he's known as the lead vocalist for Queen.

that many parents are upset. I'm just the only one brave enough to say it."

Nothing would change her mind, so the next day at school, my principal and I sent home a survey to all of my students' parents asking if they had watched the video or if they had any issues or concerns with the lesson itself. Then, we surveyed all of my students anonymously to ask:

1. What was the main idea of the video we watched?
2. Did they have any questions about the video or our discussion?
3. Were they confused at all about the topic of the video and/or discussion?

Surprise, surprise! Absolutely no students had any questions or confusions about the video or discussion...other than Becky. In fact, they not only understood the purpose, but they commented on how thankful they were for the opportunity to have an honest discussion about suicide. Being kids from poverty, almost all of them knew someone who'd died from it or at least attempted it.

Only 50% of parents returned the survey, but of those, not one had an issue with the video or discussion outside of Becky's mom. Some of them had watched the video beforehand and were happy to see that the school cared enough to engage in heavy topics.

In other words, the issue was Becky and her mother.

When we tallied up the results, the mother wanted access to everything the students and parents wrote, which was a major FERPA[4] violation. She was denied access to all the surveys, but Dr. Thomas did provide for her the statistical

---

4. FERPA is the Family Educational Rights & Privacy Act, which protects the privacy of students in terms of what information is released about them as minors.

data showing that only 0.006% of my students found the video confusing.

For me, I wanted to tell this mother to stuff that data up her ass. A good principal would have, of course in a more professional manner, but instead, Dr. Thomas told me that next semester, I should "stick to talking about drugs like everyone else."

I was told never to show or discuss any "It Gets Better" material in any classroom again, despite it being on the list of approved lessons provided by Texas's Department of Education[5].

Because we were required to submit each lesson and a variety of forms to our principal each time we did one of the D.A.R.E. lessons, there wasn't a way to circumvent her order. It was my first interaction with bigotry at this school and served as a reminder that hate often rules Texas with an iron fist.

If you were skipping the content discussing suicide, it's now safe to pick up reading at this point.

As a member of the queer community, having your existence declared a "lifestyle" is both insulting and traumatizing. I didn't choose to be queer any more than someone chooses to be born with green eyes or an extra finger. It's a part of me determined by a mix of hormones and cells like anything else. Being queer isn't new. It's existed since humanity first crawled out of the muck. Homosexual relationships occur across the animal kingdom, yet we don't pass laws regulating which animals can be together.

It amazes me what queer teachers suffer through, especially in red states. If I walk into the average classroom, most teachers have photos of their families proudly displayed on

---

5. At least it was approved at that time. With all the anti-LGBTQ+ laws being passed in Texas, I'm pretty sure it's been pulled at this point.

their desks. No one tells them to keep their marriage in the closet and remove their photos from the views of children. But if you're queer, goodness forbid you have a photo of *your* family on *your* desk.

"The students might see!"

"We can't advocate that lifestyle in school."

Being queer is synonymous with being dirty, with being… wrong. Which is odd considering that most members of the LGBTQ+ community are at *higher* risk[ii] of being victims, not perpetrators. In fact, 80% of rapes, assaults, and abuse[iii] is committed by cisgender[6] heterosexual men who are married and with their own children, not members of the queer community. Some argue that queer folks are pedophiles, but fewer than 1% of pedophiles[iv] identify as members of the LGBTQ+ community.

In other words, the rationale for why people like me need to "keep it in the closet" is hatred and fear based and nothing more.

I found it similar being a non-Christian teacher. My colleagues were allowed to openly wear crosses as symbols of their faith in the classroom. Under the First Amendment, so was I, but while I was a student teacher, I made the mistake of one day wearing an ankh to class. My necklace wasn't obtrusive as it was a small, hematite dangle barely visible with my sweater's neckline, but a student spotted it right away.

"Is that Satanic?" she asked.

I shook my head. "It's an ankh. In Egyptian mythology, it's considered the key of life and stands for life itself."

Being atheist doesn't mean that I don't appreciate symbology or have morals. I love the concept that having one life, we should live it to the best of our abilities and help everyone we can. But for this student, the idea that there are other beliefs out there was unacceptable. She told her mother,

---

6. Cisgender means folks who identify with the same gender they were assigned at birth.

who told other parents and so on until word reached my principal and my university.

I was told I could not wear any jewelry to class as it might be a distraction.

No other student teachers were given these rules. No other teachers had to hide their jewelry away, and I guarantee that had it been a cross, nothing would have been said or done against me. Every student teacher who taught at that school was hired by that school at year's end except for me.

In fact, the principal made it clear that he chose not to hire me because I was a "problem." He recommended I move to a "more liberal state" if I was going to be one of "those people" and still wanted to teach.

Welcome to the Bible Belt.

Having grown up in the church, my understanding of queerness comes from an idea that real love is not a sin. Christianity itself dictates that Christ is love, so how could it be? I'm not going to step on my soapbox on this as there are amazing ministers out there who've said all of this much more eloquently than I ever could, but I'm still amazed at the number of people who profess to follow love, yet so easily choose to ostracize others rather than demonstrate the core tenet of their beliefs.

Even worse when they are parents.

No one is born choosing their birth parents—we get who we get—but the number one task for a parent is to love their child(ren) for all that they are. Tossing your child out or cutting off contact with them for being themselves isn't love.

I will admit that in writing all of this down, I worry about my relationship with my father were he to read this. I know his viewpoints on homosexuality and gender. He made it very clear growing up that if I were ever to bring home a date who was a person of color or a woman, their faces would be introduced to a brick wall, and I would never see the light of day again.

As I'm typing this, my wife is beginning her transition

into who she has always been. As for me, I've been openly nonbinary for five years now. I don't bring it up in conversation with my father, but if he were to dig enough, it's out there. I'm not in the closet. But he doesn't know that my former husband is now my wife. It's not his business, so I've never spoken openly about it to him.

Will he disown me?

Will he make another sad attempt to "save me?"

Will he misgender and deadname my wife the way he does me?

Will he understand that love is love is love, or will this be the end of the shaky relationship we have?

Will he still love me?

I don't have the answers, which scares me if I'm honest. I'm fighting to rediscover my voice, and I won't allow him to silence my wife, let alone me. Without the answers, all I can do is write and hope that my struggles help someone else know they aren't alone.

And if you need a new family, a chosen family is just as good. Consider me your Auntie Raven or even your sibling, but most of all, know you are loved.

IF MY EARLY childhood taught me anything, it was that life isn't fair. Some of us are born of privilege, and contrary to popular belief, this doesn't mean we don't have struggles. It means that society works in such a way that is supporting of us, even when we're unaware of it. Being white, I didn't experience the inherent racism of being a person of color. I faced other adversities—especially being nonbinary, queer, neurodiverse, and disabled, but my skin color wasn't something I had to worry about.

But at seven years old, unfair was a word used to blame the world for all its sins. Why were we so poor? Because life is unfair. Why didn't I get the new toy I wanted? Because life is unfair. Why didn't my mother love me? Because life is unfair. Why did my father hit me?

Because life is *unfair*.

I was fortunate enough to have many friends in elementary school. Young me wasn't different enough to send them running home in fear, so I spent my weekends and summers staying with my friends as often as I could. For one, it was more fun than being alone, but also, it was safe.

It's odd to use that word—safe—because at seven, I was blissfully unaware that my home life wasn't normal. I thought every parent called their child stupid. I thought every kid got smacked in the face or had their fingers squeezed until they broke.

You can't stand up against what you don't know, but at seven, I understood that my friends' homes were calmer, quieter, and friendlier.

Most of my friends had two parents, and those who didn't, their parent seemed…different. When they grew angry, I didn't feel the urge to flinch or hide. My friends didn't bury their tears and thoughts. They shared with their parents in a way that spoke of a deeper relationship than I had with my parents.

I was never going to be "best friends" with my mother.

I was never going to be "Daddy's girl."

Life wasn't fair and thus, I didn't get to have those types of relationships. Jealousy screamed inside me as I yearned for what my friends had. It wasn't something I wanted; it was something I *needed*.

The phrase "life isn't fair" felt like an excuse and a copout. If we were able to make choices—be they right or wrong—choices that would guide our lives, what had I done at so young an age to bring this outcome upon me?

Questions haunted my childhood. I dreamed of parents who didn't yell at me because I didn't understand a math problem, of parents who could teach me how to style my hair or take me to get a manicure, and of parents who listened when I spoke, even if it was rambling garbage that fell from my tongue.

In our home, children were to be seen not heard. They were to be hit and often, otherwise they would be spoiled. Of course, that required a father who was home long enough for any of this to apply. During my younger years, between school and various jobs, he was rarely home, and if he was, he slept. Looking back, I see a father who was too young and too tired to be what I needed.

He tried. There are certainly memories I hold dear, those moments when I was given a glimpse of the relationship we might've had under different circumstances. The lost potential stings all the more, bitter reminders of what would never be.

If child me were standing in my office today, I think she'd be happy with what I've accomplished and built with my life. With the chosen family I've created from my wife and my friends, both of whom love me for all that I am. Here, I am safe. I am happy. I am loved.

Even knowing all that, there are days where I wonder why some of us don't get the type of parental relationships we deserve. As a teacher, I certainly encountered many students whose parents were beyond worse than mine, so I understand that even with my adversities, I have privilege. When you've made a dozen phone calls to Child Protective Services in the course of a year, it wears on you—the weight of what teachers do, and the bravery required to advocate for children.

It wasn't until high school that I found people who would advocate for me, so I understand the importance of being there for others. I've already written about the day I realized I needed to escape my home situation, but the escape wasn't a process that happened solitarily.

I met my first openly gay couple in high school as I hung out with the geeky goths and students labeled as 'freaks.' Constantly othered and bullied, we huddled together in a group we called family, and it was this family that helped me leave. Three friends, among them my wife, volunteered to help me escape.

When my father found out what I'd been planning, he moved us to a different city four hours away—still in Texas but far enough away from the people he saw as 'bad influences' to prevent me from leaving, or so he thought. But I grew up during the launch of public Internet. AOL was the top dog, and email the newest buzz word. It was through a mix of email and snail mail that we made our plans and over the holidays, while my father visited family, I stayed home and packed. One morning, my chosen family loaded up a moving van I'd rented and off we drove.

The growth I did during those years and the bravery I held when I left astounds current day me. So many victims never manage to leave their abusers, much less make a good life for themselves. The help I had was instrumental, but also, I think I'm made of stronger stuff.

Fighting to exist is hard work.

So when I think about child me and everything I went through to get to where I am, I want to give her a massive hug and tell her that cliche as it sounds, it does, indeed, get better.

CHAPTER
SIX
NOT THE TEACHER

> *No one can make you feel inferior without your consent."*

ELEANOR ROOSEVELT

WHILE I'M out as a nonbinary person now, when I was teaching, I was still publicly identifying as female. Mostly because this was Texas but also because I hadn't realized that being nonbinary was a gender identity. At the time, I believed gender to be binary, despite science proving otherwise. Gender is a mix of chromosomes, anatomy, hormones, psychology, and culture. It's not simple and it's not binary[i]. I could write an entire book on this topic alone, but instead, I'll leave the source in the footnotes. It's a great article that talks about intersex people and why gender isn't as simple as male/female.

My first day at Rogers Middle School where I was teaching computer classes was an interesting lesson on misogyny and how rampant it is even outside of tech. Because I was a late hire, I missed most of the summer's professional development. I hadn't met the other technology teacher at my school or the other computer teachers across the district. While my classes were the computer software, programming, and business side of computing, my colleague at Rogers taught classes that were more a mix of shop and robotics with a little 3D printing mixed in. As someone who helped run the robotics program at the school where I student taught, I figured I would get along great with this new colleague.

I was sitting at my desk in my computer lab prepping for my first day at this school when an older, robust man strode in with complete authority. No knock. Just swung open the lab door and trounced in like he owned the place, which immediately set me on edge. He glanced around at the posters I'd hung up and the various supplies I'd unpacked before finally turning towards me.

"Oh. I'm sorry, I was looking for someone else," he said with a frown. "I guess Mr. Oak is absent today, but I'm Mr. Milt. I've never seen you sub here before but if you run into any trouble, my extension is 1234. I can be down here to help any time."

I stared at him. When I didn't immediately respond, his frown grew deeper.

"Hello, Mr. Milt. I'm Mrs. Oak, the computer teacher." I could almost see the wheels turning in his head. "Are you the other technology teacher?"

He nodded.

"Great. Since I'm not a sub, I think today will run just fine, but I'll let you know if I need anything."

Finally, he spoke again. "You're a woman."

"I am."

If he'd frowned any harder, his wrinkles would have popped.

"I was expecting…well…"

"A man?"

"Yeah."

"Sorry to disappoint, but if it helps, I have a Masters in computers so I promise I know what I'm doing."

At this, he turned and slunk out of my lab with a baffled expression on his face. This guy couldn't believe I was female. The idea of a woman teaching computers rocked his world so much, it might as well have been California's "Big One." You'd think I'd grown horns and turned bits and bytes into water.

Several other teachers—all men—made similar mistakes. It doesn't help that most autistic people have young faces. Even at thirty, my face convinced people I was barely legal as I was often carded for R-rated movies and on the rare occasions I purchased alcohol. Despite this, the assumption that only men could work in tech is such bullshit, and I expected better from my fellow educators.

Teaching is predominately a female-centric field, much like nursing, though high schools are a tad more balanced. While technology is a male-centric field, it would've been simple to ask me if I were Mrs. Oak, the new computer teacher, especially since the school website and the sign outside my class both stated I was a Mrs.

You know what they say about assumptions…

That's not to say that Mr. Milt and I didn't get along. He spent the next week apologizing every time he saw me as he realized what an ass he'd been. We worked well together and often planned ways to incorporate each other's lessons into our own classes in small ways. He was one of the few folks at Rogers Middle School that I considered a friend and one of those who respected my work and intelligence, once he realized its existence. I suspect he was a tad neurodivergent himself so that helped us understand each other's idiosyncrasies a bit better.

Our first district-wide professional development for all technology teachers was a sausage fest to put it bluntly. I expected it, and again, too many teachers assumed I was in the wrong area. When I asked what room we were meeting in, district staff tried to send me everywhere *but* to the tech group.

97

The number of teachers who refused to believe I could possibly have an advanced degree in computers was unreal. As this was the 00's, I worked hard to use my classroom website and implement emerging tech into my classroom. Often, this caused my principal to question whether what I was doing was "safe" as she would contact district higher-ups to confer about technology's uses.

I'd be dragged before a board comprised of men who'd drill me on what I was doing and why, but also how I planned to keep students safe on the Internet. They treated me like I was an oblivious old educator who didn't know how email worked, and when I explained to them in technical jargon the ins and outs of my lessons, I became a different kind of target.

A threat.

They didn't understand what I was saying. The idea that I knew more than they did frightened them, and they banned or blocked me from using simple tech that now is standard in every school across the United States.

I was ahead of my time as a computer teacher, but I suspect that had I been a man, they wouldn't have questioned a damned thing. I'd have taught the way I was meant to and carried on without issue. As more video gamers realize that women have been a part of video games forever, perhaps more folks in the tech industry will realize women have also been in computers forever. After all, it was a group of women who put men on the moon[1].

I suspect Ada Lovelace[2] would also like a word.

---

1. This topic is what the book and movie *Hidden Figures* was about (great movie by the way). If you want to learn more, look up Katherine Johnson, Dorothy Vaughan, and Mary Jackson, all female engineers that worked at NASA.
2. Augusta Ada King, Countess of Lovelace, was both a mathematician and a writer. She's most known for her work on Charles Babbage's general purpose computer, the Analytical Engine back in 1837 and is considered the "mother of modern computers."

HEY, did you see that car yesterday at—SQUIRREL!

If you're neurodivergent like me, you probably got that joke. If you're neurotypical, aka normal, you might not have. My brain doesn't function "normally," or in the same way that most people's brains work. Besides having ADHD[3], I'm also autistic and have panic/anxiety disorder, which is to say that my brain is very, very unusual. My calendars have calendars, and my lists have lists, which have lists. If you walk through my home, lists lay everywhere, as frequent as tissue boxes and cat toys. To the casual observer, my home looks cluttered, but for me, it's necessary. If I can't see something, it doesn't exist. It's a lack object permanence that can result in my buying another loaf of bread because I've forgotten we have one tucked in the cupboard. Everything has a home, but those homes are out in the open rather than hidden.

If I'm juggling a train of thought and something or someone diverts me, the thought unravels and I lose both what I was doing and what the interruption was. When I lie down to sleep, my mind hops from thought to thought as it problem solves what it perceives as problems, even when they're not. There is no need to solve the angle of a character's arm in my recent artwork at 4 A.M., and I certainly *can't* solve world hunger then either. If I try and push it aside, it invades my dreams as my mind tries to work through whatever has its attention when I drift off.

I see a T-Rex on my desk[4], which reminds me of the last time I watched *Jurassic Park* and the term veggie-saurus, which makes me think about how food manufacturers are creating better vegetarian options these days than they did

---

3. Attention-Deficit / Hyperactivity Disorder or ADHD is disorder that causes difficulty with focusing or paying attention, controlling impulsive behaviors, and can be overly active of mind and/or body.
4. It's a pen holder.

when I began teaching. But rather than those thoughts following that logical trail aloud, I'll look at my wife and say, "This T-Rex...there are better options these days."

In my brain, the logic is sound but to the world around me, I speak in tongues. Gibberish. While it comes across less often when I'm writing, it does happen as my editors have been known to leave notes trying desperately to decipher my train of thought and utterly failing.

Being neurodivergent has caused no end of stress and chaos throughout my teaching career. When we're in school to learn how to be a teacher, we're taught what to do if we suspect a student of having some undiagnosed learning struggle. We're also taught how to teach in a variety of ways in order to reach all learners, including those with neurodivergences, so we'd understand when we spot it in our colleagues. If anything, it's the exact opposite. They love you until they don't.

I'm only tolerated while I'm useful.

For example, I usually end up as the default notetaker during school meetings because I have an auditory memory. In the way that some people can look at a book page and see it word for word in their minds[5], I can do something similar with conversations. If listening to a lecture, I can recall what was said word for word for about ten minutes, sometimes longer. That means that when I take notes, I can rewind and fast-forward as needed to ensure that I dictate what was said word for word, and I don't need to use shorthand to do it.

This is helpful as I'm not the only neurodivergent teacher out there. Some people struggle to take notes or remember what words were spoken a second ago. Because I was already taking notes for myself and my ADHD brain, my principal at Rogers Middle School asked if I'd be willing to share these

---

5. This is called a photographic memory or eidetic memory. Mozart, Nicolas Tesla, and Leonardo da Vinci are said to have had it. Lucky them! According to Psychology Today, only 2% of people have this.

notes with any colleagues who miss the meetings. I love being helpful, so I was willing and able!

When others saw how detailed my notes were, word got around and before too long, everyone wanted copies of my notes. Dr. Thomas, my principal, okayed me to share the notes via email to everyone on staff. The plus side to this is that few people forgot anything important as they had a nice set of notes to remind them. The downside to this, as I learned the hard way, is that no one in administration wants notes that are word for word what was said during a school meeting.

At first, my actions were helpful. A teacher asked a question that didn't portray our school in the best light, which made it into the notes, and now, I was a problem.

Again.

I don't know how the laws work in other states but in Texas, any documents created at school are a matter of public record, the exceptions being student records, which are covered by HIPAA[6] and FERPA. At any time, a parent could submit a request to see my grade book, my lesson plans, and any emails I sent using the school's server. Any private information covered by FERPA and/or HIPAA would be marked out, but otherwise, they could openly read our emails because we were public servants and everything we did and said was a matter of public record[7].

In emailing out copies of our meeting notes, they became a matter of public record, including the inappropriate question asked by my colleague.

At this point, Dr. Thomas asked me to send my notes to her first so she could "edit" them to ensure nothing inappropriate was emailed to everyone else. Of course, by emailing

---

6. FERPA covers most student records, but anything medical gets covered by HIPAA, the Health Insurance Portability & Accountability Act.

7. Note: I am not a lawyer. This is just how it was explained to me during teacher trainings.

her, they were still public record. Oops! She wasn't very tech savvy so this thought didn't occur to her.

If it was inappropriate, why'd I add it to the notes to begin with?

Part of being neurodiverse, or neurospicy as some folks call it, is that I don't always understand what's appropriate. I don't always read tone well or catch whether something was said in jest or in all seriousness. First and foremost, I'm typing these notes for me. Reading back what was said—including the unnecessary bits—helps my auditory recall. I can then replay the meeting in my head like a TV show, which helps me catch the nuances and tones that I might have missed the first time.

It's a survival skill built up over my life to fit in better, but it's also an accommodation.

Being me, I know that I can be overly blunt. I try hard not to be, but my brain doesn't have some of the same filters that normal brains do. I tend to think and operate from logic and less from emotion, but once emotions get involved, they're intense. If something doesn't logically make sense, I tend to slam against it in order to force it into my brain's file system, so to speak. This is fairly common for autistic people.

This also means that it's easy for others to misunderstand what I've said and why I've said it. I can tell a friend that I "hate her sweater," in a joking manner as we both joke about Ugly Sweater Day and if she's not someone who knows me well or knows I'm autistic, my words cut rather than being a joke. Conversations are logic puzzles for me.

When I have a meeting with any supervisor or person of power, I take notes. I also email a meeting summary to the people in question so I can ensure I understood everything correctly *(and didn't misread the tone)* and that I was understood by everyone else as well. Some people like this style while others find it a trap. Such was the case of my administrators at Rogers Middle School.

The admin team at my second school were not good

people. Some teachers become principals to help, but some do it for the power. Some never left high school bullying behind and use their position to create their own little fiefdoms[8].

In our school, like many businesses and schools, we had a catch-all email set up for ease of use. We could send email to one address and that email was sent to everyone who worked in our building—from teachers and admin down to the janitors and lunch ladies. Some schools used this to share humor, as teaching is rough job, and our school was one of them. Problem was, the rules on using this All-Staff email address varied by who you knew and how "in" you were with the bosses.

During my first year at Rogers, a 6th grade English teacher shared a joke about autocorrect with All-Staff. It got a laugh out of Dr. Thomas and a few staff members. This type of email usage happened maybe twice a week, so fairly often. In March, I decided to share a funny newspaper article about technology. I don't remember the details of the article, only that another techie in the district had shared it with me. It was funny, so why not share?

Almost immediately, Dr. Thomas emailed me to state that All-Staff was to be used for important and approved information for our school because not everyone "had the time to sit around and find funny things to share." The implication that as a computer teacher, all I did was sit around and surf the net was not only insulting, it was wrong.

This is where my neurodiversity screws things up.

What she said didn't logically make sense. No other teachers had to get permission to share their funnies—I know because I asked them—but I did? Why? If the catch-all email address was to be used for important messages only, why were other teachers using it to share humor? So doing what I

---

8. A fiefdom was a domain controlled by a feudal lord during medieval times.

do best, I turned around and asked her. Via email of course. With attachments of other teachers for an example.

Her response? "Because I said so."

If you know anything about neurodivergent people, you know how much we *hate* that phrase. It makes no logical sense and places us in a position of either doing what's fair or breaking logic to people please, the latter being something we suck at. I'm also a gifted person with a super-high IQ, so the ethical quandary of doing something nonsensical "just because" is bonkers to me.

I followed her rule for that first year and once my contract was renewed, I tried pushing the boundary a second time to the same outcome.

Asking around, several colleagues mentioned that Dr. Thomas had her own clique at Rogers. If you weren't in it, the rules for you were different. You didn't get invited to participate in potlucks or holiday parties—well, you did, but you weren't expected to show up.

Unlike East Valley, Rogers lacked a proper teacher's lounge. We had a small room barely large enough for a copy machine and our teacher in-boxes. With no room, no one ate in any lounge together. Most ate lunch alone at their desks or with colleagues in various classrooms. Core subject teachers shared planning periods together, but as an elective teacher, my schedule never meshed with theirs. No one invited me to join them for lunch. Whether it was because of our schedules or because they chose not to, I can't say for sure, but many of the teachers felt I was too much.

I was extra.

Seeing the inequality of rules at Rogers, I spent any down time I had deciphering these new, unspoken rules. Hard enough to do if you're neurotypical. Near impossible to do if you're neurodivergent.

I was constantly stepping in dog shit so to speak and sticking my dirty foot in my mouth. No matter what I said, I pissed off somebody in admin, be it my boss, Dr. Thomas, or her vice principal, Mr. Smidt.

Mr. Smidt was a special kind of hell for me because he was the type of man who only respected other men, or women who fell in line. He particularly didn't like that I was a writer. Words are my power and when I had questions, I used those words to keep myself safe. If I couldn't get the necessary support from parents or admin to deal with a problem student, my emails were detailed for everyone's protection. Again, I didn't want any misunderstandings and I certainly didn't want to miss an important detail. Ending up with another situation like Coach Rage, or worse, a parent like Josh's in my new school district, was something I fought to avoid.

One year, a student of mine hacked into the district's gradebook. He didn't change any grades as he had only done it for bragging rights. Of course, he was a colleague's child which made the situation sticky. When I reported my evidence of this to the appropriate people, the student was punished by having his computer access revoked for six weeks. In an email sent to my boss and the district's technology liaison, I pointed out that by hacking into the gradebook, this student had exposed all of my students' private information. That under FERPA, we were required to notify parents of this data breach. Measures needed to be taken to ensure this couldn't happen again.

While the district was already working on the second part, Dr. Thomas was none-to-happy about my mentioning parents and the school's liability. She didn't want to notify the parents —it's a lot of work and "gives them information they didn't need." In other words, by alerting them to what had happened, they could sue the district if they chose to do so. If she hid what had happened, the district could fix the problem with no one the wiser. By emailing what I had, which was now a matter of public record, she couldn't hide the event anymore.

I'd forced her to do the right thing.

The first time this happened, she chastised me. The second time, she threatened to write me up for insubordination. The third time, I got that write up in my file.

Honestly, I wasn't doing this to spite her or make life harder. I was trying to cover my own ass while ensuring the right and fair option was taken. I'm a rule follower by nature...until I'm not.

During my third year at Rogers Middle School, doctors discovered that my spinal issues were worsening and I'd need to have two major surgeries in an attempt to delay further degradation. The recovery would be lengthy, during which I wouldn't be able to stand more than thirty seconds at a time. Standing and walking are major components of a teacher's career, and once I knew the details, I typed up the details for my bosses.

I explained what was happening, what dates I would be out, and when I returned, what accommodations I'd need. One of those accommodations meant that I couldn't perform lunch duty. Since elective teachers taught subjects not subject to testing by the state, we were given fewer classes in order to cover various duties across the building such as lunch duty.

During a time we could have been educating students, we were tasked with walking around the cafeteria to ensure no fights broke out.

Glorified babysitters.

Because my logic had pissed off my principal one too many times, my duty had recently shifted from general lunch duty to lunch detention. That's right, I didn't get to walk around chatting with kids. My job was to monitor kids serving detention. They'd line up silently in the hall, and once all the other students had received their lunch, I'd escort my group through the noisy cafeteria to get their lunches. Food acquired, I'd escort them back to the hallway where they were forced to sit on the floor and eat in silence during what little time remained. No one wanted to be there, let alone me as lunch detention was humiliating and miserable for all involved.

Post-op, I'd need to sit and elevate my feet, which didn't sound possible outside of my classroom. My doctor agreed, which is why I emailed my bosses to find a solution. An easy option would have been for Mr. Smidt, the vice principal, to cover lunch detention. It was more fitting to his job description than mine and would give him an opportunity to bond more with the students most at-risk.

But doing so meant he didn't get to enjoy lunch with the rest of the administration staff—the nice hour long lunches they enjoyed behind closed doors while teachers scarfed their food down in twenty minutes, if that. I understand that administrators have a rough job, at least if they're doing it right, but filling in where they're needed is a part of it. At Rogers, if a duty or job could be shoved off on a teacher or staff member, it would be. When teachers wrote referrals, more times than not, students were right back in the classroom causing issues within the hour. In my teaching career, I worked with five sets of admins and these folks were the laziest and most useless by far.

I don't say that lightly either. Their "solution" to my surgery and accommodation needs was to have me do lunch duty anyway—just sitting down in the most uncomfortable chair possible. We're talking the hard plastic stackable chairs used in most school cafeterias. When I stated that I wouldn't be able to walk the students down to get their lunches, stand in line with them, and escort them back—you know, due to all the walking and standing, they said I could send the students alone.

With no one to watch them. Brilliant idea there.

When these students escorted themselves, they acted like typical middle school students. Rather than silence, they chatted, joked, tossed food at others, and generally made a nuisance of themselves because *they could*. Other elective teachers and staff members in the cafeteria complained and rightfully so.

Did the admin involve themselves at this point?

Of course not. In fact, they called me down to a meeting to complain that I wasn't doing my job. I asked them how I was supposed to sit in a chair in the hallway, *and* walk students to and from lunch when I was under doctor's orders to limit all walking and standing?

The answer? I needed to stop making things "difficult" for them.

In other words, all of their troubles were my fault. How dare I have a birth defect in my spine requiring so many surgeries? How dare I need help? They thought I enjoyed being disabled, that I chose to be this way in order to be a pain in their ass.

Because they both seemed unable to recognize disability and accommodations, I typed up a detailed email reiterating my doctor's orders as well as information about my disability and what types of accommodations could be made. I gave input into ways to ensure lunch detention moved smoothly and safely for all involved. I wanted everything in writing because if they didn't work with me, I'd be filing a complaint for their failure to follow the ADA[9].

Mr. Smidt replied first, from his home computer as it was after school hours. He hadn't intended me to see his reply, but in his frustration or hurry, he clicked the REPLY-ALL button, so his private message meant for Dr. Thomas's eyes only was also sent to me.

Why does she always have to write a damned novel? Can she not just get to the point with anything? Is this a woman thing?

---

9. Americans with Disabilities Act of 1990 is a civil rights law that prohibits discrimination based on disability. It's also requires employers to provide reasonable accommodations for employees with disabilities.

Yep. My detailed email, detailed in order to guarantee I received accommodations I was legally entitled to, accommodations he was refusing to provide, sent this little man into a tizzy. In his mind, I was the problem because I was a woman.

My first move was to share the email with my wife.

"I'm not overreacting here, right? You see what he said?" I asked.

"Uh, no. That's…that's sexual harassment."

My second step was to call my teacher organization. In Texas, we aren't allowed to have teacher unions. It's not legal. Our teacher organizations are fairly useless but one perk they provide is access to attorneys. After reading the email, my new attorney called me that Saturday.

"You can ask for an apology but that's about it. You could do more, but how many bridges do you want to burn here?"

If I decided to sue, I'd be blackballed by every school district in the state and could potentially lose my teaching license. It was unlikely we'd ever make it to court because the district would settle. Even then, without proving damage had been done, there was little worth suing over.

While not exactly correct, these folks had no teeth so I figured the attorney thought he was doing me a solid.

I decided to reply to the email myself since my attorney was fairly useless. My reply said:

"I'm pretty sure you didn't intend for me to see this email. It was probably meant for Dr. Thomas only, but you hit the reply-all button. Darned email, right? Either way, this was not an appropriate response and my teacher organization and attorney have now seen this email."

Come Monday morning, I had a response from Dr.

Thomas asking me to report to her office the moment I arrived at school.

Mr. Smidt was waiting in her office, his face beet red, and when I arrived, he refused to meet my gaze. I took a seat across from Dr. Thomas and waited. At first, no one spoke.

"Raven, I just want to tell you how sorry I am that you saw that email. I've spoken at length with Mr. Smidt about how the reply buttons work to ensure that this doesn't happen again," said Dr. Thomas.

That's right—the apology wasn't for *what* was said but for the fact I saw it at all.

Mr. Smidt kept his eyes on the door behind me and pretended not to see me. "I'm sorry for my role in this."

"I just want to state that I wrote a detailed email because I wasn't receiving the accommodations I need in order to do my job. It wasn't because of my gender or because I'm a writer."

Dr. Thomas nodded. "I understand but in the future, please keep all emails limited to 1-2 sentences."

She waved a hand to dismiss us both. If I could have raged down the hallway, I would have. There is no way a teacher can do their job and limit all email lengths like that. Documentation on students' behaviors and grades alone are longer than a sentence or two. I was being punished for keeping detailed documentation, plain and simple.

Nothing was done to change or fix my accommodations so I took them as I needed to, and if the students misbehaved, so be it. It wasn't my problem anymore. When colleagues complained, I told them to take it up with the boss. Rather than do so, my colleagues decided I was a pain in the ass.

The ostracization had begun once again.

I could have done something. I should have done something. But fear rooted me in place and yet again, I allowed my administrators to walk all over me.

The first rule of teaching: clone thyself.

The second rule: learn teleportation. The earlier, the better.

The third rule: trust no one.

THESE ARE the rules I learned at Rogers Middle School. I'm not sure why this is an expectation, only that it is one and failure to comply means uncomfortable meetings, notes in employment files, and sometimes contract non-renewal.

My computer lab held thirty-five computers. Rather than leave one or two open in case of computer failure[10], my classes were often packed with a student on every computer. That means thirty-five students in one room. It doesn't sound like a lot until it is. Sometimes, I'd begin a semester with forty students. When I asked how I was supposed to work with more students then computers, admin waved their hands dismissively until I went away. The schedule would be fixed a few weeks in but by then, the students who remained were behind due to the never-ending game of musical chairs we played.

Since I taught six classes, math says I had 210 students in one semester. While one of my classes was a year long, the others rotated at the semester break, so throughout the year I taught closer to 385 students.

In a typical classroom, I might have had anywhere from five to ten students needing specialized instruction or accommodations. Most of the time, they didn't come with an aide as their learning disabilities weren't profound enough for that, so I was expected to help my computer gifted students who finished work early to further enhance their education, help any students with general questions that arose during work

---

10. Which happened more often than not.

time, and provide one-on-one help to those struggling students needing accommodations.

Any teacher will tell you that it's not possible.

We all do our best but students can and do fall through the cracks. To make matters more challenging, computer work comes with risks that aren't a part of the general subject classroom—or at least they weren't before COVID[11]. When I was in the computer lab, I could keep an eye on what each student was doing.

The computers in my lab were laid out in a U-shape, meaning I could always see their screens. Also, we used a computer program that displayed each desktop's monitor on my computer, so even while taking attendance, I could see what they were doing. This helped keep them on-task, but it also helped catch those students who wanted to watch YouTube or play a video game rather than working on an assignment.

In a good school, the administration will roam the halls in between classes to help keep kids moving towards class and out of trouble. It's often how to prevent kids from vaping in school bathrooms *(which is a huge problem now)* and fighting in the hallways. Walk through a school and you'll see teachers straddling their doorway, one eye on the hall and the other, watching the students inside their classroom.

In many schools, hallways aren't wide enough for students to line up and wait to enter a classroom or if they are, lockers get in the way, so most teachers allow students access to their room from the moment the students arrive. If it's a particularly difficult class, administration being in the hall means a teacher doesn't have to keep one foot in both

---

11. With online schooling during lockdown and most schools providing laptops to all students, this has shifted. At the time I was teaching, the only times students had access to computers were in the computer lab or via phones, which were not allowed in class. This was also before TikTok and students being glued to their phones 24/7 so again, some of this has changed.

worlds. They can stay inside the room to keep an eye on the kids before class begins.

But in a school like Rogers Middle School, where our admin were rarely anywhere but their offices, teachers were "required to be in outside in hallway between classes." No door straddling here. Failure to serve this duty meant marks against the annual evaluation, which could lead to all manner of disciplinary actions.

As a computer teacher, being in the hall meant I left myself liable to lawsuits and criminal charges. If I were outside my classroom, I couldn't see students computer monitors. It didn't matter if I asked them not to log in to the computer until class began. If they chose to break that rule, how would I know?

I brought up this concern the first time I received a mark for not standing outside my computer lab in between classes, and I was told that my priority was to the students in the hallway first. If I had "good classroom management," students wouldn't do anything wrong when not being watched. Oh, the irony…

At this point in my career, I'd been a teacher for seven years. My classroom management was spot on, but none of that mattered if I wasn't in the classroom. During the first quarter, I stood in the hallway while a student logged on in my lab. He pulled up YouTube and found porn that wasn't blocked by our safety programs.

Several students huddled around the screen to watch. By the time I entered the classroom, everyone had settled back at their desks. It wasn't a mystery as to when I'd be back as our passing periods used bells. Bell rings, close the video, log off, and people scatter.

The first time this occurred, I had no idea. I was in the hallway. Word reached me when I was called into a meeting with both school and district administration. Apparently, several kids in the class had reported to their parents that porn was being watched in my classroom. Because of the

Internet tools deployed by the district, they were able to track the user and video being watched, confirming the who, what, when, and where.

"Where were you when this took place?" That was the first question asked by the district's technology staff.

"I was in the hallway."

"Why weren't you in the classroom?"

At this question, Dr. Thomas shifted in her chair and glared at me. I ignored the look and answered honestly, "My principal requires all teachers to be in the hallway between classes."

Technology staff drilled into my boss about why I was needed in a hallway with ten other teachers. Why couldn't they monitor the students while I watched the computer lab with $100,000 worth of tech?

District staff brought up the same concerns I'd voiced at the beginning of the school year. Watching Dr. Thomas try and explain herself was entertaining.

Students' ability to sideline blocked sites was always going to be a possibility. No "online protection" program is perfect. My being in the hallway had allowed students to circumvent safety measures, opening up the district up to lawsuits by parents whose children were exposed to pornographic material. Access to such material broke several federal laws and opened the door for the parents to also sue me because I didn't stop it.

It didn't matter that I couldn't.

The district made it clear to Dr. Thomas that I couldn't be in two places at once so a work-around would have to happen.

At first, I was told that my students would have to line up outside my door until the tardy bell rang. Then they could enter the room with me and thus, be supervised. While our district wasn't poor, our network connection was. Logging in could take anywhere from 1-6 minutes depending upon how many students were attempting this at the same time. Standing outside in the hallway led to lost instructional time.

I pointed this out and when my boss shrugged, I brought it up to the district's head of technology. By going over my boss's head, I got slapped with a count of insubordination in my file, despite my explanation that district policy made the head of technology my boss as well. In district training, I'd been told to go to them with issues that couldn't be solved at the campus level[12].

The district explained to my boss that no other computer teachers were losing class time due to what amounted to "poor campus management," and since my classes were high school classes, I had to follow high school policies.

I no longer had to stand in the hallway, nor did my students.

Dr. Thomas about popped a brain cell. Her school having poor campus management? She steamed.

In private, she whispered to me, "This isn't over. If you go over my head again, you'll be out of this district so fast that your head will spin."

Being my first year in the district, it wasn't great that my boss wanted me gone.

By my second year, the former technology head had retired. As soon as news reached our school, Dr. Thomas's rules were back. I would be in the hallway between classes no matter what. Two weeks into school, I emailed her to ask why the band instructors and gym coaches weren't required to be in the hallways between class.

"Too many liabilities and expensive equipment," she said.

I asked one of the campus technicians tasked with keeping our machines running about this in person and was told to "let it go." It was a battle I'd "never win." When I reiterated my concern about being sued or potentially jailed when shit hit the fan, I received a shrug. The district knew of the issue,

---

12. Gotta love school politics!

115

but my boss had friends in high places, namely, the superintendent. Their families vacationed together, and nothing I said was going to change problematic policies as long as Dr. Thomas was the principal.

That night, when I arrived home, I dropped a lot of f-bombs. How was I going to do my job and keep my students safe when my bosses were dead set against my doing so?

During the second semester, a fight broke out in my lab. Because of noisy students slamming shut their lockers, I couldn't hear the fight from my place in the hallway. Middle schoolers like a good fight, so there was a delay between its start and when a student made it out to tell me about it. By that time, a computer monitor was smashed and two students were bleeding. A rival gang member had spoken ill of someone and before anyone could blink, fists were flying. Both students were suspended for a week, but the damage was done. Students didn't feel safe in my classroom without an adult in the room.

Parents complained and when met with silence from Dr. Thomas, they elevated their concerns to school board meetings. The district met with Dr. Thomas privately and afterward, I was told to stay in my classroom as the other teachers could handle any hallway disruptions.

As teachers, we weren't allowed to get between fighting students, so I privately questioned the idea of us "handling" hallway disruptions to begin with. If a student was loitering, sure, we could shoo them towards class, but most of what they wanted us to watch for were events we could do nothing about. Events that needed our administrators.

Where were they?

After the dust settled, we were told at the next faculty meeting that all teachers would be in the hallways again, including *all* elective teachers and coaches. While I had little to do with this change, my colleagues blamed me for it, especially the first time a band instrument went missing and a locker room fight broke out.

Frustrated by what parents saw as a lack of supervision, they complained again and rightly so. Our policy regarding hallways changed yet again. Coaches were to rotate the watch with one in the locker room while the other watched the halls. Same with the band instructors seeing as there were two of them. For teachers like me, we were told to hover in the doorway and watch both. Again, this ignored the fact that I couldn't see all of the computers from the doorway.

Another porn site was pulled up and another excuse made as to why I was needed in the hallway.

Before events could escalate, the birth defect in my spine rendered me unable to stand for the five minute passing period. Reluctantly, I was excused from being in the hall and my lab returned to being a safe space.

Despite my medical issues being valid and backed up by a team of doctors, every time my annual evaluation rolled around, I was dinged for not being in the hallway and for not standing enough during class.

I wonder if I'd been wheelchair bound if they would've made those same determinations? People forget that not every disability is visible, yet they still exist.

Something tells me that Dr. Thomas would've been petty enough not to hire someone disabled in the first place, including me, had she known.

CHAPTER
SEVEN
THAT'S SO GAY

I am no longer accepting the things I cannot change. I am changing the things I cannot accept."

ANGELA DAVIS

DURING MY TIME at Rogers Middle School, I served as the dreaded Yearbook Advisor. I say dreaded because it's usually a job no one wants. Lots of hours for a tiny stipend. I was in charge of the yearbook at my previous school and with my background in graphic design[1] and art, I can genuinely say it's a task I loved. Yearbook was an extension of my artistic self and allowed me to share that with my students.

At East Valley, my yearbook crew was highly motivated and could be trusted with expensive camera equipment. Yearbook was a club that met after school, so they chose to be there. At Rogers, yearbook was a class with attached state learning standards. This excited me! An actual class? That excitement lasted until the first day when it became obvious yearbook was used as a dumping ground for problem kids

---

1. Odd fact: I completed my first paid graphic design job at the age of fourteen for a large hospital needing a new logo. Go me!

with no interests in any electives. Some well-meaning counselor hoped that yearbook might help these students connect with their school. Maybe encourage them to take pride in it and with that, they might improve their behavior.

Allow me to laugh. Loudly.

This tactic works for some, but as a whole, it doesn't do anything other than frustrate all involved. Within the first quarter, one camera was stolen and two more broken. Most of the students refused to complete classwork, let alone homework, which led to a sit down between the school counselors and my principal. During this meeting, I laid out the realities of yearbook production—the hard work and long hours involved in creating such a book and how I needed students who wanted to be in the class.

I have no trouble teaching kids labeled as "troubled teens" but yearbook wasn't the appropriate class for it, not when students needed to be able and willing to attend school events before and after hours in order to take photos.

The administration chose not to listen to me that year. "Try and help them improve," was what they said and try I did. That yearbook was entirely made by me as what few photos they took were only of their friends or themselves flashing gang signs.

Having survived my first year at Rogers, year two of yearbook looked drastically different. Students now recognized me. Many had taken my computer classes and learned that yearbook was a possible elective. When it came time for students to choose their classes for the next school year, the counselors found an entire crowd of students clamoring to join yearbook.

No more room at the inn as a dumping ground.

Parents commented on how much better the yearbook was with me in charge. Prior years' books were quite amateur, but with students interested in learning, I taught them solid design skills. They created over ¾ of the book themselves and it looked amazing. It goes to show that motivated, educated students who want to do something, can and will. Most people thought I did the entire book myself, but I was proud to say that I didn't.

At both campuses, pages submitted to the yearbook company for printing had to be approved by school administration. This was especially true at Rogers as kids would throw gang signs and other hand gestures into photos. Sometimes it was something I could edit out in Photoshop, but occasionally, Dr. Thomas would ask me to substitute a different photo.

The first three years of creating yearbooks, she and I butted heads about who to include. From my point of view, I wanted to include all students as I believed in equality, but she often asked me to pull photos of our "behavior problem" students. She felt they didn't deserve to be in the yearbook.

It's ironic considering my first yearbook crew at her school. Dr. Thomas wanted behavior problem kids on the yearbook staff so that they might develop school pride and thus, behave better, but when it came to including them in the book, nope. Take them out.

I don't think she understood how to work with at-risk teens at all.

In fact, if a kid attended our school for the first semester but transferred to the alternative school due to behavior problems, all evidence of their attendance was removed from the yearbook as if they'd never set foot inside our doors. Parents and students alike hated this and complained often. If a student moved, they missed their friends and wanted those memories included. Perfectly logical, but my hands were tied. I could follow her orders or lose yearbook completely.

One year, our football team was smashing the competition. I'm not a sports person, but I guess we were heading towards some sort of championships. One game in particular would determine this, so I attended to ensure we got some amazing shots[2].

We won the game and afterwards, lots of the players were doing the typical "we won" camaraderie of body slamming, high-fiving, etc. Two players, both students of mine, wanted to pose for a picture, and when I agreed, they tossed their arms over each other's shoulders and smiled for the camera. It was a great shot of two Latinos, sweaty and happy with their win.

The photo came out perfectly, so my crew and I placed it front and center on the yearbook's title page collage. This particular spread featured sporting events from the first half of the school year, a year full of wins for us. Because of how the book printing industry works, especially the world of yearbook printing, the first half of a yearbook is submitted fairly early. In our neck of the woods, our deadline was January. The last half was due in April, and the printed books would arrive towards the end of May[3].

This meant sitting down with administrators before the holidays to discuss the pages. In November, we gathered in my computer lab around a large table full of page proofs or printouts of what the pages would look like inside the book. My bosses and the school counselors spotted a few pics we needed to change out due to the usual issues, but otherwise, the admin were happy with the book. Then Dr. Thomas picked up the title page and stared at it.

"Is something wrong?" I asked.

"You need to remove this photo." She frowned and pointed at the photo of the two football players posing after the game.

"Oh. Both of them are good kiddos. What's up with it?"

Without hesitating, she said, "They look too gay."

---

2. Action shots are difficult to take. While my students tried, they weren't always successful in capturing moving football players.

3. Because of high school events that happen later in the year such as prom and graduation, their printing schedule is different, which is why they don't receive their books until summer.

Folks, I figured I'd misheard her. "I'm sorry?"

"They look gay. Their arms are around each other's shoulders."

"Yes, in school spirit, in camaraderie. There's nothing gay about that. Even if there was, so what?"

Mr. Smidt, the vice principal, sighed but remained silent. Everyone in that room knew who was boss.

"Raven, you live in Texas. This city isn't Austin. We can't have gay kids, even gay looking ones, in the yearbook."

Bile burned my throat. Not that she knew I was queer, but she already had "gay" people in the yearbook. "Dr. Thomas, I'm pretty sure you have gay students here. That aside, these two aren't gay. No one's going to look at two kids posing like this and think they are anything other than friends who just won a game—"

"If you want to keep your job, you'll remove this photo." With those words, she trudged out of my computer lab, leaving the rest to follow in silence.

I sat there in shock for a few minutes before I called my wife. Her outrage practically burned my phone. "She can't do that, can she? Make you change the book?"

"Dr. Thomas has done it before, though not for this reason. She can absolutely force me to change it. But I'm not going to."

My wife was silent for a moment before she said, "You might lose your job."

"I might, but I'm so done with the homophobia in this school. Hell, in this state. Fuck 'em."

Lucky for me, my wife is amazing. She always has my back so when I made this decision, she was one-hundred percent behind it.

I didn't change the photo. I sent those pages to the printers and clicked the box stating I had principal approval on all pages[4]. By the time the books arrived in May, there'd be

---

4. Yes, that's a real box many yearbook printers use. Too many times they've

no way to change it and if she fired me, I'd sue the pants off her and enjoy every minute of it.

I swear I'm not an antagonistic person by nature. Most of the time, I'm a live and let live type, but LGBTQ+ rights are human rights, meaning that we have the right to love who we love. We should be able to get married and divorced just like everyone else and all that comes with it. Queer folks are human—full humans. We are not partial citizens or partial people and as such, we should have the same rights and opportunities as straight people.

This is a hill I will die on.

There are many tales I could tell of the homophobia and transphobia in Texas, especially from Dr. Thomas, enough that I could write an entire new book on that topic alone. For years I'd allowed her to show her homophobic ass to the world and at this point in my career, I was done. Something in me had snapped.

Once home, I told my wife that we needed to prep for leaving Texas. "If we stay here, I'm going to get arrested. If one more redneck shithead throws anti-queer shade at me, I'm going to deck them. Hell, it might be my boss that I hit. I need out."

Preparations began to save money and consider our options, but in the meantime, I had a job to survive. By year's end, the yearbooks arrived. Parents and students loved them. Another hit for the Rogers Middle School yearbook crew.

A few days passed before Dr. Thomas noticed the image. "I thought I told you to remove this picture."

"Hmm, I did. Maybe the wrong file was uploaded. Have you had any complaints?"

"None."

"Then I guess all's well that ends well," I said with a smile.

---

been sued when something pornographic or violent ended up in a printed yearbook.

Life was already difficult for me at Rogers as my bosses hated me. They didn't understand my neurodiversity and hated that I understood and enforced my rights when I could. They hated that I knew more about technology than they did and used those tools to ensure I was protected from their bigotry and bullying.

But that year, my ability to give a fuck got up and went. I refused to be pushed around. Standing up for what was right became a battle charge that lit a fire in me. I no longer cared if I was fired. In many ways, I hoped it would happen. I craved the opportunity to take them down.

My wife could see this change in me and worried. While I'd made the right decision to stand up against my bosses, neither of us wanted me placed in a position where I could be arrested, so that summer, the job search picked up in earnest.

We'd always wanted to move to Washington State, particularly the Seattle area. When we were both in college, we visited Seattle as we'd considered transferring to the University of Washington, but we couldn't afford out of state tuition, let alone the cost of living. With my wife working in tech, we were now in a much better place financially and our dreams solidified.

Not everyone can escape. As two white people, our privilege helped tremendously, though leaving came with its own share of difficulties. Would I be teaching in Washington? Would my certification transfer or would I need to return to college for a third time[5]? If we moved, our friends would remain in Texas—a state I would never set foot in again[6]—but moving ended up being one of the best decisions of our lives.

---

5. The answer is no, my certification wouldn't transfer as Washington State sees Texas education as the joke it is. If I had continued teaching, I would've had to return to college for at least one year to take additional courses and become certified all over again.

6. Because I'm trans nonbinary and my wife is a trans woman, it is no longer safe for either of us to visit Texas. Doing so could mean great harm to us both from transphobic people and laws.

In Seattle, we found acceptance and pride. We found love and so many people who loved us in return for all that we are. Washington is not a paradise. Prejudice and bigotry exist here, too, as it does anywhere, but the differences are astounding. When I talk with people here about my experiences in Texas, they're shocked.

Often, they can't believe events like this can happen. In some ways, Seattleites live in a liberal bubble, unaware of how hate-filled areas of this country are[7].

Leaving in that photo was the first step for me in rediscovering my voice, something that had been silenced so much throughout my childhood and adult life. Moving to Seattle gave me the vocabulary to define myself, and now, to give voice to all that shaped me.

In some ways, Dr. Thomas did me a favor.

Her bigotry chased me out of the classroom and out of Texas, but in doing so, I found a home and myself.

---

7. Though this bubble seems to have popped with the election of Trump.

CHAPTER
EIGHT
BANG BANG

> *You can waste your lives drawing lines. Or you can live your life crossing them."*

SHONDA RHIMES

Content Warning: *This chapter will not discuss an active shooter situation with regards to violence. However, it will talk about shooter drills and briefly mention historical events. If this is a harmful topic for you, you may wish to skip this first section.*

ONE OF THE most challenging and frightening parts of being a teacher is the threat of school violence, particularly school shootings. It wasn't even a year after the Columbine shooting[1] when I began student teaching, and at the time, we thought Columbine was a one off. We certainly didn't see it as the beginning of an epidemic.

East Valley Middle School was a sizable campus with six

---

1. The Columbine High School massacre occurred on April 20, 1999. Two students attempted to bomb the school but ended up shooting and killing twelve students and one teacher. It was considered the deadliest mass shooting in a K-12 school in US history until the Sandy Hook shooting in December 2012.

wings and two main hallways, plus two gyms and a large band hall. Like most of the school's exterior rooms, my classroom came with two floor-to-ceiling windows that folded out at waist level. As a new teacher, it gave me comfort that in an emergency, they would've been easy to climb out of to escape.

If you've never been to Texas, it's *hot*. Not just hot, but humid. Plenty of summers it was 105° F outside with the humidity of a sauna. None of this dry heat of a desert, just hot and sticky. Even worse were the days above that temperature because it meant the school A/C was going to give up the ghost. There were many Augusts I taught with a portable air conditioner in my classroom—a large, noisy beast that made teaching almost as unbearable as the heat.

Most days, it was too hot to open my classroom windows so on the rare day that the weather cooperated, most of us opened our windows to enjoy the rare breeze. Since my first period class was my conference period, I'd prep for my day while listening to the students in athletics run laps around the school. My students would often call out a quick, "Good morning, Mrs. Oak!" as they passed by my window the first lap around. After that, they were too tired to talk and run at the same time.

That first year at East Valley, Dr. Web had a unique way to inform teachers and staff that we were going into lockdown. Someone would come over the loud speaker and announce, "Teachers, don't forget about our faculty meeting this Saturday"—the idea being that we'd never have a faculty meeting on a weekend. Yet the statement was innocuous enough not to tip off any school shooter, if one were present.

Of course, this only works when you've told faculty and staff the code and what it means. Teachers were responsible for disclosing this in their substitute teacher notes so that no one was caught off guard. However, no one thought to tell me as I was the only new teacher that year.

Oops.

The first time the announcement was made, it was *not* a drill.

In the middle of a lesson, I frowned at the announcement. Since when did we have a faculty meeting coming up? I shrugged, filed it away to ask someone later, and kept teaching. A minute later, I heard police sirens approaching and turned towards my open window. A man wearing a bandana over his face and carrying a gun stood outside. He looked at me, gestured that I should close my windows, and kept walking.

Honestly, I almost wet myself in fear.

I closed my windows and locked them, drew the shades, locked my classroom door, and called the front office. That was when I learned what the phrase meant. That was when they learned they hadn't informed me.

The man had robbed a nearby bank before fleeing police. He'd been seen cutting through a neighborhood so our school was placed into lockdown to be safe. At the time he passed by my room, the local police thought he was still in a residential area. The front office alerted them to his location after I mentioned seeing him. I also mentioned that he'd had the perfect opportunity to crawl into my window and take hostages, but he'd chosen not to. In fact, he'd made it clear I should close my windows and keep the students safe. I'm not saying he was a good person being an armed bank robber but that situation could've ended in tragedy.

After the lockdown, Dr. Web called an emergency faculty meeting after school to discuss what went right and what went wrong. I brought up how often the kids jogged past my window and how, if the kids didn't realize a lockdown had been called, they would keep running around the building, oblivious to potential danger. It could take them several minutes to loop back around to the gym where a coach could explain the situation. Nothing about hiding the lockdown from the kids was going to help keep us safe.

Not to mention that they'd failed to explain their code to

me. After this lockdown, our school and district changed their policies to practice drills with students and to ensure that the language used made it clear to *everyone* what was happening.

During my time at East Valley, our admin called for a lockdown three more times. Once because it was rumored a student had a knife in his locker, which he did. He brought it to show his history teacher because he thought it was a genuine Bowie knife[2]. The other two times were because of threats of violence against the elementary school across the field from us. Nothing at all like that first lockdown.

Because my commute to East Valley was an hour long one way, I passed my commute listening to podcasts or talking with my grandmother, who thanked God every day that I didn't end up dead. She worried about the increase in mass shootings and violence. By being a teacher, I'd chosen to put myself in grave danger according to her. A combat job without the combat pay.

She wasn't wrong.

By the time I changed jobs to teaching computers at Rogers Middle School in 2007, there'd been four other school shootings: two at colleges, one at a high school, and one at an Amish school. We had lockdown drills but only once a year. It was during my last year at the school that Sandy Hook happened, and our lockdown drills changed dramatically.

Dr. Thomas worked closely with our on-campus school resource officer[3], or SRO, to shake drills up a bit. Part of the problem with middle school students and drills is that teens don't take them seriously. Their brains are still developing, so students live in the land of perceived invincibility. In other words, "School shootings can't happen here."

No matter how much a teacher tries to prep kids for the possibility, they giggle and whisper through the drills. They

---

2. Because 7th graders in Texas learn Texas History, they learn all about James Bowie, the knife fighter who died at the Battle of the Alamo.
3. SROs are police officers who are assigned to a campus for its protection as well as to deal with any student activities that could result in criminal charges.

throw spit balls[4] or make farting noises. Welcome to middle school.

We were a school full of wild children for sure. Part of our district's initiative to keep schools safe meant that emergency construction had been done over the break on every school so that all school visitors were forced to enter through the front doors, where they were routed into the front office. From there, they signed in, which included showing identification, and if necessary, were given access to the school proper. All other exterior doors were kept locked at all times. Teachers were no longer allowed to open classroom windows either[5].

Teachers had been instructed that when going into lock-down, all doors were to be locked and windows covered by district policy. Students were to take shelter under desks, in closets, or wherever else they could that would hide them from view. Any students in the hallway were to take shelter in bathroom stalls. Teachers were not to try and pull them into our classrooms as that could endanger the lives of those inside our rooms. The grisly instructions were frightening enough, but no one covered what to do if we weren't in lock-down yet.

I was teaching my 6th grade students how to navigate a word processor program when someone started tugging on the exterior doors outside my lab. Since my lab was located at the building's rear, it sat near two double doors that led to parent pick-up. They were locked until school's end when students used them to exit the building.

Since I knew they were locked, I didn't think anything of the noise I heard. We often had parents who forgot the new policies and tried entering through those doors before walking or driving around to the building's front doors.

Someone used their keys to unlock the door, which meant

---

4. Yes, those are still a thing.
5. I couldn't reach the ones in my computer lab anyway as they were tiny windows up near the ceiling.

it was a faculty member, and I carried on teaching. I knew we were supposed to have a drill that day, but it was scheduled for the afternoon. It never entered my mind that they would change it without telling us.

Silly me.

I realize that in a true active shooter scenario, there isn't usually any warning, but with drills, I expected to know what was what. This particular class of mine held a small group of eleven-year-olds. As this was September, they more closely resembled 5th graders than actual 6th graders. East Valley also served as a school for disabled students and as such, half of my students in this class were also deaf. Two ASL[6] interpreters were present with me as they translated my instructions into sign language. I also had three special education students in the class, one of which came with his own paraprofessional aide[7].

As I taught, several of my 6th graders cried out, and I glanced towards the door to see a man dressed all in black step into my room. A ski mask covered his face, and he carried some sort of assault rifle.

My heart dropped into my stomach.

Before I could move, he swung the gun around, pointing it first at the kids and then at me. "Bang, you're dead," he said, then he ducked out of my lab.

Because we weren't literally shot, I figured out it was part of the drill, or I hoped it was. I called the front office to report an armed intruder while the other adults in the room tried to calm panicked children.

How do you explain to special needs kids that it wasn't real? That they weren't going to be shot dead?

As I hung up the phone, the announcement was made that we were having a "lockdown drill."

My principal and the officer charged with keeping us safe

---

6. American Sign Language

7. For the curious, that's twenty students and four adults in the room.

thought it would get the point across best if the SRO looked like a school shooter. If he scared the kids enough, maybe they'd take drills seriously.

As my kids cried and trembled in groups under the computer desks, I locked my door and covered the windows. My heart raced, both from fear and fury. We could hear the SRO pounding on doors and yelling about dead kids as he strode down the nearby 8th grade hallway. Every time he made noise, my 6th graders screamed.

They were absolutely terrified and inconsolable—and rightly so.

How dare they traumatize children like this?

I understand that school shootings happen. Sandy Hook resulted in the deaths of elementary school kids. School shootings are serious and these lockdown drills important, but there are ways to practice them and talk about these topics without terrorizing everyone. As a teacher, I already worried about tornados hitting our school[8]. I worried about school violence because we were teaching known gang leaders' kids. We had teen pregnancy, drug abuse/use, alcoholism, and gang violence on the regular so a school shooting wasn't exactly out of the question. It was a *possible* event.

Having an officer walk in, disguised and armed, scared me and I'm an adult. I still have nightmares about it, and I haven't been a teacher for over a decade. How many of those 6th graders had nightmares back then? Do any of them still?

Parents threw a fit about the drill. Most of the students in other classrooms didn't see him because they were already in lockdown. They were frightened a bit but not like my kiddos. This was the same class period with the mother who had complained about our talk regarding suicide. She led the way on reporting what happened to the district. Unlike the *It Gets Better* video, the other parents were ticked that their children had been brutalized by a police officer, especially since most

---

8. Which has happened a few times in my teaching career.

of these children were of color. Their relationship with the police was already shaky as many of them had faced racism, harassment, and worse at the hands of local cops.

After the lockdown was released, I sent for the school counselors as nothing I said could calm my kids. There were four adults in the room, all in shock, and completely unprepared for how to calm twenty children in a panic. Our two counselors were appalled at the damage done.

I don't know what happened on the back side of things, but soon after, the district emailed staff to make it very clear that in the future, lockdown drills were to be age appropriate and follow district policy. The next week, our SRO came into my 6th grade class in his normal police uniform. He gave a gruff apology to the kids for "scaring them."

To me, he said, "You failed."

Further, he had a list of "rules" for me.

1. My classroom door should be locked and closed at all times.
2. The blinds should always be down over all classroom windows.
3. If I hear someone trying to enter the building, call the office.
4. Train my students on how to handle school violence.
5. If an intruder enters my classroom, fight back.

The list went on but I think you get the point. He didn't apologize to me at all and smirked when he left my classroom.

One of my students signed something too rapidly for me to understand, and the interpreter sighed. "He said that the officer is a bad man and it's not your fault."

My students erupted with similar comments. None of them bought his lousy apology.

"If you'd tried to fight, he would have shot you. How'd he expect you to do anything against that gun, miss?"

Even my traumatized students could see the problem.

Since I left teaching, school shootings have rocketed. In fact, the year I left had thirteen shootings[i]. Every year since then, the numbers have increased—the exception being in 2020 when schools closed for the pandemic. That year, there were only twenty-two. The "only" in that sentence is almost as traumatic to me as the lockdowns. Twenty-two is twenty-two too many. It's February 2024 as I write this and already, we've had thirteen school shootings this year. **Thirteen**, and it's only February. Last year, the total number was eighty-two.

You didn't misread that.

I'm not going to get into a debate about gun rights, but something we're doing as educators and parents isn't working. Something society is doing is failing these children.

Teaching used to be a professional people aspired to, and in many countries, it still is. In many countries, teachers are well-paid and respected for without teachers, you wouldn't be reading this and I wouldn't be writing it. Teachers are the creators of every job in existence. We ensure that children grow up to be intelligent, curious citizens. Parents play a large role in that too, but as some found out during the pandemic, it's not as easy teaching as they thought.

Every time I hear about another school shooting, after my initial shock and grief, I'm glad I'm not a teacher anymore. It's too deadly.

While I miss my grandmother, I'm glad she passed before Sandy Hook happened and gun violence erupted across the United States. She would weep with relief that now I work from home as a full-time writer rather than a human shield.

If you skipped the first section, it's now safe to resume reading.

I've talked about lunch detention at Rogers Middle School

before, though not in this much detail. It was a chore, but more than that, it revealed a cruel indifference towards children that resulted in my notifying the media as a whistleblower.

Plenty of data exists about the ties between crime and poverty[9], so it's no surprise that it was often our poorest kids assigned to lunch detention for behavioral issues. Most of these students received a free or reduced lunch. When serving their lunch detentions, Dr. Thomas didn't want them to enjoy it as it was a punishment. She and Mr. Smidt redesigned lunch detention to give these students a bland lunch.

I'll get into this more in a moment, but I want to point out that using food as a form of punishment on children is wrong. Using food as punishment on food insecure children is even worse.

For some of these kids, their only meals came from our school. Many kids in our cafeteria would hop table to table to collect unopened milks and cereal packs from other students who didn't want their food. Then, they'd bundle it all up in their backpacks to take home and share with their siblings. The idea of limiting what these kids can eat is cruel. In my opinion, it falls under "cruel and unusual punishment," which is against the Eighth Amendment of our Constitution.

Since there are federal nutritional guidelines in place dictating what students could be served, the administration couldn't feed the kids garbage. If they could've arranged it, I think they would have done so in a heartbeat. Instead, students received: one plain hamburger: patty and bun only; one regular milk; one vegetable side like broccoli or corn.

They couldn't choose which side they wanted as they did when not serving lunch detention. There were no accommodations for food intolerances, allergies, or special diets, like

---

9. I am not saying that only poor people become criminals. Plenty of data also exists indicating how racism and bigotry influence those in power to make assumptions, which often results in what we call the school to prison pipeline. You can read more about that here: https://www.learningforjustice.org/maga zine/spring-2013/the-school-to-prison-pipeline

being a vegetarian or needing something halal[10]. They couldn't have chocolate milk as that would be "too fun" and they'd "enjoy it too much."

One concern I voiced about this was for those students whose parents paid for their lunch. If a mother gave their child $10 to choose what they wanted to eat, but because of lunch detention, the school forced them to purchase a $3 hamburger and milk, that would have pissed me off as a parent. In fact, some could argue such a thing fraudulent as the student didn't choose to buy that food and was forced to do so under duress.

"It's detention. They'll live," was the response.

"But what if a parent has a problem with it?" I asked.

If looks could kill, my boss would have just slain me. "What they don't know won't hurt them."

The implication after those words was that I had better not tell them either.

Most of the time, the kids in lunch detention tried to eat. They'd take a few bites and give up. But mostly, they didn't bother at all. They'd drink their milk and that would be it. One day, I asked one of the students why no one ate the hamburgers. I'd noticed that even in the cafeteria, students chose a different entree and avoided the burgers if they had a choice.

The student laughed. "You mean the hockey pucks?"

I frowned.

"Watch, miss." He picked up the meat patty in his hands, leaving the bun behind. Then he tapped it against the floor.

I'd expected it to crumble or fall apart. What I did *not* expect was for it to make a clanking noise. I walked over and held out my hand. "May I?"

He passed me the patty and when I held it, it was rock solid. Mind you, it wasn't frozen. This wasn't a case of being undercooked or unthawed, but a patty that was old and stale.

---

10. I'm not even sure most Texas school administrators know what halal is.

I gave it back to him and looked at the rest of the students. "Is anyone else's patty hard like that?"

They all nodded.

"It's why they're called hockey pucks, miss."

Every last patty was rock hard. Some edges were chewable if one tried enough, but the majority of the meat was inedible.

Later that day, I emailed Mr. Smidt about these hockey pucks. He assured me that while the patties weren't from that day, they had been refrigerated and cooked per health and safety standards. In other words, excuses. Or he didn't believe me.

The next day, I "borrowed" one of the patties and when lunch duty was over, I delivered it to his office. This time, he promised to "look into it."

Truth of the matter is that nothing changed. I suspect that he and Dr. Thomas were not only aware of this, but had intentionally been serving bad food to the lunch detention kids. When I asked my 8th grade students how long the "hockey pucks" had been around, they could remember them from their 6th grade year.

This wasn't a one-off instance or an accident.

I tried to talk to the cafeteria workers, but they don't get paid enough to buck the system. They weren't about to rat out their bosses and lose their jobs, so I gathered what information I could and sent it to the local media from a dummy email account.

There was a gap between that point and when reporters began calling the school district about potential health code violations, but when shit hit the proverbial fan, Mr. Smidt visited my classroom during my conference period, demanding to know if I'd spoken to the media.

"As a representative of this district, you can't talk to them without district approval," he said, and I almost laughed in his face.

Remember when I said my ability to give a damn had fled?

"I have no idea what you're talking about, but just so you know, teachers do have First Amendment rights like every other citizen of this country."

He opened his mouth, face flushed red, and I held up a hand.

"Perhaps someone wrote 'a damn novel' that paid off?"

With those words, he left my room. If he came after me, I had no issues telling the media about his email and he knew it. Dr. Thomas and he would do their best to crush my spirit and make my job a living hell, but I didn't see how it could get much worse.

Due to media scrutiny, our school did have a surprise health and safety inspection, which did find a number of issues in the cafeteria. The district came down on my bosses for potentially exposing them to any lawsuits, which the faculty figured out when the district released a public statement ensuring everyone that our cafeteria was being reorganized to better meet the health needs of our students.

They didn't care about feeding students garbage. They only cared about being sued.

Lunch detention was still in full effect, and while yes, the district caved and allowed my bosses to continue to serve boring food, the burgers had to be edible and any special food needs had to be met with alternative choices.

It wasn't perfect, but it was better than nothing at all.

They gave me permanent lunch duty as a punishment, but at least the students were eating again. Note to all administrators: Don't put an advocate in charge of something as punishment unless you want them to release the skeletons in your closet.

CHAPTER NINE
OWNING UP

Experience is simply the name we give our mistakes."

OSCAR WILDE

WHEN IT COMES to students with profound special needs, I will own up to carrying some baggage due to a few incidents growing up. It's not something I'm proud of and it's certainly something I worked on throughout my teaching career, but to pretend it doesn't exist would be hypocritical of me.

When I was perhaps seven or eight years old, I often accompanied my father to his college campus, either because I was sick and couldn't stay home, or because it was a school holiday for me but not for him. Being a single parent is challenging. Being one who couldn't afford or find a sitter is even harder. During this visit, we ventured into a building I hadn't visited before. My father was a research assistant for a professor studying special needs students with Down Syndrome and other forms of profound intellectual disabilities. All of the subjects were adults, and while my father mentioned to me that they might act differently, he also promised me that I had no reason to be afraid.

While he discussed something with his professor, one of the special needs men in the room grabbed me. He pulled at my long hair, which gained the attention of others. A few other men tried to pull off my shirt, and I screamed. While the researchers moved quick, they weren't quick enough as the man tugging my hair slapped me. Hard enough to leave a handprint behind.

We immediately left the building, and while my father apologized for what happened, he didn't explain it.

For a long stretch of childhood, profoundly special needs people sent me into fight or flight response. Young me didn't understand that intellectually, they didn't comprehend what they were doing or that it was wrong. I was different, and they were overly curious. After meeting some of the special education students at my middle school, I relaxed some around those with special needs, at least if they were my age.

High school science classes taught me more about their disabilities, and I completely stopped expecting them to attack me. So much so that I began babysitting a high school student with profound special needs. Being my helpful self, I wanted to give the exhausted parents a break or a night off.

What I didn't understand at the time was that while this young man's IQ meant he couldn't understand or process at a normal level, he still held the hormones of a teenaged boy. Unlike his mind, his body was not delayed. He was much taller and stockier than me, and I found myself in a situation where he attempted multiple times to touch me inappropriately.

When I mentioned this to the parents, they apologized and said that he didn't know what he was doing. While I can believe that and know that can happen on a logical level, the experience scared the hell out of me. I stopped babysitting for them and some of my previous trauma resurfaced.

As a teacher, I knew I'd encounter students with profound needs, but I also understood that most of them would be in their own classrooms. Any students with disabilities present in my computer lab were more likely to be my deaf ed students, English language learners[1], or students with ADHD and/or autism. I felt capable of teaching such students without falling into a panic attack.

My second year at Rogers led to a conundrum for me with regards to my special needs students. With the exception of my 6th grade Intro to Computers class, my classes were high school credit classes. They were meant for accelerated students to get ahead and earn high school credit before entering high school. At other schools in my district, this was understood, but at Rogers, this was ignored in order to place students who had nowhere else to go[2].

It's a teacher's job to ensure that with work and effort, students can be successful in their classes. A teacher becomes limited in that job when everything is stacked against them, which is where I found myself that second year.

Petey, a student with both mental and physical disabilities, ended up enrolled in my first period class. His physical disabilities meant that he came with adaptive technology like an enlarged mouse and keyboard. He struggled to see and suffered from severe tremors in his limbs. Even with the adaptive tech, his hands would swing wildly, and he struggled to type at a speed of three words per minute[3]. He struggled to speak and had significant intellectual delays as well.

Most accommodations for students with dyslexia, ADHD, and such are easy, but it would be nigh impossible for Petey to type with any sort of speed, let alone create and manipulate spreadsheets, databases, and computer code. Even if he was physically able to operate a computer, he often stared at the screen with little comprehension. He often drooled on his desk and the computer equipment, which left his germs

---

1. Or what we used to call students with English as a Second Language or ESL.

2. Sound familiar? I'm looking at you first year yearbook class…

3. Average is around 40 wpm. Prior to my disability advancing, my best was 120 wpm. On a good day now, I'm around 80 wpm.

everywhere and posed a risk since moisture and electronics don't work well together. Petey came with an aide, and while she did her best to help him and clean up after him, her hands were tied as well. I didn't understand why he was in a high school accelerated class.

If he was going to be included in general education, placing him in my 6th grade introduction class would have been a better placement. I brought this up to the school counselors but was told that he needed to be with other students of his grade level.

While I understand the purpose of inclusion and have always been an advocate of it, there are some situations where it doesn't make sense. For example, they would never place Petey in a shop class. Safety issues are a consideration in placements, so his electives were limited to those where he could be safe and successful.

In talking with my subject matter colleagues, they agreed that their counselors would not have placed a student at his level in their advanced classes. When I brought this up, I was called into a meeting with the school counselors, Dr. Thomas, and the Special Education department head.

When interviewing for this job, I'd been honest about my experiences in my past with students more profoundly disabled than Petey. I used it as an example of an area of improvement that I wished to work on as a teacher. However, my boss had shared this information with Ms. Jodi, the SPED department head. The moment the meeting began, she explained that I couldn't use my "prejudice" as a reason to have a student removed from my classroom. She lit into me like I'd used the "r" word.

For the record, I abhor that word and anyone who uses it.

I may find myself sometimes startled by some special needs students, but I don't hate them. I'm mentally and physically disabled myself[4], and honestly, they are some of my favorite students. Some of my deaf-ed and autistic students tended to be geeky and nerdy in unique ways that I identify with.

No matter how much I explained to them my rational concerns about Petey's ability to be successful in an accelerated high school class, the folks in the room had already decided that this was a "me" problem. They assured me that while he wouldn't receive high school credit, in my class he would remain. If I had problems accommodating the lessons for his needs, I could ask the special education department for help.

Which is what I did.

Ms. Jodi learned to hate me that semester as not one member of the SPED department had any idea how to do anything more than surf the web and answer email. My students were learning business computing skills and programming—topics far beyond most of the school's staff. Their department didn't have a clue how to help me help Petey, so he failed my class.

Technically, he didn't fail. From a numbers perspective, yes, but as a student receiving accommodations, they adjusted his grade after the fact to pass him. The next semester, Petey was in my class again[5]. They thought taking it a second time, he might find more success.

He did not.

His physical limitations meant that he physically couldn't keep up with the pacing needed to work on a computer. His mental disabilities led to a complete lack of understanding on what he was seeing. He could watch a video and understand some of it, but honestly, I think he enjoyed videos because of the colors.

---

4. Not that being disabled means one can't be prejudiced against those who are also disabled. It happens.

5. The 7th grade class was one semester only and served as a prerequisite for other full year classes I taught.

Several members of the special education department began to attend my class in hopes that if they learned the skills, perhaps we could all work together to better help Petey, but after a few weeks, they were as lost as Petey. They didn't have the foundations to comprehend the assignments. A few of them moved to my Introduction to Computer courses where the common thought was, "Mrs. Oak needs to teach this class to all the teachers in the building."

They were probably right.

When Petey's 8th grade year came around, he was back in my first period class—the high school level course—but this time, the SPED team had a new plan. "Just have him type."

I found a great online program used by our elementary schools for teaching touch typing and sat Petey down in front of it. Even with his oversized keyboard, he averaged about 4 WPM that year, but at least it was a skill set he could work on and mostly understand as he did well with pattern recognition. Also, his speed *had* improved so he showed progress.

During my last years at Rogers, I noticed that my classes were less of a dumping ground as they had been and wondered if both the experience with Petey and the special education department's attempt to take my classes had led to some sort of "Come to Jesus" talk at the administration level.

Petey was a sweet kid. I wasn't afraid of him, and I didn't dislike him. If I'd had him in my 6th grade class, I would've enjoyed it, but both admin and the SPED department failed that kid. They set him up for failure in a class where he had no hopes of success, which is something teachers across the United States experience on a daily basis.

With students who don't speak a ton of English, math and technology are often subjects that serve as a universal language. Much of technology is iconology based, meaning we click on pictures to do tasks, and what isn't, can often be inferred or translated. The majority of our school's population was Latinx, and they taught me how to translate technology terms in Spanish *muy rapido*[6]. I created a word wall[7] with all the jargon from our courses in both English and Spanish because that's an accommodation I can do. It's something that can help those students succeed as they learn both English and my classwork.

But not everything can be simplified or changed. There are some skills that require a foundational knowledge. Petey should no more have been in my advanced classes than he should be placed in medical school. The lesson in this that I feel they missed is that it's okay for not every student to be college bound. Some students won't be able to take any class they want, and that's also okay.

We push all kids to go to college, often at the detriment of blue-collar jobs. Ask any appliance repairperson how many apprentices they have these days. The numbers are depressing. Most of what we consider as skilled blue-collar labor is made up of people close to retirement. Schools don't teach enough of the trade classes anymore.

Shop and automotive classes, home economics, and other electives have fallen by the wayside in order to prep kids for state tests. We push them to try for college and some of them fail out in the first semester.

That's not to say that students who want to try for college shouldn't, but there is a realistic expectation that students who are college bound have a certain skill level so that they can be successful. There is no shame in being a plumber. Hell, plumbers make twice as much per year than I ever did as a teacher. Certainly more than I do as a writer.

When I think about Petey now, I hope his typing speed has improved, but I understand if it hasn't. There's nothing wrong with being different, with being special, and the

---

6. Very quickly.
7. For those who are not teachers, it's what you think it is: a wall with vocabulary words on it.

sooner we recognize that education isn't a one-size-fits-all, the better it will be for students like Petey.

NOT EVERYTHING at Rogers was a disaster, I promise. As I mentioned before, I loved my deaf-ed students. They were goofy kids who loved learning about computers, and I loved learning more sign language from them as I taught. They gave me my own name sign[8] and taught me how to sign technology words.

One of the lessons I taught in my 6th grade class involved a spreadsheet program commonly used for a variety of business purposes. In fact, I use one these days to track how many words I write per day, month, and year. Many of us in the self-employment world use them to track income and expenses for taxes. Using a spreadsheet program such as Google Sheets® or Microsoft Excel® means understanding how rows and columns work. It's a nice tie-in to math class and for my intro classes, we used the game Battleship® to learn it.

Fingerspelling, or the ASL alphabet, is a skill I've had since elementary school (*go Girl Scouts!*), but I've never known how to sign numbers. Watching the interpreter call out the letters and numbers meant I picked up counting as a new skill. When I'd call out, "C6" during the game, I would sign it along with the interpreter. The students loved that I made an effort to learn more of their language, but they also loved that they didn't need to hear to be included.

---

8. When referring to a person by name, you typically fingerspell it in ASL, or American Sign Language. A name sign is when a sign is used instead of fingerspelling and it's an honor to be given one. Not everyone in the Deaf community is given one either. No one gives themselves their own name sign in the Deaf community. By Deaf culture traditions, name signs are only given by a person in the Deaf community.

When my wife and I first moved to Seattle, I'd retired from teaching in order to write full-time. However, one of our cats suffered a major illness that required several surgeries. Having moved across the country and bought a condo, we found ourselves struggling with vet bills, so I worked part-time for a stretch.

Where I worked was an amazing place as it was a non-profit organization called Sight Connection. They worked with Seattle's libraries and eye doctors to better accommodate blind people in a busy city. They connected them to Braille and audio books, helped teach them how to use assistive technology so that they could use computers and cell phones, and they helped treat the medical side of issues like macular degeneration[9].

I absolutely loved working with this group and meeting so many people who were either blind or losing their sight. But more than that, I learned about the various assistive technologies that didn't exist ten years ago, some of which could have potentially helped students like Petey. Seeing how much medicine has changed through the decades has been an eye-opening experience, but it all began for me with my deaf education students and their desire to teach the teacher.

SINCE I'M OWNING up to my own faults and flaws, I feel I would be remiss if I didn't address something that's been bothering me throughout the writing of this book. Something gnawing on me like my cat with a catnip toy. Memories are tricky as they can make you smile while simultaneously ripping you apart. Writing a memoir is part storytelling and

---

9. Macular degeneration is a disease that affects a person's central vision. It's often seen in folks over 50, those who smoke, or those with high blood pressure. Unlike cataracts, there is no cure for macular degeneration.

part reflection, and what you see isn't always what you expected.

Reaching back, I can see all of the places where I failed my students because of a lack of action, times when I should have stepped up, not just for me, but for them. Times where I chose the easier option because I was…afraid.

Doing the right thing isn't easy. If it were easy, everyone would do it, right?

I've always lived with the best of intentions, but intentions mean little without actions behind them. Too many times I've held onto my excuses as a shield.

If I do this, someone might physically harm me.

If I do that, I might lose my job.

If I do this, someone else may get hurt.

I can rationalize my way out of anything, I swear. Would losing my job have hurt? Absolutely, but by not speaking up, others potentially suffered. Towards the end of my teaching career, I was emboldened by the fact that we were planning to leave Texas. The risk to my job was less, so it was easier to make the better choice and stand up against injustice and prejudice.

Again, if doing right by society wasn't risky, everyone would do it.

It's easy to dictate[10] to others what they must do in the face of hate from a place of privilege. I'm self-employed and living in a very liberal state where it's less likely I would be harmed by speaking out. My wife can live as a transwoman in Washington State with less chance of being beaten to death for it. Our state is unlikely to pass anti-trans legislation, unlike Texas. My being nonbinary doesn't place me at huge risk the way it would have in the south. I'm not saying it's perfectly safe here, but we both recognize the privilege that protects us.

I'm not punishing myself for those moments, as every

---

10. I've tried not to do that in this book, but if I have, I apologize.

experience and decision has created the me that exists today, nor am I recommending that anyone reading this beat themselves up over their own past inadequacies. There's a difference in acknowledging your past and drowning in it.

When this book rolled out of me in the rush that it did, I recognized certain patterns throughout my life that have dictated which direction I've turned at various moments. As I know that many teachers find themselves in a similar boat these days, it's important to recognize when to jump ship and remember how to swim.

Part of finding one's self and voice is acknowledging one's whole self, which includes those flaws we'd rather hide or pretend don't exist. I'm not proud of the ways I've hidden, nor am I proud of the baggage I carry. Some of it isn't mine to carry, yet I allow it to weigh me down out of fear.

Fear is what keeps us from ourselves.

It's also what causes people to other each other. It's easier to see someone different and run screaming to the hills than it is to make the effort to get to know them and their story. Why do our differences matter in all the wrong ways?

I am proud to be a disabled, queer, nonbinary writer and artist. What makes me different is what makes me unique and what makes me, me. None of these identities should give anyone pause or reason to hate, any more than someone wearing glasses or eating meat should. But fear takes root and locks our feet in place, preventing us from growing and learning.

Knowing what I know now, if I could go back and stand up in those moments when I didn't, I would—without hesitation—but sadly, time travel doesn't exist[11]. Moving forward, all I can do is acknowledge my role in this timeline and work to change the things I cannot accept.

---

11. At least not to our knowledge.

Age: 6
Grade: 1st

When I grow up, I want to be a
riter, and a teacher + music
My hobbies are
riting, reading, singing,
drawing, swimming

Scanned image from the scrapbook Grandma Elle got me so long ago. I couldn't spell "writer" at six, but I got the point across.

Me (age 3ish) and my Grandma Ruth, both of us wearing frilly, pink Easter dresses before heading to church.

*Me (age 4) with a doll I got from my maternal grandfather. I
didn't know him well but this doll was from his home in
Mexico. I called her "My Old Lady," and my Grandma Ruth
(paternal grandmother) hated her. She threw her away, likely
because the doll was Hispanic, and my Grandma Ruth hated
Hispanic people.*

Me (age 4) with my paternal grandfather, who died when I was really young.

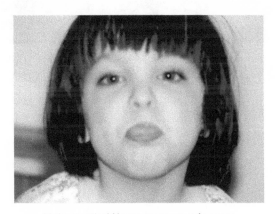

Me (age 4 or 5) sticking my tongue out at the camera. Typical me pose.

Me (age 4 or 5), sitting beneath the dining room table at my Grandma Ruth's house in Michigan. I liked hiding beneath furniture.

Me (age 4 or 5) in a new Easter dress. Still sporting a bowl haircut.

FROM LEFT TO RIGHT: an unknown cousin I met once, my great-aunt Dot, my Grandma Elle, and me (age 7), all sitting on my great-aunt's front porch in Oklahoma.

Maguire Village, circa 1988. This village that raised me has since been torn down.

This is my 9th birthday. My father wasn't home so the upstair's neighbor made me a cupcake for my birthday and invited me over so I could blow out the candle.

Me, age 10 I believe, at a friend's house.

Me at Halloween, age 11. My father made me wear a skirt over my leotard because otherwise I looked "fat."

Me (age 11) outside at Maguire Village. Yes, I'm wearing socks with my jelly shoes.

Me (age 12) not caring if my clothes match.

Me (7th grade) standing in the band hall at school, where I spent most of my time.

Me (age 14) standing on a friend's porch. I don't have many photos of myself from middle school because I thought I was too fat. Having a large chest didn't help my self-esteem.

My mother and I. This picture is from the first time I met her on one of the rare instances that she was sober.

Garland High School's
Writer's Guild
1994-1995

W ishing to be
R ecognized for
I ncredible
T ales & for
E ntertaining
R eaders of
S ci/Fi, Fantasy & Fiction

G roup of
U nbelievably talented
I ndividuals with
L asting
D etermination.

"Changing the World with the Written Word."

This is the back of our high school Writer's Guild club t-shirt. The poem says:
Wishing to be Recognized for Incredible Tales & for Entertaining Readers of
Sci-Fi, Fantasy, & Fiction. Group of Unbelievably talented Individuals with
Lasting Determination, which spells out WRITERS GUILD. Then it shows
our motto, "Changing the World with the Written Word."

PICTURED: Me and my wife (prior to transitioning) at our high school senior prom. We are such babies in this photo, though I was already living on my own at this point. My wife was a ward of the court and would soon move in with me.

Me (1999) performing on the piano one of my compositions at my college's annual composer's concert.

Me (2000) recording my CD, Walls, Boxes, & Jars *in our home studio. Of course I'm sticking out my tongue at the camera.*

The mural I painted in my first classroom. The three characters rotated what they said based upon what we were studying at the time. Here, Mario is commenting on parts of speech while the Goomba and Yoshi are giving writing advice.

More classroom art—this one featuring the main character from the game Karamari Damacy. *He's rolling up "dead words," or weak writing words so he can throw them away.*

The first day of school (2012) from my last year teaching.

*One of the first things we did upon moving to Washington
was go visit Mt. Rainier (aka Mt. Tahoma).*

Once I moved to WA State and got published, I became known for my constantly changing hair color. Here, I have fire-colored hair.

Me reading from Class-M Exile *at my second book signing at the University Book Store.*

My wife (pre-transition) and I at our favorite local convention, Norwescon, in 2018.

My wife (pre-transition) and I dressed up for Halloween. She was Space Ghost (from the Cartoon Network cartoon) and I was Ms. Marvel.

This is the face of long COVID. After massive weight loss (unhealthily), I can see the rash on my chest from the random hives I get now as part of Mast Cell Activation Syndrome.

CHAPTER
TEN

BLESS YOUR HEART

Only do what your heart tells you."

PRINCESS DIANA

IF YOU'VE EVER LIVED in or visited the South, there's a common phrase that's used like a double-edged sword: *Bless your heart.*

The first time you hear it, probably uttered by some wiry-haired granny at the grocery store, you might think it the equivalent of saying "Bless you!" when someone sneezes, but most the time, the phrase is meant as the biggest fuck you an old, Christian woman can dredge up. Southern grannies are a force unto their own. The same hands that kiss your cheeks can blister your skin with their words alone.

As I've said before, words have power.

While the phrase can burn like the sun, it's when folks in the south turn their silent disapproval on you that you need to worry.

That was me my last year teaching.

To close friends, I was on fire that year, burning out at both ends as I sought any way to escape both my job and Texas. Don't get me wrong—I loved teaching. Still do. I loved the students and watching the metaphorical lightbulb go off in their minds as they made connections between the subject matter and their own lives, but the administration and lack of support was killing me.

In between dye jobs, I sported a full head of gray hair by thirty. My blood pressure was elevated for the first time in my adult life, and my doctor had warned me that I needed to have less stress in my life if I wanted to keep living it. Trying to fight for my own existence, let alone that of my students, wore me down to a sliver of who I was.

While I may have shared my inner thoughts with close friends, at work, I shut down. Previous me went into wit-sec[1] as I hid everything that made me who I am. I stopped being friendly with anyone at work. I didn't share my weekend plans or news about my cats. I didn't discuss the newest book releases, not even the weather. When asked questions, I answered in as few words as possible, and I stopped documenting anything in emails. Radio silence was the game plan as anything else would cost me everything.

Behind my silence, I channeled my fire into what I called emergency relocation. Could we afford to move and to where? How much would we need to land in our beloved Seattle? What did it cost to move across the country and how would we handle the cats? The second week of school, my wife received an interview at a major tech company in Seattle, WA, and it took everything in me not to cheer. There was no point as she didn't have a job offer yet, just an interview, but it was the beginning of change for us.

By mid-October, my wife was on her last round of interviews. Either she would get the job or not. The wait between last interview and *knowing*, reminded me of waiting for medical news. My heart lived in the pit of my stomach and time crawled with the intensity of the sun. It was the first

---

1. Slang for the Witness Protection Program. I didn't really go into it as this is a metaphor.

week of November when a job offer was extended. Even better, the pay was double what she was making in Texas.

Suddenly, our dreams were a reality.

The company would pay for relocation. They'd pack up everything we owned, move us to Seattle, pay for several months in temporary housing while we searched for a place to live[2], and once found, they'd unpack us in our new home. They paid for our airline tickets, including those for our cats, and paid to drive our vehicles up as well. The price of relocating us was somewhere around $60,000—at least the way they handled it. My wife received a signing bonus and company stock.

Of course, they wanted us in Seattle pronto. We'd have to sell our house from Seattle as they wanted us there in two weeks. In other words, long enough for us both to give notice and get the fuck out of dodge.

Teacher me hated abandoning my students, but this move was needed and desperately wanted. It meant devoting myself to a full-time writing career. I wouldn't have to hide anymore. I could finally be me.

The bitter person deep within wanted to quit in all manner of childish ways—from cussing out Dr. Thomas and Mr. Smidt, to leaving dog shit on their desks as both of them were steaming piles in my opinion, but in the end, the future was an unknown. Not to mention that even amidst the fire, I'm a good person at heart.

I wish I could say I was completely without pettiness, but at thirty-four, I didn't have it in me to be *that* grown up. After the contracts were signed and everything solidified, I scheduled a before school meeting with Dr. Thomas where I notified her that my wife had received and accepted a new job offer meaning more pay and a much better life.

---

2. They even paid a tour guide to drive us around, introducing us to all the neighborhoods and giving us realtor help.

"We're moving to Seattle in two weeks, so this is my notice of intent to leave my position."

Keep in mind, finding computer teachers worth their salt is *hard*. Substitute teachers taught my classes for over a year before Dr. Thomas found and hired me, so leaving in November, mid-year, was leaving the school and district in a serious predicament. More than likely, a sub or multiple subs would take over my classes while the search began for a new me.

"You can't up and leave like this. You're under contract," she said, her voice shaking.

"A contract that can be broken under state law if a life changing event occurs, such as a spouse's job change, family illness, childbirth, and so on. I know my rights."

"I'll have your certificate for this."

I laughed. My wife and I had triple checked, and there was no way she could harm my credentials with the way I gave notice, but at that point, I wasn't sure I cared. Seeing her squirm helped make up for all the punishment she'd put me through.

"I'll inform my students and their parents this afternoon and will leave all of my lesson plans and files for whoever takes my place. It should help make the transition easier." None of this was required, but I chose to do so because of my students. Dr. Thomas could and should suffer but not them, not if I could help it. In leaving both lessons and files behind, I cemented my rights to leave amicably, at least as far as the state was concerned.

Her lips were thin slits as she glared at me. There was nothing more she could do and little else to be said. Instead, I patted her hand and said, "Bless your heart. I hope everything works out for you."

Then I left her office.

As I said, I'm a good person, but at thirty-four, I could also be petty.

Notifying the students and their parents was one of the

most difficult tasks I've ever experienced. They cried. I cried. It was a freaking waterworks show, and while they would miss me, my students understood. They weren't oblivious. They'd seen the hell I'd suffered in my years at that school. Amongst my colleagues, there was an obvious sigh of relief. They wouldn't miss me.

The smart computer teacher who "made waves" was leaving, not just the school but the state. Oh happy day! Of course, they failed to realize that escaping them was as joyous an event for me as it probably was for them.

For twenty-four years Texas had done its best to silence those of us living as our authentic selves, the rule-breakers and rebels, the queers and the creatives, and those willing to stand up for what was right. When our plane crossed the Texas border, every fiber in my body relaxed into a pool of relief, and let me tell you, that pool was Olympic sized.

Having been gone for twelve years, I'm still writing and fighting to find me amidst all the trauma left behind, but I breathe easier at night knowing I escaped.

To those who would have it any other way, well, bless their hearts.

CHAPTER
ELEVEN

FAT: A FATE WORSE THAN DEATH

Love your body because you only have one."

AUTHOR UNKNOWN

LIFE CONTINUES no matter where you're living, or at least one hopes so as the alternative sucks. I would be lying if I said that Seattle is perfect. The job that brought us here lasted 2.5 years and left my wife with PTSD. It's common in the tech industry for companies to use and abuse workers, and this company was no exception. Was it worth it? For us, yes, but it left scars in its wake.

Not long after I arrived in Seattle, my health slalomed off a mountaintop, which is saying something considering the mountain ranges around us. Appointments with my primary care physician and a few specialists gave no answers as my blood work was clean as a whistle. Besides severe joint pain and fatigue, my eyes and mouth were bone dry. We're talking waking up with my eyelids dried stuck to my eyes. Using my fingers to pry them apart damaged my corneas, and my eye doctor suggested I see a rheumatologist for something called Sjogren's, an autoimmune disease related to Lupus. It attacks and dehydrates cells all over the body. My tongue would stick to my teeth and gums in a similar manner and without my mentioning my eye doctor's suspicions, my dentist pointed out that I might have Sjogren's.

When I brought it up to my doctor, she sent me to an ENT[1], or an otorhinolaryngologist[2]. They weren't interested in my bone aches or fatigue, instead focusing on my ears, sinuses, and throat. My salivary glands, or parotid glands, were swollen and infected. They weren't producing saliva *(hence, dry mouth)* because there were stones inside them[3].

They thought that if we treated this, everything would be fine with my body, and I could return to normal activities. First we tried antibiotics, which did nothing. I warned them of this as I grew up with severe allergies and as such, I've taken *a lot* of antibiotics to combat all the ear and sinus infections throughout my life. At this point, many of the typical ones don't work, but they tried them anyway. Then we graduated to more aggressive antibiotics, followed by steroids like prednisone. When that didn't work, my ENT said I was beyond her abilities and I might need to try an rheumatologist[4].

If you have cancer, Seattle's an amazing place for treatment. Between UW School of Medicine and numerous hospitals, the city has an elite set of specialists, but when it comes to certain areas like rheumatology and endocrinology, we're the Sahara Desert.

The cost of living here is intense, and while the tech fields pay very well, the medical fields don't, or at least that's what rumors say. When people talk about running through doctors until they found the "right one," you can guess correctly that they live in Seattle.

---

1. Stands for ear, nose, and throat specialist
2. That's a serious mouthful. Now I see why we call them ENTs.
3. Just like a person can get bladder or kidney stones, you can also develop tonsil stones and salivary stones. Fun times!
4. For those keeping count, this is now three specialists saying I need to see a rheumy.

The first rheumatologist didn't ask me my symptoms. He talked over me, made assumptions, and generally was a complete asshole. When he walked into the room, he saw a fat woman and decided that my symptoms were mostly in my head. What wasn't mental, must be related to being over-weight—despite the fact that I've never had high blood pressure, high cholesterol, or anything else to indicate my health was in trouble[5]. He ran a few blood tests and when they came back normal, he shrugged.

"I'm going to send you to an ENT since your symptoms seem to be central to that region."

I explained that I'd already seen an ENT, and that they were the ones who sent me to him.

"Well, let's get a second opinion. The ENT I'm sending you to is one of the best," he said, and off I went to round two.

This specialist was an older, skinny man who frowned as he read through my intake files. "I'm not sure why you were referred to me," he said as he set down his laptop. "I'm an ENT, yes, but only because I have to be to be a plastic surgeon. All I do is nose jobs. You say your rheumatologist referred you to me specifically?"

When I nodded, his frown deepened.

"Yeah, I wouldn't know where to begin with this. Unless you want a nose job? Though honestly you don't need one."

I left that appointment infuriated. How in the world could that ENT be one of the best if all he did was perform plastic surgery? Had this rheumatologist sent me there on purpose, or had he genuinely not known this specialist's credentials? Either way, this appointment placed me back at square one.

Like many who suffer from chronic conditions, I ran through specialists like water in an attempt to find a specialist worth two cents who could diagnose me. I found another

---

5. For the men in the reading room, this is common. Doctors are very dismissive of women's symptoms, especially if they are at all overweight.

rheumatologist, though this one wanted me to stop taking all of my allergy and asthma medications. She was convinced they were the cause of my symptoms because the pharmaceutical companies were "out to get us." Considering the severity of my allergies and the fact that I've needed those meds since childhood, stopping them would be a bad idea. When I explained to her that without them, I would go into anaphylaxis[6], she didn't believe me.

"No one has allergies *that* bad."

Tell that to my medical records[7].

Anyone who encouraged me to stop taking major medications without having the full picture wasn't a doctor I would repeat seeing. Perhaps the rheumatologist was right. Maybe this was upper respiratory based. After more research[8], I found another recommended ENT and made an appointment. There was a three month wait where I added another symptom to my repertoire: fevers. My body ran a low grade fever on and off for over a year. Any physical activity that raised my heart rate cranked the fever into the 100°+ F range.

This ENT specialist walked in, glanced at me, and completely ignored my chart. He didn't look inside my ears, nose, or throat, but nodded as I rattled off my symptoms. I felt a moment of hope because at least the man appeared to be listening to me. When I finished, he gave one final nod.

"Parotid or salivary glands tend to get clogged easily

---

6. Anaphylaxis is a life-threatening allergic reaction that can cause the throat to swell shut. When it happens, sufferers have moments to use an epi-pen and get to a hospital or they could die from an inability to breathe. It can also cause a dangerous drop in blood pressure, fast and weak pulse, skin rash, nausea, vomiting, and other body reactions.

7. I am severely allergic to everything. Truly. Even to allergy shots, which are supposed to help decrease allergies. I should have been raised in a bubble.

8. People with chronic conditions often have a second full time job: medical researcher & advocate. Mostly because doctors don't stay up on the latest in medicine and also because if we don't prove we know what our bodies are telling us, they won't listen to us, especially those who are female or female presenting. It's even worse if you're nonbinary or transgender. Some write you off immediately as attention seeking or hypochondriacs.

when we eat lots of fatty foods. Once clogged, they can get infected, and infections can lead to fevers and other body reactions. I think if we could get you to lose the extra weight and eat healthier, you'll find all your symptoms go away. Would you like a referral to a weight management clinic?"

Please excuse me while I mentally punch a wall.

I will admit that research listed in the National Library of Medicine does make a connection between obesity and salivary glands. However, he had no idea what I ate on a daily basis, what exercises I performed, or anything else related to my weight. He made quick assumptions without an examination in order to get me out of the room quicker.

When I filed a complaint with the doctor's office, nothing came of it. I was told he was "retiring soon," and they were "sorry" I'd had a negative experience. They then asked me if I wanted to see a different doctor at their practice.

How about no.

If you think being different makes you invisible, try being fat. Society treats fatness like it's the worst thing you can be—a fate worse than death. Nobody wants to be fat because you are invisible in ways no one else is. People only see you if they want to deride you or make you the butt of a joke. Too many fat women have died of cancer or other life-altering diseases that went undiagnosed because of the fatphobia in medicine. It's a topic that comes up in panels at medical conferences because some doctors understand the need to change how physicians view patients. In fact, in the past ten years, weight discrimination has risen by 66%[i].

Many studies have shown that doctors treat fat patients differently. They often assume they are fat by choices they make and thus are lazy[ii] and less deserving of empathy[iii].

I have been a vegetarian since my teens. While I do enjoy chocolate, I've never had an overly large appetite. In fact, I tend to eat about 1400 calories on any given day, which is well under the 2000 calories in a person's recommended daily allowance. The food I eat is varied and mostly healthy.

Growing up in poverty meant I did grow up eating too much food from a box or the microwave, which continued into college as I was still poor. Once my wife and I felt financially secure enough, we bought lots of fruits and vegetables[9] and changed our diets. We both stay hydrated, and as a vegetarian, I do my best to ensure my protein comes from a variety of sources. My blood is checked regularly to ensure I'm not suffering from any deficiencies and other than my sun allergy[10] making Vitamin D a challenge, I'm fine.

Rather than continue down the path of ENTs, I began researching rheumatologists as both my eye doctor and dentist were positive my issues were Sjogren's. I found one rheumy that seemed decent enough, and during this appointment, she ran a more intensive set of blood tests than the first one I saw. In it, she found massive inflammation markers and other elements that pointed to an autoimmune disease. I tested negative for every kind she checked, but a fair number of people do, as seronegativity[11] is a known phenomenon in the world of autoimmune disorders. In fact, up to 50%[iv] of all Sjogren's sufferers are seronegative. While my blood work was clear of the antibodies, my symptoms fit Sjogren's perfectly, and thus, I was diagnosed with Sjogren's Disease.

From start of symptoms to diagnosis took two full years and over a dozen different doctors. It shouldn't have. Finding someone to listen to me who was willing to run the correct tests shouldn't have been a multi-year quest to throw a ring

9. Personally, I love cooked broccoli. I could eat cooked broccoli with every meal. I can't express to you how much I love this vegetable. Though I will admit, I can't stand it raw.

10. Yes, this is a real allergy. It's an immune system reaction to sunlight called PMLE, or Polymorphous Light Eruption. I tend to develop a skin rash or hives, migraines, nausea, and general malaise. I've had this since elementary school so I tend to take a lot of Vitamin D daily to help ensure I get what my body needs.

11. Seronegativity means having a negative serum reaction when checking for a disease's antibody. In people with Sjogrens, up to 50% of all cases are seronegative, including me. This means that while I don't have the antibodies yet, I probably will.

into a volcano. While this rheumatologist is passable, she is not well versed in Sjogren's. There have been many times where I've had to send her research articles on the disease in order to get the comprehensive treatment that I need.

Even on medication, my symptoms continued to worsen, and I decided to further educate myself on my disease[12] and look into a second opinion, provided I could find a decent rheumatologist. I joined various online groups and communities for people with Sjogren's who live in the Pacific Northwest. This is where I learned that our area is a desert in certain specialties. There are three amazing rheumatologists located here, but they can't accept any new patients because they don't have the time as there's only three of them.

I learned that there are two specialty centers for Sjogren's in the United States—one at John Hopkins on the East Coast and another at the Mayo Clinic in South Texas. Both have waiting lists years' long[13], and neither accept patients into their highly-specialized centers who are seronegative. So for now, I have to wait until my blood work catches up with my body.

During my diagnosis, my rheumatologist ordered a test known as an EMG[14], which is a test to measure how muscles respond to nerve signals. As part of my symptoms, I have peripheral neuropathy[15] in my hands, legs, and feet. Sjogren's attacks the sheaths or linings that protect nerves in the body and as such, the nerves end up damaged. With my neuropathy, I have severe numbness in my extremities as well as

---

12. Sjogren's used to be called a "syndrome," but under that medical distinction, too many doctors failed to take it seriously, despite its connections to Lupus, which is quite the serious autoimmune disease. Recently, the Sjogren's Foundation fought and won to have it medically reclassified as a disease, so if you see references online to Sjogren's Syndrome, they are out of date.

13. I'm not exaggerating.

14. Not related to the heart. That's an EKG. EMG stands for electromyography.

15. Neuropathy occurs when the nerves outside of the brain/spinal cord are damaged.

weakness and sometimes sharp stabbing pain in my toes. I can walk but sometimes my muscles collapse out from under me due to a miscommunication between my brain and my nerves.

This test can measure the severity of my nerve damage and sometimes identify the sources of it. At the time of testing, I didn't have diabetes or anything else that would cause the neuropathy. Between that knowledge and the test results, they could determine that in addition to my peripheral neuropathy from Sjogren's, I also had major fiber neuropathy. Further testing pointed to major spinal damage as the source. Knowing about my life long spine issues and countless spinal surgeries, this wasn't a surprise, so I filed the information away in case I'd need it later[16].

Because blood work is sometimes iffy, my rheumatologist also sent me for what's known as a lip biopsy. In some people with Sjogren's, certain cells can cluster in mouth tissue underneath the bottom lip. Research states that this is to be one test of many used in diagnostics, but it isn't always conclusive. For example, if the doctor doing the test isn't practiced at it, they may not collect enough tissue to test with.

I was sent to another ENT[17] for the lip biopsy. The test worried me as I'd heard people talk about how painful it is and how complex recovery can be. The doctor who did my test was ancient. I wrongly assumed that meant he would be practiced at this procedure, but instead he was incompetent as hell. His hands shook as he sliced open my mouth from my lip to the lingual frenulum[18]. Even with numbing meds, the pain shocked me like dipping my toes into hot lava. Once open, all he had to do was collect these cell clumps. When he

---

16. And I would.

17. I swear I've seen half the ENT's in the Seattle area.

18. I had to use this word because it's way too cool not to! The lingual frenulum is a small piece of tissue that connects your lips to your gums. You have another one--it connects your tongue to the floor of your mouth. Cool, huh?

looked at my mouth, his first comment was, "Wow! I've never seen a more perfect example of Sjogren's in a lip biopsy. These clumps are huge!"

He gathered what he needed and stitched me up. For days, my mouth screamed. It wasn't until two weeks later, around the time the stitches would come out, that over-the-counter pain meds gave me some relief. The ENT who did my biopsy was on vacation, so my follow-up appointment was with a different doctor, this one older than the first.

I pointed out to him how red and inflamed my incision was, but he waved me off. "Everything's healing as it should. Let's get those stitches out."

If I thought the incision hurt, it was nothing compared to having stitches yanked out of inflamed tissue. On the first stitch, I kicked the doctor. It wasn't intentional, but it hurt enough that my body reacted. This made him less than excited to remove the rest, though he tried.

"This last stitch is difficult. Your skin's stuck to it, so this is going to hurt."

He said this as if the previous ones had been pain free. Just a note that if your skin is sticking that much to stitches, perhaps you shouldn't remove them? I tried to mention this, but he pulled on the last stitch and my vision went dark for a moment.

"All done. Put some ice on it when you get home."

Blood coated my teeth the entire drive home. When I walked in the door, my lip area was very swollen. My wife took one look at me and off we went to minor emergency.

When the doctor saw my mouth, he paled. "What did you do?"

"I didn't do anything." As I explained my lip biopsy and appointment to remove the stitches, his eyes grew wider.

"Those stitches weren't ready to come out. Also, your incision site is infected."

Unlike the ENT, he numbed my mouth with topical lidocaine before injecting more lidocaine into the tissue. I didn't even feel the needle, he was that thorough. While he cleaned up the wound, a better look caused him to gasp.

"Did you know you still have partial stitches in here?"

The ENT had removed my stitches too fast and most of them had snapped under my skin, leaving partial threads inside.

"I suspect that some of this inflammation is your mouth reacting to the stitches. It's treating them like a foreign object. Rather than promoting healing, your body is trying to expel it. Might be why it's infected too. Breaking up the stitching like this didn't help."

Two hours later, my wound was cleaned and the partial stitches removed. By the next morning, most of the pain and swelling was gone. My body didn't like those stitches at all[19]. A few days later, the results of the biopsy were in.

Inconclusive.

The technician's notes stated that not enough of a sample had been gathered so they couldn't definitively test it for Sjogren's. All that pain and for nothing. I was told that if I chose to, I could repeat the test to see if a larger sample could be obtained, but no way was I going that route. For months, scar tissue built up inside my mouth.

The ENTs recommended I "massage" the area to break it up and acknowledged that it might never go away. While I took their advice, I worried because looking in the mirror, the lump of scar tissue was visible. It looked like I was pushing my tongue against my chin in an odd fashion or that I had a facial tumor of sorts. Every time I picked up my flute or clarinet, it hurt to play as both pressed against the scar tissue. Setting my mouth in the proper position or embouchure caused further pain.

It was six months before the scar tissue dissolved. There's

---

19. Remember my comments about living in a bubble? My body *hates* foreign objects, enough that I can't have any piercings of any kind. When I try, my body tries to expel those too and failing that, my skin grows over the piercing in an attempt to heal. My body's special, that's for sure.

still a small knot there if I push on it, but it's no longer painful. Considering how my body holds onto scar tissue like it's a chocolate bar[20], I wasn't about to repeat the test.

Because of the results, my rheumatologist wondered if maybe Sjogren's was the wrong diagnosis. She stated that while all my symptoms fit, the lip biopsy was negative. I pointed out that the lab report didn't say negative but inconclusive. Those are two different terms in medicine. She agreed, but still the question mark over her head remained.

I asked her what else it could be.

"Because your blood work is clear, we don't know. It could be any autoimmune disease. It doesn't change how we're treating it since your medication is working, but for now, we wait and see."

I *hate* being told to wait and see. To me, it's like throwing in the hat.

"But the medication isn't doing enough. My neuropathy is getting worse. I've been labeled a trip hazard, and my pain management specialist had insurance approve mobility aids for me, right down to the handicapped placard. I don't want to end up unable to walk because we didn't do something when we could have."

"There's nothing more we can do."

If I had a nickel for every time I've been told this, I'd be a rich, rich writer.

When folks with chronic issues get told this, they get desperate. I've seen folks rub oil on themselves, do yoga, eat only asparagus for weeks, and all sorts of uneducated attempts to feel better. From a scientific perspective, most of it's junk and any benefit is merely placebo, but people will try anything when they're scared and in pain.

I'm not immune to this as I decided to return to the first rheumatologist. His name kept recurring in local support groups as a decent doctor of general rheumatology. I'd been

---

20. Also a sign of autoimmune diseases.

hoping for someone with more Sjogren's experience but maybe he knew something more. My first experience with him had been negative, but maybe with notes from those who came after him, he'd be more inclined to look into my health. Maybe he'd find *something*.

Anything.

He didn't. In fact, I don't think he understood how rheumatology worked at all.

"There is no such thing as seronegativity. If you had Sjogren's, you'd be born with it. We'd see it in your blood work. Since we don't, I can't say that you have this disease."

"That's...that's not how this works," I said.

His tone sharpened, and I pulled up some of the articles I've referenced in the footnotes, articles that agreed with my knowledge on the subject. He dismissed these peer-reviewed articles, stating they were wrong. When I quoted the John Hopkins' Jerome L. Greene Sjogren's Center, *the* leading center on Sjogren's research in the nation, he laughed.

"If you believe them, you should go see them. I don't think I can help you anymore."

And with that, I was fired by my own doctor[21].

Welcome to the world of the disabled and fat: a fate worse than death.

Content Warning: *In the following, I will be discussing body dysphoria and eating disorders. If you need to skip this section, I understand.*

THIS TOPIC IS a toughie for me as I have a long history with body dysphoria, eating disorders, and child abuse. Even

---

21. Yes, I'm still trying to find a good rheumatologist in the Greater Seattle area. If you know one accepting new patients, ping me!

at forty-six, some of these struggles remain with me. They're topics discussed in therapy sessions, along with the trauma I suffered in childhood. Most of it relates to my paternal grandmother and my father's innate fear of death.

While she lived, my grandmother struggled with her weight as many women do. She gave birth to five children and was married to a man who never once understood how to show his emotions. For all that he was a quiet man who said very little, she loved him deeply, so when he died suddenly of a heart attack, the loss was life shattering.

I've been told that I loved my grandfather, that I used to sit in his lap as we put together puzzles or watched TV, but I have no memory of him. I have memories from before him, albeit a bit fuzzier now with age, but my time with him is gone. I was sitting in his lap when he had his heart attack and died.

The widow maker, they call it, because that's what it does. Like many men of his generation, he smoked heavily and developed emphysema. My jobless grandmother found herself with a house full of bills and no idea what to do. She found work, but without a high school diploma[22], she was limited in her options. Her job paid minimum wage, so she could pay her bills but not by much. Between work and grief, my grandmother gained weight—a lot of weight—and once gained, it was nigh impossible for her to lose it.

While she definitely took solace in food, genetics also played a role in this. Two of my aunts struggled with weight throughout their lives. While my father was rail thin as a teen, his thirties hit him hard as he gained the typical "Dad bod."

I'm not a psychologist, but between the early loss of his father and watching his mother and sisters struggle with weight, my father developed an unhealthy relationship with fat. In his mind, fat people were pariahs and brought it upon

22. These were different times. Women often didn't finish school in order to marry and be housewives.

191

themselves. If they were fat, it was entirely their fault and they deserved the bullying and shaming that came with it. While he believed this, the idea only applied to women and certainly not him.

In elementary school, I was a small kid until around 4th grade when puberty kicked in. Rather than seeing it for what it was—hormones—my father became deathly afraid that I was going to grow up as the worst thing I could be...*fat*. Each evening, while he sat in the house chowing down on an entire box of donuts[23] or something else equally unhealthy, I was sent outside to run laps. I wasn't allowed to come inside unless I'd run a certain number or the sun set, whichever came first.

After an entire day of school, playing outside, and generally running around like the child I was, come supper time I was hungry and tired. None of that mattered if I hadn't run those laps. Rather than model for me healthy eating or finding a sport I enjoyed that we could do together, my father taught me the worst lesson possible.

Exercise was a punishment, and food was the reward.

Food scarcity is real. When you're poor, using food as a reward rather than a necessity is not the way to a healthy food relationship, let alone one with exercise. To this day, I *hate* running. Even if I weren't disabled, you couldn't get me to run in a race if my life depended upon it[24]. Since most of my weight gain was hormone driven, running wasn't going to change the fact that I was growing into a woman. Lesson for any men reading this: breasts don't go away by running laps.

Of course, society's views of fat didn't help as even my grandmother joined in. She continually called me "husky," a term that to this day gives me a panic attack. On the rare

---

23. I am not kidding. The man wouldn't know healthy eating if it smacked him in the lips.

24. I truly hope the zombie apocalypse never happens because if it does, I'm so screwed. You know the #1 rule to winning against zombies right? Cardio.

occasion that I received new clothes, they came via shopping trips with my grandmother who thought buying me boys jeans would be a win. Not only were they cheaper, but they were made for "children my size."

I've seen the photos from my childhood, and I was not fat. I was kid-sized and kid-shaped. But fear that I might somehow balloon into a massive creature large enough to take down buildings in a single stomp was enough for them to rag on me every chance they got.

When people discuss how eating crappy food is cheaper than eating healthy, believe them. My father was a fan of fast food dollar menus and anything that could be microwaved— at least once we owned one. As a general rule, I don't like fast food, but it was fast and cheap—two requirements of single parents everywhere.

The rule of our house was eat garbage, but don't you dare gain weight.

I hit a growth spurt in middle school and slimmed out, but the size of my chest hid some of that. Being the late 80s, early 90s, society was deeply entrenched in diet and exercise fads that meant skinny was in. I remember wishing I could wrap my chest tight enough to make it disappear. Boys didn't want to date me because I was an interesting person. They only wanted a chance to potentially ogle my breasts[25]. The nickname Dolly got lobbed around the band room and for a length of time, I couldn't hear the name Dolly Parton without wanting to cut off my own breasts.

Having grown up near the ocean, I spent my gradeschool years swimming like a fish, which gave me toned muscles and strong thighs. I loved skating and biking and spent many summers doing both. Biking five miles in the Texas heat was nothing to me, and yet my father obsessed about my weight.

---

25. Not that they were given that opportunity. Even if I'd felt comfortable showing skin, I wasn't allowed to and didn't. The only ogling they got was through shirt fabric.

In high school, I received the dreaded letter home from the school nurse declaring me overweight and at risk for everything from heart disease to death. Heady stuff for a teenager with body image issues.

In the United States, medicine still relies on BMI[26] to calculate obesity, even though the creator of the measurement has long since agreed that the science behind it was never intended to be used on everyone. In fact, someone with lots of muscle can have the same BMI as a fat person. Can you imagine calling a body builder obese?

Ninth grade left me heavier than a regular BMI said I should be, but I was a very active ninth grader. I marched in marching band, which included four hour daily practice sessions in the hot Texas sun, as well as weekly games with half-time shows. I still biked and often visited the local skating rink where I'd skate for hours with friends. While I definitely had a soda addiction[27], it was diet soda, so I wasn't guzzling high fructose corn syrup on the daily.

Freshman year, I felt fat. The nurse said I was. My father said I was. Even my grandmother, who was more like a mother to me, said I was. I was a short teenager amidst puberty with a lot more muscle mass than many of my friends.

When I look back at photos of myself, I wasn't fat. I was female.

By junior year, I was done feeling fat. I understood that my father was abusive, but I couldn't see how his fat-shaming me was a part of that. I believed society when it said that

---

26. BMI, or Body Mass Index, was created over 200 years ago by a mathematician from Belgium. It was developed solely based on white men from Europe and doesn't take into account activity level, biological sex, race, ethnicity, or genetics, which all play roles in health. Source: Katella, K. (2023, August 4).

Why you shouldn't rely on BMI alone. Yale Medicine. https://www.yalemedicine.org/news/why-you-shouldnt-rely-on-bmi-alone

27. Who didn't in the 90's?

people my size were going to ruin the country and cause the health care system to collapse.

I'd seen my grandmother gain weight too and how some of it affected her health. There was no part of me that wanted to be her, so I decided that I would watch what I ate. Maybe if I lost weight, I wouldn't have to flee home. Maybe my father would learn to love me more, and I could have the relationship I'd always wanted with him—one that was safe. One that meant he loved *all* of me.

When he moved me away from my support system, aka my friends who were helping me to leave home, that was the bullet to my self-esteem. I decided that working two jobs while going to school would keep me too busy to notice I was hungry.

Anorexia worked. Between the physical labor of working and not eating much, if anything, I dropped down below what BMI says I should be at for someone assigned-female-at-birth with a height of 5'2". Like most people with an eating disorder, I wore baggy, oversized clothes in an attempt to hide most of the weight loss. It helped that this was during the 90s grunge era so wearing plaid shirts and baggy jeans was in fashion.

You'd think for a man so obsessed with my weight that my father would notice, but he didn't. He continued to make comments about how I was going to end up like my grandmother if I didn't "watch out."

I've heard many tales from women about how cruel mothers can be with regards to their daughters' weight, but my father's obsession—and it *is*[28] an obsession—found ways to needle into my skull. If we went out to eat at a restaurant or someone's home, I was hyper-aware of everything I swallowed.

---

28. I'm using the present tense here because at 46, he still obsesses over my weight. He calls it "concern for my health" but let's name it for what it is—his attempt to control me.

Were they watching me? How long would they judge me for being fat if I had another piece of bread?

To this day I struggle with thoughts like this, especially if I'm eating alone in a public place. If I'm out with my wife, sometimes she has to remind me that it's okay to have dessert.

My father's nitpicking, his constant criticism of my appearance, and his absolute dread that I'd end up a "fat cow like [my] grandma" left scars across both my flesh, my brain, and my heart.

At age 17, I weighed 114 pounds and wore a size 3 jeans. More skeletal than healthy, but I'd done it. I'd beaten BMI. Yet none of it mattered to my father who still viewed me as fat.

When my friends arrived over the holidays to break me out of my home, they were shocked by my appearance. It wasn't until I took a good, hard look in the mirror that I realized what they saw. BMI may have said I was healthy, but I'd lost so much muscle. I was gaunt and pale. Unhealthy. A blood test showed me to be anemic and deficient in most vitamins and minerals.

Let that sink in for a moment. The only way I'd been able to reach the weight that BMI stated was healthy for my frame was to starve myself and when I did so, there was nothing healthy about it. I'm stating this because this was a lesson it took me a *long* time to learn, too long to be honest, and I think it's a lesson more people need to hear.

I shared an apartment with one of my rescue-team friends at the time. Alone in my own place, I still struggled to eat. My father wasn't there to watch me, but I felt his eyes on me anytime I opened the refrigerator. If I ate a slice of cheese, what would he think? What would my friends think? Inside my head, voices taunted me.

"That cheese has fat. You don't want to be your grandmother, do you?"

"If you eat that cookie, you'll gain weight. Look how skinny you are now. Why mess that up?"

No one spoke these words aloud. No one was judging me but me, the message having been drilled into my head since first grade. I stayed unhealthily thin through my senior year. In fact, my prom dress had to be taken in because of how much weight I lost between buying it and wearing it. The most annoying bit of weight loss was that even at my skinniest, my breasts were still enormous. Lost weight never changed them as genetics decreed they would make me Dolly Parton no matter what I did.

I hated them. I wanted to chop them off and be done with it.

There was nothing good about them: they hurt my back and shoulders, they gave me the wrong kind of attention, they made my frame disproportionate, and I could see no reason for me to enjoy having them. I didn't realize at the time that some of my body dysmorphia was brought on by the fact that I'm nonbinary. Lacking the vocabulary to address this meant I figured I was broken. Everyone always commented that I wasn't normal so maybe they were correct.

My wife and I were good friends throughout high school, brought closer together when her mother died, which happened around the same time I realized that my home life wasn't normal. We began dating senior year and slowly, she worked on helping me restore my self-esteem, though it wasn't until college that I felt more comfortable eating.

Between genetics and the flip-flop I'd given my metabolism with anorexia, my change in eating had the expected effect—I gained weight. It didn't help that being on my own meant I could eat whatever I wanted. It was as if something had snapped in me and all of the horrible foods I hadn't been allowed were suddenly on the table like a feast. Everything from cheesy pastas to slices of cake, I enjoyed it.

The first year of college, I walked into my workplace to overhear a colleague talking about me. "She's gained so much weight. Maybe she should lay off the cookies."

My insides deflated as I ran into the restroom. Looking in

the mirror, I felt fat. Hearing someone say what I'd always worried people were saying threatened to undo the healing I thought I'd done.

The reality is that disordered eating works in both ways and like an alcoholic, it never goes away. You're always struggling with an eating disorder. It may have been months or years or decades since it affected you physically, but the mental scars remain.

My wife and I began using the college gym to work out and vowed to eat better, which is a challenge when you're poor college students. I lost some weight and gained back much of my muscle mass, but my body stubbornly decided that it liked the size I was, which is how weight gain works. In fact, weight gain is controlled by "hormonal and metabolic dysregulation[v]" which is often outside of a person's control.

While I wasn't eating healthy by any means, much of my weight gain was related to the above. Even when I shifted from starvation mode to eating again, it was never a case of me eating an entire cake or a box of donuts like my father did. Despite my exercising and eating better, most of the weight stubbornly remained.

With the growing severity of my spinal defect, being as active as I wanted to be dwindled in my twenties. Teaching is a physically challenging job as you tend to be on your feet for 8+ hours day, constantly bustling around a classroom or school. Lots of reaching up high and squatting beside working students means that the job can require a certain level of mobility, something I was quickly losing.

By the time I hit thirty and the hormonal shifts that come with that, I struggled to bike or swim, the two activities I loved. Every visit to the gym ended in my being injured. Torn rotator cuff, broken fingers from falling, twisted ankles, and more. Having crappy state insurance meant my doctors weren't the best. They had no idea what was wrong with me, certainly not that I had EDS[29], meaning all of my joints were hypermobile or too flexible.

Living with EDS means that movement is dangerous for me and has to be done in a tightly controlled manner because if I move too quickly, my joints dislocate. I've been able to pop my hips in and out of their sockets at will since I was seven[30]. I can dislocate my shoulders by leaning on them and pop them back into place as easily. My ankles roll with the weather changes, so walking in unfamiliar or sloped areas can lead to major damage. Toss into the mix my neuropathy, which worsened each year, and I was a mess.

No one was ready to say I was disabled as no doctor wants to make that diagnosis, but I was well on my way. Of course, if you don't exercise, you gain weight. It didn't matter that most days, I ate no more than 1300 calories. My body decided that more weight was what I needed.

I spent most of my thirties hating myself and the way I looked. Shopping for clothes became lessons in trying and failing to control my panic attacks, but as the age of Internet shopping blossomed, I sighed in relief. I'd never have to embarrass myself with entering a store in person again.

Leaving the judgmental teaching profession behind helped a great deal with my self-image and self-esteem issues. Living in the Seattle area as a full-time author helped more. Here among my geeky, nerdy, and sometimes queer peers, I can live as myself. It's expected to dress differently and shops up here have a better range of sizes. Giving voice to my full identity meant growing comfortable in my own skin for the first time in my life.

My wife has always loved me, no matter what size I am or how I present myself. She loved me as a woman, and she loves me just as much as a nonbinary queer. While I appre-

---

29. EDS stands for Ehlers Danlos syndrome which is a hereditary connective tissue disorder.

30. I used to think it was fun and did it to freak people out until I grew up and realized my hips hurt from doing that so much. Oops!

ciate the hell out of her for that, loving myself is a necessary part of our relationship too. Weight loss and gain is part of living, but it's a complex topic for me, even now. I'm forty-six and while I'm mostly happy with my size, there are still days when little whispers rage in my head to try and tear me down.

Anxiety is good at that—the tearing you down bit. The ability to think of all the what-ifs is a great talent as a writer but not so much as a person with panic-anxiety disorder. Being creative means my imagination is *very, very* good, but that also means I can not only picture a possibility, I can walk around inside it like it's happening. I can smell the smoke, I can taste the blood from biting my tongue, I can hear the screams, and worse, I can feel the emotions of the moment. Again, great when I'm writing. Not so much when my anxiety is asking me if I look fat.

These are the struggles people like me deal with, but it's worse when those struggles bleed into the medical profession.

Every time I have an appointment to see a new physician, they double check my blood pressure. Every time. The first time the numbers come up, they think they've made a mistake. By their thinking, there's no way someone fat can have excellent blood pressure. So they check it a second time and when the numbers are the same, they ask if I normally have blood pressure in the normal range.

Yes, Dr. Biased, my blood pressure is normally 105/60[31].

They often ask what statins I'm on, to which the answer is none. They ask when the last time I was checked for diabetes was and when was my cholesterol last checked. I have those numbers checked annually. I've never had high cholesterol and my heart is healthy too.

That's when they give a double-take and scroll rapidly through whatever computer history they have. If they're connected to any major hospital in the area, they'll see my

---

31. If I could insert a facepalm here, I would.

current list of medications as well as the blood tests and physicals. They see I'm not lying and yet, their brains can't figure out how I'm healthy.

But being fat, medical treatment is an exercise in patience and frustration. I'm the patient who goes in for a cat scratch and gets told that if I lost weight, it might help me. This was the case when I scheduled an appointment for a cough I'd developed. As someone with autoimmune issues and allergies, I don't tend to get sick, at least not in the normal sense. While people run through colds and flus, I don't. By definition, having an autoimmune disease means that my body fights too hard. In fact, it fights itself in its rush to keep enemies at bay.

So when I get sick, my illnesses tend to be related to my overactive immune system. I get sinus, ear, and upper-respiratory infections stemming from my body attacking its own cells. When spring hits and everything grows, my allergies are at their worst. I tend to spend most of spring wishing it were winter as I sneeze my way through it. Congestion tends to aggravate my asthma, which in turn can lead to coughing. This illness was severe enough that I managed to break a rib coughing. The ER could do nothing for the rib but suggested I follow up with my doctor for some cough medicine.

My doctor could see the chart from the ER where they'd taken an x-ray of the broken rib. In it, you could also see my lungs, which showed no signs of bronchitis or pneumonia, the latter of which I've thankfully never had. She pulled up the imaging and pointed at my lungs.

"I think your lungs are a bit larger than normal," she said. When I shrugged, she added, "There could be something wrong with your heart."

"Could my lungs be a bit inflamed because of my upper respiratory infection?"

She shrugged. "It's possible, but with your other risk factors, I'd like to send you for an echocardiogram[32]."

Something to note, she mentioned risk factors, of which there is only one: I'm fat. As my primary care physician, she knew my numbers. With no high blood pressure and so on, there was no indication that anything was wrong with my heart. If she was concerned, most people would at least do an EKG[33] first.

I asked about this and was told again that with my risk factors, we needed to jump to the expensive, detailed test. "What risk factors?"

"Obesity puts you at risk of a heart attack and with the enlarged lungs—"

"Which could be explained by my cough."

"Yes, well, let's be sure."

Normally, I would have left her office and never returned, but Sjogren's does carry the risk of interstitial lung disease, which can lead to heart cell damage. If nothing else, I could ask the cardiologist what he thought before agreeing to anything.

When the scheduler called, she tried to be as polite as possible on the phone, but her tone made it clear what the cardiology department thought about my doctor.

"Dr. Heart[34] reviewed the imaging and doesn't see anything in your records to indicate the need for this test, but your insurance company approved it, so we'd like to schedule a consultation first where we'll do an EKG[35]. If at

---

32. Echocardiograms do more than EKGs as they are cardiac ultrasounds and show blood flow through the heart, any narrowing of blood flow, electrical signals through the heart, the speed of blood flow, and so on. It's a very detailed and expensive procedure.

33. An ECG/EKG, or electrocardiogram, shows how a heart is beating by measuring electricity from the heart. It can pick up some heart abnormalities and is usually the first test done to check for a heart condition.

34. Obviously not his name.

35. Told you it should've come first!

that time the cardiologist thinks you should have an echo, then we'll schedule that at that time."

The cardiologist I saw was a polite young doctor who chatted with me at length about my health history as well as how often I exercised and what I ate from day to day. He was very thorough before running the EKG, which was perfectly normal.

"I don't see any reason why this test was ordered. Did your doctor tell you why she placed it?" he asked.

"She said my lungs were slightly enlarged and since I'm fat, I must have heart issues. Well, she more implied the second part, but you get the idea."

He shook his head. "I don't like to speak ill of colleagues but your lungs were inflamed by your upper-respiratory infection. You labs are great, as is the EKG. I would suggest you find a new primary care doctor.

"Tell you what," he said while closing his laptop. "Since you have Sjogren's and your insurance has approved this, let's go ahead and do the echo with contrast. It'll give us an established baseline of your heart so that if your autoimmune disease progresses, we'll better catch any heart damage that occurs. It'll also prove your heart's fine should any other doctors question that."

"And I can watch! I've never seen what my heart looks like before[36]."

We scheduled the procedure and two weeks later, they injected contrast into me and hooked me up to a multitude of electrodes. The technician used an ultrasound wand on my chest and boom, there was my heart! The test lasted about an hour and gave me a complete visual of the organ keeping me alive. Not only was the electrical current strong and healthy, but my aorta and other vessels where unobstructed. Everything from blood flow to rhythm and strength was perfect. The technician mentioned she rarely sees hearts that healthy

---

36. Leave it to me to be geeky about my heart.

in her line of work because they don't usually do echocardio-grams on healthy hearts.

In other words, my primary care physician was fatphobic as fuck in her decision to call for an unneeded, expensive test like this. She made no comment to the results, nor did she apologize for her assumptions. After the results were sent to her, I called the office to explain I was no longer a patient at that office or of hers. I made it very clear as to the *why* and filed it as an official complaint.

She's still a doctor there, meaning they didn't care one bit that they charged my insurance company several thousand dollars for nothing. At least I got to see my heart. While I can look back now and remember how cool it was to see blood flowing in me, my former doctor's judgments didn't help my body image issues.

Every time I see a new doctor, my anxiety spikes as I wonder whether I'll get what I need out of the appointment or whether this will be yet another doctor who sees someone fat and decides I'm not worth it, leaving me to wrestle with my anxiety the rest of the day. Is it their opinion that I'm too fat to deserve decent health care?

What if I become one of those statistics—one of those fat people who dies of some horrible cancer that wasn't caught because everyone wrote off my pain and symptoms? It happens more than the medical community likes to admit.

It's bad enough to judge myself. I don't need it from the people I trust to keep me alive and healthy.

CHAPTER
TWELVE
NOT ALL DOCTORS

> *Wherever the art of Medicine is loved, there is also a love of Humanity."*

> HIPPOCRATES

NOT EVERY DOCTOR is an asshole[1].

One of my doctors in the Seattle area was a pain management doctor. Usually when folks talk about pain management, they do so with disdain as most folks in pain management expect that we're drug seeking, and even if we're not, they're under stringent federal and state regulations in regards to prescribing pain killers. My guy, who we'll call Dr. Jack, was the most patient doctor I've ever met in my entire life. I wish on a daily basis he was a rheumatologist.

My first appointment with him took almost two hours and was one of the most thorough appointments I've ever had. He dug into my entire medical history and every diagnosis in the hopes that it would help him treat me and my pain better.

---

1. I was recently part of a study on this exact topic, though I believe it was worded more along the lines of medical biases by physicians rather than doctors are assholes. I like my title better—yes, I totally went there. Subnote: if you don't get the joke, don't sweat it. My sense of humor is sometimes odd.

"If I know the details, my help can only be more accurate."

When he found out that I was a writer, he visited my website where he discovered I would be a guest at a local convention. Dr. Jack bought tickets for the geeky convention and showed up with his kids. Not only did they enjoy themselves, but Dr. Jack attended one of my panels and visited my table, where he bought not one but two of my books.

This was a doctor who went out of his way to connect with his patients so he could better understand their needs.

In other words, he was a true doctor[2].

With him, I didn't have to fight so hard to advocate and educate. I could be the Raven who hurt and sought help. I could be vulnerable and let someone else take the wheel for once. He didn't tell me that everything would be better with weight loss. He didn't lecture me on how to eat or how to move. In fact, he fought with my insurance company multiple times to get medical massage therapy covered so that I could experience some relief from crippling pain.

During his treatment of me, he was the one who convinced my rheumatologist to order the EMG test and seek out the causes of my neuropathy. While he was sure that Sjogren's was a part of it, he suspected there might be more, and he was correct.

The technicians reading the EMG reports noted major spine damage causing major-fiber neuropathy in my hips and legs. Post-EMG, Dr. Jack ordered an MRI with contrast on my entire spine and hips, and the results were eye-opening.

Sometimes, when embryos are developing in the womb, nerve pathways and bone formations don't always grow as planned. When studying my MRI, the radiologists who read it discovered that two of the major nerves running through my spine were partially fused together. This wasn't something that happened suddenly. In fact, the only known cause

_____

2. Why is this the exception instead of the rule??

for this is a birth defect related to Spondylolysis, which is also an autoimmune disorder. When Dr. Jack explained this to me, so much of my life with pain made more sense.

The fusion impacts my hips and everything down to my feet. He didn't know whether or not it would lead to paralysis but at least we had a place to begin. Knowledge is power and all of that. His hope was that continuing to work on my mobility and using resources such as massage, we might keep my neuropathy in line.

This diagnosis happened at the end of 2018. I'd been fighting chronic back issues and pain since childhood, but a mix of being poor[3] and doctors who couldn't see past obesity meant I suffered for decades without any idea what was going on.

My visits to Dr. Jack also exposed that I had EDS or Ehlers-Danlos syndrome[4] and one of my legs is longer than the other. The MRI also showed some mild scoliosis[5], which was never caught in childhood. For all that he was meant to manage my pain, Dr. Jack's need to be thorough led to me understanding the connections between everything in my body.

Symptoms of sun allergies[6] tied in with my generalized allergies and asthma, pointed a strong finger at my overactive immune system and thus, Sjogren's. Various injuries and pains in childhood could now be connected to scoliosis, EDS, and the birth defect in my spine, which also bore ties to autoimmune issues.

For once in my life, my medical profile made sense.

Life couldn't allow me a Dr. Jack in my life for long, as in 2019, he was diagnosed with Lupus. The doctor who treated

---

3. Which usually means no insurance.
4. EDS affects connective tissues, much like Sjogren's does, but it specifically attacks your skin, joints, and blood vessel walls. People who have it tend to have overly flexible joints (*another reason why I fall a lot!*) and stretchy skin.
5. Scoliosis is when the spine curves sideways.
6. Thought to also be caused by autoimmune issues

so many with compassion and thorough care was now in need of specialists himself. Having the money to do so, Dr. Jack made the decision to retire from practice in order to spend more time with his family and travel to other countries where healthcare meant he might actually survive his disease longer than average.

He apologized for leaving us. The diagnosis bore a profound impact on him, and I think he knew that his colleagues weren't up to the level of care he'd always given. In trying to find another pain management specialist, his colleagues told me my case was "too complicated" for pain management and that I would need to see a rheumatologist or a neurologist.

That's another way I could be rich—for all the times I've been told I'm medically too complex or challenging. Finding a decent primary care physician who can see the entire picture is like winning the lottery.

Only I haven't won yet.

I genuinely hope Dr. Jack is living his fullest life somewhere awesome, and I am extremely blessed to have known him as my doctor, if only for a few years.

FATPHOBIA AND FAT-SHAMING IS a prevalent part of American society. It invades our literature, our ability to find jobs, and it dwells in Hollywood like a never-ending disease. When *Avengers: Endgame* premiered, discussion erupted about Thor's character and his struggles with depression and eating disorders.

For some, he modeled what they understood, sometimes intimately—grief and its ties to weight. To others, he was the butt of a movie-length joke. As someone who's fat, who has a mental illness, and has suffered from an eating disorder, I found the joke harmful. Making fun of someone who's grieving and struggling is never funny.

Below is a letter I wrote at the time in order to process my thoughts on the matter.

EAT A SALAD, aka Dear Non-Fat People of the World,

If you've seen *Avengers: Endgame*, you'll get the above reference[7] to "eat a salad" and by the end of this letter, you'll get why it bothered so many people.

While I'm going to be blunt and honest about some of the issues I've struggled with, I want to start off by saying that this is not a post to thin-shame or make people feel badly about being healthy. I no more want to do that then I would wish to fat-shame someone, trust me. Nor am I saying that being overweight is synonymous with being healthy. There are unhealthy, thin people and healthy, overweight people. Health is complicated. That being said, this is a letter to those who haven't walked this world and this life as a fat person in hopes that I can erase some of the fatphobia of society.

Prejudice isn't anything new to this world, but there's one form of prejudice that transcends skin color, sexuality, gender, and nationality—society's disdain for fat people.

For reasons beyond my understanding, one of the worst things you can in life is fat. We're hired less often, promoted less often, paid less, and worse, we're believed less by everyone from family members to doctors. What's worse is that this fat discrimination is considered socially acceptable.

It's okay to tell someone they need to lose weight.

Think on that a moment. If I told someone with gray hair that they needed to cover it up with hair dye, I'd be seen as

---

7. When Thor's character talks with his mother about his feelings, she notices his gut and tells him to eat a salad. It's meant to be a joke, but it's part of a long history of society shaming anyone who doesn't fit an ideal image of humanity.

rude. If I mentioned to a stranger that they should have Lasik and ditch the glasses, they'd tell me to fuck off and rightly so.

So why is it okay to tell others they're fat? As if we didn't know. I didn't wake up one morning with this revelation and say, "Wow! I didn't know this about myself. Why didn't someone tell me?"

Being fat is something I've dealt with for as many years as I've dealt with pain. Maybe longer. I'd like to say it began with a serious knee injury in middle school that crippled me for a time, but my genetics says it began before that as I've never been average weight.

When I look at photos of me as a child, there's nothing wrong with how I look, yet family and friends referred to me as "chunky." Being called chunky at five isn't healthy for anyone's self-esteem, and it certainly wasn't for me.

This fear of fat permeates everything in our culture, and it gives people unrealistic expectations about their bodies and whether those bodies are worthy of love. When my grandmother died, she hated her body. She died feeling like a useless burden to everyone around her. She suffered when her husband died, and it never once dawned on her that she might find love again because who could love a fat woman? These are the lessons that I learned growing up, which is part of the reason why when I look back at young me, I can see how much I hid my body. Even then, weight was a constant mental companion.

My first experiences with fatphobia in the medical field came during middle school–that injury I mentioned earlier. In 7th grade, a boy pushed me down the stairs at school. My right kneecap struck the metal-capped steps multiple times during the two flights I fell down. The doctor provided to us by our crappy-HMO explained that my continued knee pain post-fall was because I was overweight. He said if I lost weight, my knee wouldn't hurt anymore, because even at thirteen, being overweight was the reason for every plague I ever had and ever would have. The second opinion doctor called them "growing pains" and wrote me off as well.

We'd moved again by high school and with my father's new job came better insurance. My knee was a hot mess, which set my body up to move wrong. Everything I did was in reaction to pain and hypermobile joints. This new doctor agreed that something was wrong, and I was sent to surgery to fix it. Most of my cartilage was damaged or gone, knocked out of place by the fall and continued physical activity post-fall. In many places, I was bone on bone. My pain finally had a reason that made sense.

I suffered three years in the excruciating pain of bone on bone because doctors couldn't see past my fat. Most of my high school experience was spent like most teenaged young women–unhappy within my own skin.

Despite a wife who loves me, doubts about myself crept into the oddest places in my life. Every job I ever interviewed for, I second guessed myself during the interviews. Would they hire me, or would they assume I couldn't do the job because I didn't fit their ideal of how a woman should look? Just visiting the doctor's office was a chore. I had to fight for a flu test because the doctor wanted to refer me to a nutritionist to "help me lose weight" instead of focusing on the actual reason for my visit. I could be running a 103-degree fever, and the doctor would want to talk about my home exercise program. Back when I taught, students would leave me notes telling me how amazing I was as a teacher...but I'd be even more amazing if I were thin. If you ask any overweight person you know about this, they can tell you horror stories—especially women.

People think they mean well when they ask if you've recently lost weight or when they want to tell you about the new diet fad that worked for them, despite overwhelming evidence that diets don't work[i]. People also mean well when they tell people with depression to "go for a walk outside" or when they tell folks with autoimmune disorders to "try some yoga" or snort some essential oils.

What people don't realize or think about is how deeply rooted prejudice is in our words and actions. What people don't do is think about how much their well-meaning costs others—like telling your son to "eat a salad" as a way to deal with his PTSD.

As an author, I'm well aware that words have power. I've lost friends to suicide because of the power of words. Even when we mean well, we have the power to do great harm. As creators, we have an obligation to be cognizant of our true motivations for "meaning well."

When trying to get my autoimmune disease diagnosed, I lost track of the "specialists" who told me all my symptoms would go away if I lost weight. I lost track of the number who ignored serious symptoms because I'm fat and presented then as female.

When my physician ordered that unnecessary echocardiogram, my anxiety went wild. It didn't matter that an echocardiogram is nothing more than a super-fancy ultrasound. I was fighting a panic attack the entire way through the day. It didn't help that I had to go to a major hospital and walk into a cardiac unit to get the procedure.

Everyone in the waiting room was a good 20+ years older than me. They stared at me the entire time I waited for my name to be called, probably wondering what I had done at so young an age to be there. Or maybe they didn't have to wonder. Maybe they just assumed like the rest of the world that because I'm fat, I'm a walking disaster. It's taken a long time for me to love myself, especially post-autoimmune diagnosis, but this one moment threatened to undo all of that.

It was mortifying to sit there beneath their judgment, like there was something horrifically wrong with me.

Watching my heart beat on the screen was amazing, I'm not going to lie. Seeing it pump blood to the rest of my body…it's something we take for granted. The technician and nurse both tried to make it a learning experience for me since they could see my panic. For example, I learned quite a bit about what Hollywood gets wrong with regards to a pulmonary embolism. During an echo, they pump tiny air bubbles into your heart, which you'd think would be bad, but as it turns out, it's necessary. Once done, I retreated to my car where I burst into tears.

The entire procedure took two hours–straight through lunch–and as I sat in my car, I realized I didn't want to eat. The idea of food was embarrassing and felt…wrong. It wasn't until I was halfway home that I realized why. This one moment had made it easy to slip into an unhealthy style of thinking. Like an addict, food disorders are a one-day-at-a-time type ordeal, and many find it easy to relapse.

Worst part is, many people probably think skipping a meal is good for a fat person, but it isn't. Starving yourself plays havoc with the metabolism and messes with the body's ability to be healthy. It makes it harder to lose weight and easier to gain it.

The problem with that test was that it was unnecessary. Insurance will receive the results and use that as an example of yet another doctor ordering an unnecessary and expensive test. They'll use it as leverage for why they should be the ones deciding what is medically necessary instead of my doctors.

That right there is how we end up with people with cancer not getting diagnosed early enough because insurance didn't want to pay for the tests or countless other issues that have sprung up as a result of for-profit health care.

Even though I've left my former PCP behind, how many others will she harm? Folks who might not have the support network that I do? It's not just her, and it's not just doctors. Society believes fat people are better left hidden in the shadows—better unseen and unheard.

To those that aren't fat, please examine your own prejudices. Before you "mean well," think about your motivations. To everyone, be an advocate for your health. You know your body better than anyone else. You might not be a doctor, but you live with yourself every day.

On that note, I make this vow to the world:

I will not be silent, nor will I hide myself from view.

I will not allow society to dictate my health decisions, and I will advocate for better healthcare.

And no, I won't go eat a salad…unless I want one.

CHAPTER
THIRTEEN
THE CONS OF CONS

> *What writers of fantasy, science fiction, and much historical fiction do for a living is different from what writers of so-called literary or other kinds of fiction do. The name of the game in F/SF/HF is creating fictional worlds and then telling particular stories set in those worlds. If you're doing it right, then the reader, coming to the end of the story, will say, 'Hey, wait a minute, there are so many other stories that could be told in this universe!' And that's how we get the sprawling, coherent fictional universes that fandom is all about."*
>
> NEIL STEPHENSON

I'M IN LOVE.

I'm in love with my body.

It's a sentence I try to say often, but how did it happen? The falling in love part, not my body because that part I know. Honestly, I'm not entirely sure how I learned to love my body, but in accepting myself, I found myself, if that makes sense. Settling into the Seattle area and being self-employed meant I could dye my hair and cut it in a way I'd always wanted.

Growing up, I'd avoided short cuts because I'd been told they'd make me look fatter. The one time I took the risk, the Super Cuts "stylist[1]" gave me the flat haircut from hell. It was horrible and at that time, I vowed never to have short hair again.

In Seattle, I took a risk with a stylist, who like most, is a hair artist. I sport an asymmetrical cut these days, where one side of my head is shaved, the back is similar to a pixie cut, and the other side has one long swoosh of hair in a reverse or inverted bob. Looking in the mirror, I look good.

I've had green, blue, purple, teal colors as well as fire hair[2] and rainbows, meaning every color at once. While my natural hair color is closer to black, I've never felt that it fit me.

It felt…boring. Normal.

I'm not your usual writer and artist, and at this point, my ever-changing hair color as become part of my brand. When people look for me at a convention, they look for my hair first. In terms of clothes, I'm a geek. I love fandom, especially the many worlds of science fiction and fantasy. Most of my clothing either borders on cosplay[3] or fits an eclectic style straddling ren-faires or the gaming world. I have a few normal pieces of clothing, but not much as I left most of the boring outfits behind when I left teaching.

I hated looking normal back then. Being my own boss means I can wear whatever I want. Some days, I write in pajamas—geeky pajamas but still pajamas. I have writing related tattoos and plan to get more. I have a jewelry cabinet

---

1. I put this in quotes because these poor folks made minimum wage and hated their jobs. They gave crappy cuts to cheapskates who didn't want to pay a living wage.

2. Think bright reds, oranges, and yellows like flames.

3. Cosplay stands for costume play. You'll see a ton of cosplayers at Comicon and other conventions where they dress up as their favorite characters from a variety of books, TV shows, movies, comics, and so on.

full of geeky accessories, and when I have the time and money, I sport geeky nail art as well.

Who I am is more than just appearance, though it helps when I physically appear the way I mentally see myself. Holding my first published novel in my hands made my dreams reality, so success also affects my body relationship. I'd transitioned from teacher to author, a feat I never thought would happen. Recognizing my queerness and my gender identity gave me a confidence I'd been lacking as well.

So yes, I'm in love with my body.

Despite all of this, I still find myself vulnerable in spaces I don't expect.

I love the Seattle area and the freeness it gives me to be myself, but my first exposure to the writing community up here was a conference that labeled itself as a general writing conference, meaning for *all* writers. The conference's title alone was very nondescript and its webpage gave no indication that this was *not* your typical writers' conference.

There were opportunities to pitch your books to editors, which excited me since I'd just finished writing *Amaskan's Blood*, Book I in my *Boahim Trilogy*. I signed up for several time slots to pitch my book in hopes of finding an editor willing to buy it for publication. As a new attendee, I managed to miss being added to all the mailing lists and social media groups associated with the conference, so I showed up the first day expecting to have my brain explode with new information.

The conference took place at a local hotel, and I sat in the hotel lounge having arrived a tad early. There I met several other authors who were excited to discover I was a "newbie" to both the area and the conference itself, and when I say excited, I mean *excited*. Albeit lightheartedly, they fought over who would "adopt" me as their shadow for the con. The winner would show me the ropes and make sure my experience was the "best ever!"

I don't mind optimists—truly—but there's a level of cheeriness that some folks have that borders on annoying, not to mention exhausting. My mentor exuded an almost cloying level of happy that had my skin crawling from the get-go, but when in Rome... so I slapped on my best "YAY!" smile and off we went into the conference hall.

From the moment I walked in, I knew this was not a writing convention for general genre writers as the first people to greet me were five "firefighters" wearing nothing more than a thong. They were ripped and slick with oil like they'd just walked off a porn set, and they gathered around me as they set up a little welcome dance.

As someone who's demisexual, I'm being polite in saying this was *not* comfortable for me. Even if I were a romance writer, objectifying people like that is not my bag and certainly not at a professional conference...or what I'd expected to be a professional conference. When I turned around to leave, my mentor finally ripped her gaze away from the eye candy long enough to realize that I was trying to flee the group.

"What's wrong?" she asked.

"Um...I thought this was a writing conference."

"It is."

I'd been to several professional writing conferences in Texas and none of them featured strippers or entertainers like this. I said as much, and my mentor couldn't hold back her laughing.

"You write romance, my dear! Why would we have a stuffy event like that when we could mix work *and* play?"

"But I don't write romance."

My mentor halted, her face falling. "What do you write then?"

"I write science fiction and fantasy."

"Oh, so your romance is in space?"

It took a few minutes to explain to her that no, I don't write bodice-busters in space, and when I said I wrote SF/F, I meant it. There might be a few romantic sub-plots but as a general rule, no, I don't write in the romance genre.

Genre fiction has rules, folks. People who pick up a sci-fi novel expect certain elements in the plot line. If they pick up a book expecting a roaring space adventure, and instead find a plot focusing on whether two people hook up, then the author has failed to meet the reader's expectations. It's called a bait and switch, and it's not cool to do that to your readers. If the book's marketed as a romance novel, readers expect a happily-ever-after ending and a plot focused on the character(s)' relationship. Where the story takes place is just frosting at that point.

My genre fiction would never be marketed as romance. Ever.

Once my mentor understood that, her eyes grew large. "I'm not sure you're in the right place. Is there another conference happening here this weekend? How did you find this conference?"

I explained how I found them via a simple Internet search. I also mentioned how nowhere on the site did it mention this was a writing conference for romance writers. It specifically stated the conference was for *all* writers.

My mentor dragged me to the registration table where I divulged the story for a second time. This resulted in them calling for the Woman in Charge, aka the leader of said local romance writers.

"Well, how different is writing sci-fi really? It's just romance in space, right? I'm sure you'll be fine. We offer a wide variety of panels on a variety of topics so find what works for you and enjoy the conference!" Woman in Charge shuffled off to enjoy a few other "firefighters," leaving me to wonder what in the hell I'd gotten myself into.

"I'm not sure how useful I'll be as a mentor. Do you mind if I leave you to it?"

And just like that, I was abandoned at a romance writers conference where I spent my first day dodging the strippers and listening to panels that offered nothing for me as a SF/F author. Some would argue that writing is writing is writing, but the reader expectations by genre matter. How one develops a female lead character in science fiction is drastically different from a romance novel, especially if one's writing erotica or bodice busters, as most of these women were.

As far as I could tell, I was the only nonbinary person attending, and certainly the only non-romance writer. One of their guests of honor—a fairly big name in the genre—joked at my expense about my chosen genre of writing.

Throughout various panels I heard:

"Everything is about people. About relationships. That means all genres are romance. Just because you write about people[4] fucking in space doesn't make it special. It's still romance."

"If you don't write romance, why are you here?"

"Ah! You write about magical people fucking in space! Even better! See, everything is about romance!"

"What's demisexual? Wait...so you don't find our firemen hot? Oh honey, you just need to find the right man... You're married? Well, he's obviously not doing *something* right!"

Yep, she went there.

Even panels on using social media to find readers were out of date and irrelevant as they focused on finding *romance* readers. With everyone trying to tell me that I was doing something wrong by writing SF/F, or worse, that I was wrong for not wanting "hot, oily men" all over me, I was ready to leave.

The only reason I didn't was that I had my pitching sessions with two editors and an agent coming up on the second day. I'd paid extra money for those events, so I

---

4. The term used wasn't the word people, but it was so offensive a term that I'm not going to type it out.

decided to stick it out despite being very uncomfortable. Perhaps I would get *something* out of the experience.

A panel on the inclusion of queer people in fiction came off completely tone deaf and was little more than queerbaiting[5]. The panelists reminded me of a bunch of straight, white women talking about how woke they were because their nanny was gay or of color. Their idea of depicting people like me was insulting and inaccurate. Their thoughts on how gay sex worked were worse. Several writers spoke excitedly about including their first token gay character in some new book. I abandoned ship halfway through that panel.

My wife and I stayed up late into the night discussing day one of this conference. She felt I should demand my money back and abandon the pitching sessions altogether. "If it's a romance conference, the editors will be looking for romance books. This is useless to you," she said around 1 A.M, and she was right.

Both editorial pitches went as she'd predicted. The editors loved my ideas and my characters, but they were looking for romance. "If you rewrite this as a romance, I can publish it. Do you have any interest in reworking it?"

My answer then and still is no.

I don't mind romance happening in a book—that's not a problem—but I want books that explore themes and issues beyond who's hooking up with whom. I want to explore why prejudice continues to permeate society, despite all of our advances, and what I think that will look like in the future. As a writer, I love creating worlds and exploring how life would differ with magic. Not everything is about sex or even love.

---

5. Queerbaiting is a marketing technique used in fiction where creators and writers hint at characters being LGBTQ+ without actually saying or showing it. This idea of representation is meant to keep queer viewers or readers engaged without alienating homophobic viewers/readers.

"There are more things in Heaven and Earth, Horatio, than are dreamt of in your philosophy."[6]

In other words, there's more to this world than meets the eye, and I, for one, like to explore that concept.

Pitching my novel to the agent went the same way. "If this were romance, I could sell this, but you'd have to rewrite it. There's little romance at all and well, there's too much death in the book. Romance readers don't want people to die[7]."

After a ton of pressure to change genres and rewrite my novel, I attended one last panel, this one focusing on finding good editors, proofreaders, and beta-readers. It was during this panel that I found an editor, specifically one willing to work with folks outside of romancelandia[8]. I snagged her business card on the way out the door.

I did *not* return for day three.

While they aren't my cup of tea, I have nothing against romance books. What I *do* take issue with is objectifying folks and forcing people into uncomfortable situations without acknowledgement or apology. That conference was everything a conference shouldn't be and from my observations, the attendees enjoyed it. They laughed at me, at my feeling discomfort, and in doing so, were active participants in sexually harassing me because I did not consent.

In the same way that cosplay is not consent for others to ogle, attending a conference isn't either. I didn't ask nor want the attention of strange men. It was no different than being cat-called on the street.

---

6. A quote from Shakespeare's play, *Hamlet*, Act 1 Scene 5. In it, Hamlet's friend, Horatio, states that he doesn't believe in ghosts, despite having seen one. Hamlet responds with this quote, suggesting that the human imagination is limited. There is so much we don't know, haven't discovered, and don't understand.

7. Unlike epic fantasy, where characters die to serve the plot every day ending with a -y. Just ask George R. R. Martin.

8. A common nickname for folks who write romance.

Romancelandia, or the community of romance writers, has a lengthy history of being problematic with evidence of outright bigotry[i] in their awards[ii] and board of directors[iii]. This is true within many areas of fandom, including the SF/F field, but to see it openly supported in the way that I did was not an experience I wish to repeat. My being a nonbinary demisexual should not have been at odds with attending what was supposed to be a professional writer's conference.

I responded to many emailed surveys asking for my feedback on the conference, and I was blunt and honest… in other words, my usual self. For me, the firemen were unnecessary, which I made very clear in my feedback. No one should be forcibly danced with in that manner without consent. They didn't ask first, which is a major problem. The bigotry present by not just attendees but guests of honor was another. Since my expectations and theirs didn't mesh, the conference organizers refunded a quarter of my entrance fee. They figured since I attended two of the three days and kept the pitching sessions, they deserved some of my money.

Someone listened, since the next year their entire website had been reworked to make it clear what kind of conference they were. The Romance Writers logo was firmly placed at the top of the website as well as a note about who sponsors them.

No more confusing the newbies, though I suspect they're still objectifying folks.

THIS TALE IS a complicated one to write about because at the time, I was too star-struck to rationally understand what happened. It's only been in retrospect that I've seen the events for what they were. Isn't it always the case that we comprehend best after the fact?

Content Warning: *I'm briefly going to discuss sexual abuse here. If it's harmful for you, skip the next paragraph.*

Growing up, there were many who shaped who I am as a writer and creative. Teenaged me loved one writer in particular and endeavored to follow in their footsteps. Since then, some of the writers I grew up reading have exposed their asses as problematic people undeserving of my praise or my money. For example, Marion Zimmer Bradley. Her daughter, Moira Greyland, accused her and her second husband[9] of sexually abusing her and other children. The accusations claimed that MZB knew about her husband's predilection for molesting children and participated in it before their divorce in 1990. Other potentially problematic authors include Piers Anthony, Orson Scott Card, J. K. Rowling, and Mercedes Lackey.

Thankfully, the author I wanted to emulate most as a teen has not shown herself to be a horrible person. This author shared her birthday with my grandmother and oddly enough, both died the same year. During a convention where I was a guest panelist, one of her children was also a guest. This person, John, had grown up to be a writer like his mother, and I'd mentioned to several folks that I'd love to meet this colleague of mine and talk to him about his mother's influence on me.

As a writer, I love the idea of giving back to the community that raised me as a newbie author, and in this case, to comment on the massive impact this writer had on so many, myself included.

When I first met John, I was signing a book for a reader when he walked up to my table and introduced himself. My feelings about John's mom were tangled up in my emotions

---

9. MZB's second husband was convicted child abuser Walter Breen, who also wrote in defense of pederasty and was a NAMbLA activist. He served multiple sentences for child molestation and died in prison in 1993.

about my grandmother. The flood of emotions that erupted from me startled us both. John resembled his mom so much. All I saw were his mother's eyes, eyes that always held kindness in their photos, a kindness I often saw in my grandmother. In that moment, I shifted from professional author and colleague to someone mourning a great loss.

John handled it as well as he could considering this random writer was crying on him. He managed to make me smile before leaving my table, but I found myself completely star-struck and embarrassed by the incident. An hour later, I was introducing my panel when John walked in. At first, I thought he'd intended to be a part of the audience, but as I spoke, he strolled up the aisle and up the stairs to the dais to stand beside me. He gestured for a volunteer who brought up another chair.

Suddenly, John was seated beside me as a co-panelist on my panel.

It was unexpected enough that I barely managed to finish introducing the panel before he plowed ahead with his own insight on the topic. At the time, my brain wobbled between, "Oh my god, oh my god, it's freaking John! On my panel!" and "Okay, remain calm. Be a pro. This ain't your first rodeo." I was supposed to be the moderator, but John's presence was not to be denied. He commanded the panel and dominated everyone in the room by his mother's name alone.

By the panel's end, no one had any interest in talking to me or the other co-panelists. All eyes were on John. I left the room feeling honored to have someone so *known* volunteer his time in that way—I thought he'd done me a favor—but a few days later, my brain rewound the weekend's events.

Serving as a panelist is to make connections to others, often in the hopes that they will buy your book *(or whatever work)* and continue that relationship. Because John wrestled control of the panel away from me and my co-panelists, we didn't have the opportunity to make any connections.

Everything became about him, something I've since seen him do at every convention he attends.

John was not a guest of honor at the convention in question. He'd shown up for reasons unknown to me, and being the biggest name there, he wormed his way onto a variety of panels until the convention's focus became all about him. Instead of talking about the topic at hand, my panel had become a panel about John and his mother's works. The focus had shifted, and in my stupor I'd allowed it.

Since that convention, I've watched John wiggle his way into various scenarios that place him front and center, whether or not he is meant to be. As a wealthy white man, there's a certain privilege that comes with carrying the name he does. Using that power for good is what he should be doing, but I can't help but feel that he's using it to stay relevant, to keep his name on people's tongues as his mother's works become old classics no longer in vogue.

The tactic of using others, younger, newer folks in the industry to stay afloat, is nothing new, but I wouldn't have thought someone would try it with me[10]. We never think it will happen to us until it does.

I suspect his mother is rolling in her grave at the sight of her son.

BY THE TIME THIS OCCURRED, my first book publication was three years past and several more had followed. I'd been published in half a dozen anthologies and was close to gaining full membership into SFWA[11], the

---

10. Sadly, it wasn't the last time either. Nothing is more frightening to certain old, white men than the threat of irrelevance.
11. Formerly named the Science-Fiction & Fantasy Writers of America. Entrance requires a certain number of professional sales.

Science-Fiction & Fantasy Writers Association[12]. I'd been a guest panelist at a dozen conventions, taught writing workshops at conferences, and had generally established myself as a PNW writer.

It was during a particular convention that I loved that I discovered how threatening women and nonbinary people can appear towards many white men. They perceived us as "taking over" their territory. I don't mean to give the impression that I hate white men—not at all—but there is definitely a subsection of cis-het[13] white males with fragile egos who succumb to toxic masculinity[14]. In the field of science fiction and fantasy, especially epic fantasy, many of the books and movies we've been taught are classics have been written by white men featuring white men. Think about *Lord of the Rings* or *The Wheel of Time*. The original *Star Trek*, where it was scandalous to have a woman of color[15] in a leadership position, let alone kissing a white man.

During these earlier decades, many women were writing SF/F books but getting them published was a challenge. Many women writers wrote under male-appearing or male-sounding pseudonyms because publishers didn't believe that men would buy books in these genres if it were known they were written by women. For all that we're seeing more women, more people of color, and queer writers in the field,

---

12. Membership into SFWA has been a dream of mine since I was twelve. All the SF/F authors I read at the time were members, and I looked up to them as an example of professionalism and success.

13. Cis means cisgender, which means someone's gender identity matches their biological sex assigned at birth. Het is short for heterosexual, meaning straight.

14. Folks love to act like this is a bad word but it's not. As a society, many folks grow up thinking that if a man cries, he's weak or a pussy. That he isn't a *real* man. Those kinds of ideals are what we mean when we say toxic masculinity. There's nothing inherently toxic about being a man, but there's something toxic in the raising of men to be callous and cruel to others and more importantly, themselves.

15. Long live Lt. Uhura!

there's a large crew of older white males still acting as gate-keepers.

I've known this since I began my professional writing career, but I didn't expect to see it at a convention where I'd not only been a guest multiple times, but I'd helped programming create many of the successful panels that fans enjoyed.

Because I was scheduled for multiple panels that particular year, I had to bustle to arrive at each panel on time. Bustling isn't easy for me being disabled, and it certainly isn't in the crowded halls of a convention. This was the case for this particular panel and when I arrived two minutes late, I found the room had been rearranged.

If you've never been to a convention, most panel rooms consist of two areas: the front stage or table, where panelists sit; and the attendee section, which is filled with chairs for attendees to participate or listen, depending upon the topic and style of the panel. Most times, panelists have microphones. Sometimes there's a large screen so folks in the back can see better, and often there's a free mic for attendees to use to ask questions at the end during any Q&A section.

Usually there's a moderator, who is either from the convention or one of the panelists. They sit at the table with the panelists and ask questions as needed to help encourage conversation and keep discussion professional and family friendly[16]. They also ensure that the topic doesn't slide off course and that attendees aren't asking off-topic or sensitive questions. Because of my background as a teacher, I'm a great moderator, so it's common that as a guest panelist, I'm also chosen by the convention to be the moderator of my panels. This was the case at this particular panel.

When I walked in, I'd expected the usual layout. Instead, the table up front held three chairs instead of four. The unclaimed chair, presumably for me, had been set in the

16. Unless otherwise noted. Some panels are labeled with recommended age groups.

opposite corner. A large screen projector was hooked up front and center. Since this was a panel I'd created, I knew I didn't need a projector, especially not one that took up almost half the room. Audience chairs were crowded together to make room for it, which made navigating the walkways a nightmare for anyone disabled.

Sometimes as a moderator, you can choose your co-panelists, but in this case, the convention planners did that for me. My co-panelists were three white men, all over the age of fifty-five. They had settled with their legs propped up on the table and piles of DVDs splayed across the table's top. When I entered the room, they gestured to the audience chairs as a way to welcome me to have a seat. Instead, I walked up to the table, leaned over, and said, "Hi, I'm your moderator and co-panelist."

Without missing a beat, one guy said, "We've got this, thanks."

"No, I'm your moderator. As in, this is my panel. Where's my chair?"

The second guy pointed at the extra tucked into the corner. When I walked over to grab it, one of them cleared his throat loudly. "No, no, you sit over there. We don't need you."

That's right—they had decided to relegate me to the corner like I was a child in need of a time out. Before I could react, one of the men stood up and introduced the panel, which was *my* job.

"We decided this panel idea is boring, so we'd rather show you deleted scenes from the show[17] instead."

Something to keep in mind is that when attendees show up for a panel, they attend because they expect it to be about the topic in the program book's description. To suddenly

---

17. I am intentionally not naming the show because if I do, it will become obvious which convention I'm talking about since it predominately centers around that show. I know I could name names but in this case, there are a few bridges I'd rather not burn if I can help it.

change the focus is to potentially disappoint anyone who came for the original topic. It's like buying a book that promises to be a scary thriller and it turns out to be a cozy romance. It might work out, but it wasn't what you expected[18]. As a moderator, my job was to regain control and keep us on topic, which was the first thing I attempted.

I cleared my throat. "While my co-panelist would like to show you deleted scenes, this panel is about [insert topic] and as the moderator of this panel, I would like to remind everyone of this. Let's start by introducing ourselves—" As I spoke, the ringleader, Frank, flushed.

"I don't think we need an introduction, do you, Bob?"

The second guy shook his head.

"Oh, this third clown here is Greg. We're huge fans of [show]. What say we watch some reels?"

At this, two-thirds of the audience remained silent as they turned to look at me. The rest of the attendees (*obviously Frank's friends*) erupted into noisy cheers and hoots.

Because we were in a hotel known for thin walls, this wasn't an appropriate way to react as it often disrupts nearby panels. I tried to speak, but every time I opened my mouth, Frank shouted something obnoxious to cover me up.

Looking back, I should have left the room to find a convention employee, but because of my past, when men yell and shout, particularly at me, I fly into panic mode. I fell into my chair and stared at him like someone in a trance. I tried multiple times to wrest back control and failed.

They spent the hour-long panel watching random video clips and laughing with their friends. Ten minutes in, half the audience had left. It didn't help that several clips they showed dropped more f-bombs than this book by far, and some included R-rated material of a sexual nature. This was a family friendly convention, and our panel was supposed to be all-ages. Parents were angry and rightly so. By the panel's

---

18. Otherwise known as a bait and switch.

end, the only people remaining were friends of Frank, Bob, & Greg.

One minute before the end, Frank stood up and said, "Any questions? No? I mean, we rock so why would there be?"

They gathered up their videos and left the room.

Tears gathered in my eyes as I trembled. I didn't know whether I wanted to knock Frank's teeth out or go cry in a corner. My insides warred between fury and fear. When I reached my autograph table, friends and convention staff found me an utter mess. I didn't get three sentences out before they called for a member of the concom or convention committee[19].

I explained what had happened in detail and who it had involved, only to discover that Frank was on the concom, and Bob was married to a member of the concom. In other words, the woman I talked with had no idea how to proceed. The people she would report this to were involved, even tangentially, in the incident. In the end, she decided to ask all concom members to convene.

Bob's wife refused to believe he would be so cruel and all but called me a liar. Then she claimed that because of family drama, Bob was under "a lot of stress" so whatever had happened, he "hadn't meant it." Frank was unapologetic and waved off the complaint like I was an annoying gnat. The rest of the concom was appalled, but since Frank was the head of the convention, no one was going to take action against him.

In other words, I was harassed, quite possibly because of my perceived gender, and nothing was to be done about it. I spent the rest of that convention feeling unwanted and unsafe, which is frightening when you're an invited guest. By the time the convention was over, I'd promised myself that

---

19. Basically a convention's board of directors.

unless Frank and Bob were removed from any manner of convention organization, I would never return to this con[20].

This wasn't the first time in my professional writing career that someone had harassed me, but it was most certainly the first time I'd helped them silence me. While I understand that I reacted out of a place of trauma and that wasn't my fault, I hate that to them, I didn't exist.

Most women have experienced this in their lives, probably hundreds of times, and it's why we have terms like *mansplaining*[21]. But this went beyond that as they worked together not only to stick me away from view, but to utterly silence me because they didn't believe I had anything of importance to say. It reminds me of the 1950's when women were supposed to remain silent as they cleaned and cooked for their men without thought as to their own needs.

These are the gatekeepers of fandom, and I for one, am glad they're a dying breed.

PROVIDED that I'm not overbooked as a guest panelist, I often vend[22] at conventions as a way to reach more fans. This involves me arriving at the convention center or hotel the day before, hauling several hundred pounds of books, art, and other gear into the dealer's hall or writer's alley, or whatever the event calls it, and setting up a table or three to welcome

---

20. They are still on the board and no, I haven't been back.
21. From the Oxford dictionary, mansplaining is the explanation of something by a man, typically to a woman, in a manner regarded as condescending or patronizing. I will add that it's often done by men who aren't knowledgeable on a topic to women who are experts on the topic, like if a plumber tried to explain microbiology to an award-winning biologist. Or better yet, if a man tried explaining childbirth to a mother of five.
22. This means that I set up a table in the dealer's hall or the writer's row where I can autograph and sell my books and art. It's a nice way of meeting readers.

people to the world of me. I often partner with a friend who makes amazing chainmaille, some of it inspired by my works. Her partnership helps with needed restroom and meal breaks throughout the weekend and also with the set-up and tear-down of the booth. During popular panels, the dealer's hall tends to empty so having a friend to chat with helps pass the time.

Since I'm disabled, we've figured out a system that works well for us in terms of accommodating for any disabilities. While the gear is heavy, I lean towards numerous lightly packed crates rather than heavier ones, though the latter would mean fewer crates. We use dollies and if needed, helpers, to ensure everything is done in a way that doesn't injure us. Most conventions are great at understanding we have different needs than most vendors and work with us to help ensure safety. In between panels, I sit at the booth and talk with readers and art fans, and if I'm lucky, they buy something from me.

But aren't my books in bookstores?

Yes, but the reality is that a physical bookstore can carry only so many books by so many authors. Online bookstores aren't limited by that, but the royalties an author receives on books sold through stores is crap[23]. If I sell books directly, after the cost of the book, the entire profit goes to me. Direct sales have always been the bread and butter of a creative's life, but it does mean attending lots of events where you hope you don't come off as a used-car salesperson.

Most of us being introverts, most writers *hate* the marketing side of the job. Long gone are the days of an artist having patrons who paid for them to create full-time and nothing more. Publishing houses used to do more to promote a book but now that social media rules the Internet, authors

---

23. Unless you're Stephen King or John Scalzi. There aren't many big name authors out there, but if you get a lucky break, then sure. Your royalties will rock.

are expected to handle the majority, if not all, of the promotional side. On the art side, most artists also rely on direct sales as too few art galleries and museums are willing to display work by an unknown.

During one particular convention, I found my booth near a rather worrisome vendor. In the convention circuit, we vendors become family. We tend to know who's vending at which cons, which vendors are resellers[24] vs. actual creatives, and which vendors are problematic. Usually, if a vendor shows their ass[25] so to speak, a convention won't invite them back, but sometimes, if they know the right people, they end up vending time and time again while the rest of us learn to avoid them.

I'd encountered this married couple before at my first convention as a published author. The wife had decided that I was only invited as a guest because I "knew the right people." She felt my books weren't any good and spent the majority of the convention badmouthing me to everyone she could. She'd never met me before or read my books, so it made little sense to me. When she decided to push her attack and say this to my face, I reported her to the concom. They made it clear that if she continued badmouthing guests, she would be removed from the convention.

It had been almost a decade since that one encounter, when I spotted her and her husband vending maybe thirty feet from my table. I spent all of Friday ignoring them, but on Saturday, they brought in their new puppy.

On Friday, their usual dog—an emotional support animal for the husband—was present, but he remained quiet and subdued. The introduction of the "puppy-in-training" on Saturday shifted the dynamics for both dogs.

For those not aware, emotional support animals are *not*

24. Resellers are those who buy a retail product, such as toys, and resell them at a markup, vs. the artists and creatives at a con who make the products they sell at their booths.
25. A phrase online meaning they acted like an asshole.

service animals, the latter of which undergo stringent training by professionals and additional training with the disabled people they're helping. Service animals are taught that when they're "at work," they aren't to encourage people to pet them and aren't reactive to other people or animals unless their person is having a medical emergency. They often wear vests and aren't there for other people's amusement or entertainment. This is why they tend to appear so serious and you don't see them wagging their tails much while at work.

As someone with anxiety and autism, I understand the way animals can make us feel. The idea behind emotional support animals is important, especially in mental health situations, but currently, there is no training guideline set up for them. Anyone can call their pet an emotional support animal.

Conventions don't allow animals due to liability issues, allergies, etc., but they are required by law to allow all service animals. This convention decided to allow this couple their emotional support animals, despite them being underfoot in their booth.

Midway through a Saturday, the puppy was playing with the older dog and they erupted in a bit of a snit. Typical of most animals, though certainly not proper working service animals. A customer grew nervous as the two dogs barked and bit each other, so she left. Seeing money walk out of their booth, the husband got steamed. When he turned to chastise the not-so-trained dogs, the puppy got underfoot and he stepped on her paw. Keep in mind, this man is over six feet and easily 250 lbs. That's a lot of weight on a puppy's foot, so the puppy let out a yelp. According to the husband, this startled him and triggered his PTSD.

Content Warning: *This next paragraph is going to contain animal abuse. If you need to skip it, do so.*

The husband lifted the puppy with his foot and tossed it

almost ten feet[26] across the booth. The puppy let out another cry, this one loud enough to gain the attention of everyone in the dealer's hall. As silence spread, the husband cussed out the dog and threatened to beat him. Because of the first yelp, I'd been looking in the dog's direction in time to see the husband toss the puppy and all that came after. I'm not going to lie—it was horrific. The puppy crawled under a table and trembled in a way that said this wasn't the first time he'd been treated this way.

Immediately, I reported what I saw and heard to the convention committee via the dealer's hall liaison, who surreptitiously interviewed other vendors and attendees to confirm my report, which they did. In response, the couple were "talked to." We were told that if it happened again, they'd be asked to leave.

I questioned why the police weren't called. This was obviously a case of animal cruelty and unlikely the first occurrence. Everyone was concerned about the dogs, but the concom didn't want to cause a fuss and burn a bridge with this couple. Whoever they knew or whoever's ass they were kissing, it gave them a get-out-of-jail-free card no matter what they did.

Apparently, the couple had claimed the puppy was a service dog in training. Problem was, it was the couple training the puppy, which is not something that generally happens with service animals. As I said, service animals[27] are serious animals and there are laws protecting the animals and the people who use them from discrimination. Even if the puppy were a service animal in training, they can be asked to leave if the animal is out of control or a danger to others. The problem was less the puppy, who was acting like puppies do, and more the husband's reaction.

---

26. I know the distance because at this convention, all of the booths were 10' x 10' in size.

27. You can find out more about service animals at: https://www.ada.gov/topics/service-animals/

The liaison explained that he had PTSD and often had an explosive temper, which is what the dogs were there for. While I understand that, mental illness is not an excuse to harm someone or something.

As a guest, I didn't feel comfortable pushing back on this, and in retrospect, I wish I had. I should have called the police myself, convention be damned, and made sure that this guy left the convention with a record or note of his abuse.

But I didn't.

There's a familiar thread that runs through so many of these tales, one that points to my earliest traumas. I find myself comfortable standing up for others and even myself against women, but when a male figure becomes violent, even verbally, my bravery dives for cover, and I hate that. I want to be the person who stands up against injustice and abuse no matter what.

My hope is that in telling my stories, I find my courage again so that I might never be silenced as I found myself yet again.

I should have called the police.

But then, so should have every person in that room. I guess I'm not the only one who allows themselves to be intimidated into silence.

CHAPTER
FOURTEEN
THE LENGTH OF LONG

Some days, 24 hours is too much to stay put in, so I take the day hour by hour, moment by moment. I break the task, the challenge, the fear into small, bite-size pieces. I can handle a piece of fear, depression, anger, pain, sadness, loneliness, illness. I actually put my hands up to my face, one next to each eye, like blinders on a horse."

REGINA BRETT

DURING THE COURSE of the pandemic thus far[1], I've lost a good many things to this virus, including friends and parts of my livelihood. It's complicated living as someone who's disabled and immunocompromised, but that existence used to be buoyed by a support structure of regularly seen chosen family.

I'm going to spend a hot minute talking science because not enough people are doing so. Never have I felt so silenced as I do now as people lacking important knowledge make

---

1. Thus far because despite what our government tells us, the pandemic isn't over. We've just accepted the casualties as part of a new normal.

decisions that impact not just themselves, but also me. I know some folks will argue that they're *tired* of hearing about the pandemic, that the pandemic's over and all is well, but I'm tired of being silenced, of being considered expendable by so many. Mostly, they're good people, but they don't have the facts needed to understand how harmful they're being.

If you truly believe you understand the risks that come with COVID and are still masking, then feel free to skip down to the divider where I'll pick back up talking about me, but I truly hope you'll read this next section anyway.

I'd beg you to do so if I thought it would help.

THE CDC and federal government gave up on eradicating COVID, mostly because the mighty dollar is more important than lives, and when this shift happened, people moved on and "returned to normal," without realizing that there is no return to the previous normal we had without loss of life.

This entire experience reminds me of World War II and the country we used to be. I'm not saying we should return to that time, as queers were heavily in the closet and women couldn't do jack without their husbands sneezing first, but one element of our country I appreciate from back then was our ability to join together in a critical time of need. Those who couldn't fight in the war served in the war relief in other ways, such as rubber drives and hose drives. Our country joined together like never before and maybe never will again. A pandemic like COVID could have and should have been a time like that—a time when we locked down, masked, and eradicated the virus before it could run rampant.

When polio struck, leaving death and iron lungs in its wake, our government scrambled to find a cure or a vaccine to prevent it. They didn't ask permission, but doled out tabbed vaccines to school children to ensure their protection. They later implemented the requirement that all children be vaccinated against it prior to attending public school and with the polio vaccine, we'd all but eradicated the existence of it globally[2].

The lack of science education in the American people, coupled with a weak-kneed government has led to a resurgence in diseases we once thought gone, including polio and the measles. While some people have medical reasons for not being vaccinated, such as medical allergies, they are often protected by something called herd immunity, meaning that if enough people are protected and the disease or virus dies, the unprotected can't get the disease.

Because of financial pressure, our country and others gave in too early. Unlike some places, we had the ability and means to ensure all but essential workers stayed home until a vaccine could be found. We had the ability to require the vaccine like we did with polio. Since we didn't, we're now in a cycle where COVID continues to circulate and mutate, rendering our vaccines almost useless.

I suspect that part of the issue is that people don't understand what the word airborne means. They think that if you cover your mouth when you cough or sneeze, it's all good. If you wash your hands enough, it's fine. Some of our seasonal illness work like that—you have to have contact with droplets of saliva, snot, etc. in order to potentially get sick, but airborne means something different.

Airborne means all you have to do is breathe.

Think of it this way: Sarah[3] has COVID but she's asymptomatic, meaning she doesn't feel sick. Since everything's back to normal, Sarah is grocery shopping without a mask on. She's breathing, because that's a requirement for humans to live, and when she exhales, bits of COVID hover in the air like invisible cigarette smoke. Most grocery stores don't have great ventilation—it's expensive and older buildings tend to

---

2. According to the CDC, there were 2-3 countries where it still existed in areas where immunization rates were low.

3. Made up name, obviously.

have older HVAC systems, so her germs are hanging in the air for several hours.

Long after Sarah goes home, you're visit the store. We'll pretend you're masked, but you aren't wearing a properly fitting N95, meaning that your mask doesn't seal to your face.[4] So when you inhale to breathe, you inhale Sarah's germs. If you get enough of them, you end up with COVID. That's how the virus spreads and why it's continuing to plague us. If we don't know who has it and we don't wear proper masks when around others, it will continue to wreak havoc on our populations.

Here's that science I was talking about (all with sources)—

1. Two-thirds of COVID is spread[i] from folks who are asymptomatic or pre-symptomatic, meaning they don't know they're sick.
2. Thirty percent of all COVID cases are asymptomatic[ii].
3. Rapid home tests **miss**[iii] 90% of asymptomatic infections.
4. COVID isn't just a respiratory infection. It's a multi-organ[iv], systemic disease[v] that can impact your brain[vi], heart, neurological system, immune system[vii], lungs, and more.
5. One in five[viii] American adults who've had COVID, still have long COVID or post-COVID syndrome.
6. The CDC considers COVID-19 a biosafety level 3[ix] airborne virus, which places it at a higher risk than HIV and Staph infections. With other BSL3 infections, the CDC recommends using self-closing,

---

4. The masks used by medical professionals, often called the baggy blues, are great for protecting against germs that spread through saliva, but not airborne viruses. There's a reason why movies like *Outbreak* and such, talking about deadly viruses like Ebola have people wearing hazmat suits. To protect against airborne viruses, your mask has to seal to your face and can't have ANY gaps.

double-door access to an area; showers after contact; powered air-purifying respirators; and more. The source in the footnote has a handy picture to explain this.

7. If you get COVID, your post-infection immunity lasts about 28 days[x].

8. You don't have to be unhealthy to have risks. **Everyone**[xi] infected is at high risk for serious heart problems

9. The risk of deadly blood clots is elevated for one year[xii] after infection.

10. You can infect your dog or cat[xiii] with COVID, which can leave them with brain damage.

11. Each reinfection does cumulative, worsening damage[xiv] and increases long COVID risk[xv].

12. There is no treatment for long COVID. There is no cure for long COVID. The only prevention for long COVID is not to get COVID.

13. Formerly healthy, athletic people have been bedridden for years by long COVID. Feel free to see what that looks like[xvi] in the source linked here.

14. According to the American Medical Association[xvii], getting reinfected is similar to playing Russian Roulette with your life and the lives of others.

15. Bonus, since COVID hovers in the air, you can catch COVID outside[xviii].

When I say this is serious, I want you to understand that it truly is. So why isn't more being done? Why is this information not everywhere? These are all great questions and the only answer I can think of is money. If people understood how serious a pandemic we're in, economies would grind to a halt. Without massive government intervention, people would lose their jobs, their businesses, and their homes.

Part of the push to "return to normal" came from a need to prove that we had the pandemic in check *(which we didn't)*, but part of it was because businesses were suffering from being closed. Hospital reporting is no longer a reliable way to track COVID numbers, as hospitals are no longer tracking[xix] the spread of the virus. The best way to understand your risks is to watch wastewater tracking. When folks have COVID, even asymptomatically, they shed the virus when they use the bathroom, so water companies[5] have a better account for how much COVID is out there in a particular area than hospitals do.

The reality is that until we have better vaccines and more people masking, COVID isn't going away, which creates a serious problem for all of us.

Science lessons done, so if you wanted to skip it, here's where to pick back up.

Back in January 2020, before we knew COVID was in America, my wife and I got sick with what had to be the most horrible illness either of us have ever had in our lives. At the time, no one was looking for a SARS virus, let alone testing for it, so it was thought we had some type of random virus. We were told rest, Vitamin C, and plenty of fluids. During this infection, my coughing was severe enough that it broke several ribs. While we initially recovered in about a week, the fatigue and congestion lasted for three months.

When scientists traced an infection to a Seattleite and realized it was the same virus as Asia was battling, this patient became Patient Zero[xx], a term used to refer to the source of a new spreading virus. We've since learned that COVID was likely in the United States earlier than that[xxi], and it's likely that my wife and I had it, though there's no way to confirm it.

Like the rest of the country, we went into lockdown that

---

5. You can track wastewater at this link below, as well as your local water company.

https://covid.cdc.gov/covid-data-tracker/#wastewater-surveillance

spring, but unlike most, we never left our lockdown. Because of my autoimmune disease, I take medication to control it that makes me immunocompromised, meaning that it's easier for me to get sick and when I do, it hits me harder than most.

In November 2020, there were no vaccines yet. The CDC hadn't admitted to the public that COVID was airborne, so people were using cloth masks which do not block airborne particles. That included us. Because of Sjogren's and the meds I take, I'm required to have an eye exam every six months to ensure that the medication isn't causing eye damage which could render me blind. At this point, medical facilities were open though they all required masking and many limited patients to one at a time.

My eye doctor was taking these precautions, but if you've ever had an eye exam, you know the doctors sit very close to your face when examining the eyes through their equipment. He didn't know he had COVID yet and during that appointment, he passed it on to me. His office notified me three days later of his illness and since we hadn't left the house for any other reason since the start of the pandemic, it was easy to trace the point of contact to him.

This was the beginning of my life changing yet again.

I spent all of the holiday season very, very ill. My coughing was so hard it caused vomiting. Food tasted like literal cardboard. I couldn't smell anything, or if I could, it resembled smoke or burnt toast. By the time January rolled around, I couldn't get out of bed without severe fatigue and vertigo.

For the next six months, I lived a rotation of sleeping, attempting to watch TV through severe brain fog, and doctor's appointments where they couldn't identify what was wrong with me. Everything was exhausting like I'd run a marathon, and I couldn't string together multiple sentences like this to save my life. My wife was working from home, but she had to juggle her job with taking care of me because I couldn't function.

After six months, some of my smell and taste returned, but the fatigue and brain fog persisted for over a year. During this time, I lost over a hundred pounds and struggled with massive headaches that no one could help me with. None of this was healthy, but all of it was preventable.

When our state dropped mask mandates, we continued them. While others returned to the office, my wife continued to work from home. We weren't going to the movies or eating in restaurants. In fact, we continued to have our groceries delivered to our home and used contactless pickup or drop-off for everything as the pandemic continued[6].

Like many, we've received every vaccination that's been released. We've limited our medical appointments as being anywhere with unmasked people is a serious risk. In January 2022, another medical appointment gave me COVID for a second or possibly third time. While it wasn't as severe, it reset the timer on my long COVID symptoms.

I lost my sense of taste and smell for a time and gained chest congestion and additional brain fog and fatigue. My wife thought she was free from infection until she came down with long COVID symptoms too.

At my annual physical shortly after my infection, blood work and other tests showed some of the damage caused by COVID. My shortness of breath wasn't my asthma, but appeared to be linked to COVID damage. My pancreas and liver were damaged, and despite having perfect blood work previously, I was now diabetic. There was no pre-diabetes or any warning for me. I eat fairly healthy these days, but none of that mattered when the disease decided to attack my organs.

Since then, I've seen an autonomic dysfunction[7] and long COVID specialist who ran more testing than I've ever been

---

6. I recognize that not everyone has the money or privilege to do this. I am lucky that we do.

7. Autonomic dysfunction happens when the autonomic nervous system doesn't regulate properly. This system controls heart rate, blood pressure,

through in my life to rule out *(or in)* some of the diseases and disorders linked to COVID damage. I'm lucky that I escaped mast-cell activation syndrome[8], but I learned that my brain is not communicating with the rest of me properly. Sometimes I hold my breath while awake, contributing to my shortness of breath, and a whole host of other symptoms that don't seem to fit with anything in particular.

Round two of my long COVID is slowly releasing its hold on me as I find myself able to write more these days and function for about four hours without hitting a wall. But the worst part of this entire pandemic has been the loneliness and isolation. People talk about how tired they are of masking and how their mental health needs a return to normal, but in doing so, they silence the rest of us and leave us wilting in their shadows.

If people were vigilant about masking, I could go out into the world some. I could take countermeasures such as using saline nasal rinses afterwards and carry portable air purifiers to help create a safer space. I could stick with outside events, which aren't risk free, but are safer than indoors. Since you can catch COVID outdoors[9], I could see friends who I knew didn't hang around those unmasked.

We're currently entering year five of the pandemic and in this time, I've seen my friends four times—one friend twice at our house while they were still being safe and a few friends at two COVID safe events where everyone was masked and vaccinated. Other than my wife and my cats, there's an entire host of friends and family I've not seen at all.

Some of those friends think I talk too much about COVID

---

breathing, digestion, temperature, sweating, and more, basically all of the things your body does without you telling it to do so.

8. A condition where the patient experiences repeated episodes of symptoms of anaphylaxis, such as hives, swelling, low blood pressure, difficulty breathing, diarrhea, etc. You can read more about it at: https://www.aaaai.org/conditions-treatments/related-conditions/mcas

9. Remember that science we just talked about?

and see my speech as "fear mongering," but I'm not spreading fear if I'm talking about fact. Because COVID damages our organs, I see the steps I take to keep my family safe in the same way one might view wearing a seatbelt.

Failure to do it could kill me. It could kill others too. I can't risk that.

If I reach way back into my timeline to when my wife and I were in college, I can see the path we both walked that led us to the now. Both of us grew up poor, and neither of us had traditional childhoods. We aged before our times and not by choice. Poor though we were, even as college students, we created our chosen families. These circles of friends visited our overly cramped rat-hole of an apartment because we were the fun, geeky, and *safe* place to be. Our friends could be themselves without judgment, and they knew they'd be welcome with us.

When I was still teaching, we bought a larger home than we needed on purpose. We wanted to continue to have space for others, to invite geeky "orphans" over for the holidays. Our space became a place of board games and good food as my wife loves baking. Moving to Seattle didn't change this. Our chosen family may have enlarged to include people living up here, but we were still the space of entertainers, keen on having people over regularly.

All of this stems from a need to have what we didn't growing up, to create a family where others like us could be themselves and be loved.

With the pandemic, all of this ended. The limbs were chopped off and rather than being cauterized, the wounds continue to bleed out over the past five years.

When I say that I've lost friends through these years, it's a statement with a double meaning. Some of my friends have died from COVID and COVID complications, but more-so, friends have betrayed and abandoned us because we're not willing to risk our lives in the ways they are.

Being told I'm disabled and that the damage in my spine

will never go away is heartbreaking. Being told I need to rely on mobility devices like wheelchairs and scooters when out and about is traumatizing. Though it took time, I'd made peace with my new normal because I had my chosen family and friends to hold me up. They had my back and were willing to jump in and help as needed. There's a certain challenge to being isolated in a prison not of your own making while those same people move on without you.

Personally, I can scream until my throat fails about how horrible this situation is for us and others like us, but no one's listening. Even those I considered my closest, best friends are eating in restaurants, unmasking for photos or just unmasking altogether, and taking other risks that make them unsafe to be around. People who've had major medical complications from COVID are out and about as if it never happened to them.

I don't want this to come off sounding like oh-woe-is-me, because it isn't. I'm not alone in being viewed from afar by a society that's moved on, but the choices I make to keep myself safe also keep others safe too. When folks choose to unmask, their choice endangers everyone, and I'm not okay with that. Knowing what I know about home tests and the spread of COVID, I can't be responsible for someone else dying, or even the possibility of it.

I haven't set foot in a grocery store *(or any store)* in over four years. I miss people desperately. My own mental health struggles—I think more than those moving on—as there are few people I can speak to who understand the complexities in the decision to remain on lockdown while we don't have a treatment or cure for COVID and long COVID.

Honestly, I'm not even sure how to end this chapter. This topic is important, even critical, to my ability to live. So much so that I don't feel like I *can* stop talking about it. Nor should I.

If your life depended upon it, would you?

TOWARDS THE MIDDLE of the pandemic, as my friends began making choices that would cut them off from me, I wrote a letter to them that I never shared. Mostly because it's a brutally honest and vulnerable letter, but also because I worried I would end up even more isolated than I already am. Because I refuse to remain silent, I'm sharing it now.

DEAR FRIENDS,

I think I hate you.

Maybe not all of you, but most of you. People who I've loved for a lifetime make me (ir)rationally angry. When you post photos on social media of your recent trip, your fam posing unmasked on a beach somewhere pretty, sitting sans-mask on a plane full of people, or standing in a bar enjoying a Mai Tai—I hate you.

I don't mean to *hate*.

Hate erodes the person you're fighting to become, but right now, I think it's what's carrying me through this lonely pandemic. Unlike so many others, I am what folks call "high risk." I've had COVID twice, and twice now, it's changed my life at a cellular level. This virus you so easily ignore has triggered damage, leaving me disabled and diseased.

Leaving me...*broken*.

The last time I walked through a grocery store was February 20, 2020, and it's depressing that I can recall that date. I was packing for a writing retreat and returned from it to a world forever changed, a world where I am ignored and worse, expendable. I love you, my friends, but every action you take wounds me. Of course, this isn't just about me.

When a child dies in the hospital because they can't breathe, I pause. Did you give them COVID when you removed your mask for that latte? Did you unknowingly pass it on to a cashier who shared it with others, perhaps the grandmother who died last week?

Actions have consequences. They always have, and they always will.

So I say again, actions have consequences…unless they aren't convenient, and then it's business as usual. What happened to the mentality of it taking a village? Why didn't we come together to save our cities and communities? To save the world? Why isn't everyone doing their part in the battle against evil? This never-ending pandemic is before us and all I see is me, me, me. Or in this case, you, you, you.

I'm exhausted and not just because I have autoimmune diseases. Not just because I have long COVID. I'm exhausted because people have proven time and time again that their "normal" is more important than my ability to **live**.

I suspect I could survive this knowledge if these people were strangers, but you aren't. You're family. You're my friends. You're coworkers and others whom I've known most of my life.

When I open my mouth, your ears close. No one wants to hear me talk about COVID…*again*. I am the doom and gloom that forces you to acknowledge your guilt. You know you're being selfish at the expense of others' lives. When I speak, I'm seen as trying to ruin your] fun. Some say they *have to go* to conventions and share meals with friends for their mental health, something I'm intimately familiar with as I suffer from mental health issues, too. But what about *my* mental health?

I miss friendly hugs so much my arms ache from their lack.

Once loved, my home is now my prison. As long as society puts the singular person before a community, I will remain here. The shell that is me needs connections too, but I can't. The idea of risking my life and the lives of others for stolen time isn't worth it.

Maybe it's because I understand science? Or maybe I just care more? I don't know the answers. I just know this isn't it.

This isn't the way.

In an attempt to maintain my sanity, I follow virologists and researchers online. I listen to doctors at John Hopkins, UW Medicine, and other places studying this virus and its long term effects on the body. In some ways, this only fuels my anger. When the Chickenpox virus was discovered in 1875, we knew nothing of Shingles. We didn't understand that viruses can persist in the body, wreaking havoc for years or decades until they erupt again. Ten years from now, what will we know about this coronavirus? How many people will die of heart attacks and strokes that could have been prevented by proper mask wearing and vaccination? By isolation until herd immunity was achieved?

This is why I hate you.

What this virus has done to my body has undoubtably shortened my life span. It's stolen our 25th wedding anniversary, countless birthdays and holidays, and years of my career. Worse, it's stolen friends—those that have died from COVID and those who've abandoned our friendship because the truth is too loud, too sad, and too much.

I am too much.

My friends, I love you, but every post and photo of yours I see, terrifies me. Will it be your body I grieve over next? Will I speak *(virtually)* at your funeral a few years from now when all the repeated infections catch up with you? Will I mourn the loss of ever hugging you again?

I love you so much I hate you.

So I scream and shout to whoever will listen, even when it costs me everything, because there is one thing COVID can't take from me...

You.

Only you can do that.

So please, stop. Stop going to concerts and movies and dinners. It's not living. It's a death sentence in waiting.

Vaccines and masks aren't enough now. Unless we change how we live until an answer is here, our lives will be all the shorter for it.

Please stop making the wrong choice. For the both of us. For all of us.

I love you—truly I do—but right now, I hate you.

I REMEMBER a time when writing was easier. Note that I didn't say easy. Writing fiction isn't easy. Anyone who tells you otherwise is doing something wrong, at least in my opinion. Juggling characters, settings, plot lines, conflicts, and world building makes untangling yarn seem simple, yet writing is a process that's complicated by interruptions and life events. Take for example the pandemic and my bouts of long COVID.

My readers often ask what's taking me so long to finish some book or project, and when I mention long COVID, they grow frustrated and confused. I'm not sure they understand how challenging a process writing is for me now.

When I say that I remember when writing was easier, I mean it.

I used to write lengthy epic fantasy with ease. I could keep all the character and plot arcs straight *(with the help of my notes)* and knock out a good four or five thousand words in a day. I was known by my editors as writing "tight," meaning that my work was fairly good the first time through the gate. It didn't need as much editing work as many other works did, but all of that changed with the pandemic.

For the second time this year, I've had someone reading one of my stories come back with the phrase, "This isn't up to your usual standards. It's good, but it needs work." I've had editors and early readers comment that some portion of a story is unclear or needs more description.

Me—someone known for great detail and development—needs more? I'm not saying I'm perfect as no writer is, but these are words I'm not used to hearing.

Examples are given on ways I could clean up the story, but the examples knock me off my feet. They're examples I used to give when teaching others in writing workshops. They're writing I used to be capable of before brain fog settled over me like an itchy, smelly blanket.

In the before times.

These days, my ability to focus for long periods is shot to hell. It's slowly improving but some days are better than others. Some days, four hours is what I get. Others, I'm lucky to get thirty minutes of writing in before my body needs rest. When my week is interrupted by juggling various medical appointments for myself and my wife, that focus is gone.

Poof!

So when people ask me where *x* book is and why it's taking so long, I can't help but wince. Yet another thing COVID has taken from me—my ability to work and work well. To be the professional I know I can be because that *was* me.

I'm not trying to harp on and on about the pandemic, I swear, but when your career is flipped upside down, it's important for others to understand why. When you ask me what's taking so long, you're talking to a person who is grieving their past self.

All I ask is that you be kind to the artists and creatives in your life. Hell, be nice to everyone. This pandemic leaves no one unscathed, no matter how much they believe otherwise.

If we're not losing people, we're losing brain cells. Or sanity. Or connections. Or the ability to finish a damn book on time, a book with beautiful descriptions if only our brain would remember the *how*.

I wish I could be kind and rewind this timeline, but I can't. All I can do is ask that you love one another and keep one another safe.

Be kind.

YESTERDAY SHOULD HAVE BEEN a good day. A great day. My partner had her first appointment regarding HRT[10] with a new doctor who only treats transgender patients. The doctor herself *(and her assistant)* were amazing, as was the appointment, but it was the time spent in the waiting room that colored my day.

Yesterday, I was verbally assaulted.

A old man by the name of Bob—that's what they called him when he went for his lab work—decided that I was the reason for all the pain and suffering in his life. He decided that it all stemmed from the fact that I was masked.

So I decided that it was time for another letter. I've written quite a few unsent letters in my life[11]–from contractors and movie directors to neighbors and other writers. It's my way of dealing with the emotions that come from these various encounters. Sometimes, I miss the days when letter writing was an art and receiving one in the mailbox was a reason for celebration. It didn't matter if the letter was little more than small talk. It was the idea that someone cared enough about you to slap a stamp on an envelope that made it exciting.

While email and instant messaging has shoved letter writing into the past, I'm one of those who still mails out an annual newsletter along with holiday cards through the postal service. There's something personal about doing so that I don't get from email.

On that note... I wrote a letter to Bob. He wouldn't cele-

---

10. Hormone Replacement Therapy—often used in the transgender community to transition to the appropriate gender.
11. Most of them are published on my website if you're curious.

brate receiving it had I an address to mail it to, but I wrote it nonetheless.

DEAR BOB,

You are in possession of "1 miserable life" and for that, I'm sorry. Your ownership of "fear of the unknown" coupled with the certainty that you are dying sooner than you'd like doesn't excuse you from being an asshole. Based on my interactions with you yesterday, you probably live alone, which can only add to the fear in your life, but none of this excused your verbal assault of me, not to mention all the other patients in the waiting room.

I understand that you lack empathy—404 Error[12]: Empathy Not Found—and that you lack foundational science enough to understand how viruses work, how masks work, and why masking has returned to our local hospitals. Logically, I'm not the problem here, but you decided to make me a target.

While I feel bad for you and whatever existence you crawled out of, one where you feel threatened by me and my mask, I also feel like someone should give you a swat on the ass and then maybe a hug.

Masks are required at this hospital. I know you don't like that—you made it very clear to me when you cussed me out —but they are still required. Your anger doesn't negate that. COVID rates are horrible right now. I politely asked the lab employee to follow their own rules and mask. That was between me and them. But you took it upon yourself to make it about you.

You shouted at me. You called me a bitch. You told me that your being forced to mask was "my fault" and that "all this garbage" was my fault.

---

12. Online, if a computer can't find a website, it reports a 404 Not Found error to the browser and thus, the user.

Your voice and your demeanor were threatening and violent. All thirty patients in the waiting room were afraid of you in that moment. They wondered if you were going to attack me. Honestly, so did I. While you're decrepit, you are still a white male shouting and frothing at the mouth at a short female-looking person. No one deserved to experience or witness that.

Employees should have called security on you and kicked you to the curb, but they didn't. They failed the patients in that waiting room, especially me. Maybe they didn't because they're used to it. Perhaps it's something they experience regularly, which is its own epidemic I guess—male toxicity.

More than that, I think the employees failed you too. I've never done well with men yelling at me. Childhood trauma stays with us, especially emotional and verbal abuse, and I have to wonder who failed you in your life that you felt the appropriate response in all of this was to verbally attack a complete stranger.

While I'm angry that you made me afraid, I'm worried for you. Getting "COVID three times and not dying," as you said, isn't something to brag about. I wonder how much damage your brain has suffered in those repeated infections and whether this influenced your decision making yesterday.

I truly hope you get some help.

If not, as we say in Seattle, you can eat a bag of dicks[13]. 😊

---

13. A popular food joint in the greater Seattle area is Dick's Drive-In. People joke about eating a bag of Dick's.

CHAPTER
FIFTEEN
HELP UNTIL I BREAK

> *When I was a boy and I would see scary things in the news, my mother would say to me, 'Look for the helpers. You will always find people who are helping.'"*

FRED ROGERS

ONE OF THE most challenging issues I face as someone who's disabled is people who mean well but don't really. They think they do, but their well-meaning often results in more harm than good. It reminds me of a scene in a video game I've been playing recently where a man in a wheelchair is struggling to reach his mailbox. He knows he can do it, as he's done it before, but for some reason, on this day, it's a struggle.

Living inside a body that doesn't work all the time and refuses to do what you want, means that often, we feel broken. Accepting your new normal means understanding your physical and mental limitations and discovering new ways to accommodate them while giving yourself grace during uncooperative days.

Knowing that I can't always write as much as I'd like

meant accepting that and adjusting my goals to account for it. I've always been an overachiever and perfectionist, but not adjusting my expectations is like expecting me to chop down a spruce tree with my bare hands and then being mad that I couldn't do it. In order to make it work, I need to change my approach.

In this video game, a neighbor sees the character's struggle and meaning well, she pushes the character in his wheelchair away from the mailbox so that she can get his mail for him. Those of you who know a bit about disability might know this, but wheelchairs are considered a part of a disabled person's body. Touching them without permission is a huge no-no, as it's akin to grabbing a person's body without permission. In many places, it's considered physical assault.

The character expressed his upset at being moved and having had his mail retrieved as if he was an invalid. Both parties left the situation upset, one due to the physical assault and the other because she "only meant to help."

It's an aspect of my life that's rather new to me, but one that increases as time moves on.

When my spine began its rebellion in my 20's, the number of friends and colleagues who were convinced they had the answers or a cure was unreal. These were people who genuinely meant well, but they weren't thinking about how their actions were perceived, let alone how potentially dangerous they could be.

People recommended I try yoga, because stretching muscles and gaining flexibility and muscle tone can help many people with normal spine issues. Except with EDS on board, yoga is the wrong answer. Stretching my muscles and tendons in those ways leads to dislocated joints as my muscles and tendons are already too flexible. Toss in my spinal birth defect and it's a recipe for disaster. Any physical activity not well controlled could result in my paralysis.

Others mentioned physical therapy, including a lot of well-meaning doctors who didn't have the full picture. I've spent more years in physical therapy than not and unless the therapist is someone who specializes in EDS, I end up more injured than when I begin. Again, motion for me has to be specifically controlled.

I've heard the spiels about essential oils, various vitamins and supplements, Chinese herbs, acupuncture, and on and on. The list of "helpful" things guaranteed to cure me is frightening, though I get it. People in pain want relief and desperate for it, they'll try anything.

Also, placebo is a hell of a drug.

When I was first diagnosed with Sjogren's, I ran through the same gauntlet—friends who genuinely thought they could cure my autoimmune disease through anti-inflammatory diets and "clean" eating. Sometimes Pilates. You fill in the blank, and it was suggested.

Again, these people weren't listening, especially not to me. They didn't have a full medical history nor the medical degree to suggest much of anything for me, yet they crawled out of the dirt, desperate to help.

It's a lot like being in a wheelchair. Sometimes, we don't need your help. Most of the time, we don't want it either.

One of my flaws throughout my life is that I've always been eager to help—especially when it's not needed. As someone on the spectrum, I often fail to read the room so to speak, and I don't pick up on the subtle clues that would warn me that my help or input isn't needed.

My desire to help someone sends me charging in, sword in hand, until I stick my foot in my mouth and end up swallowing it.

It doesn't occur to me to pause and ask, "Do they really need my help? Is what I'm doing actually helpful? Or is it only helping me?"

Yes, I'm one of those people I'm bitching about.

It's a struggle I'm working on, but it's a flaw. We've been taught that being helpful is a gift, that only when we help others can we help ourselves, and that's true to an extent. I'm the friend who will give and give and give until there's nothing left of me. Nothing left *for* me. I will help people until I break because that's who I am, but not every situation or person needs help or that level of help.

I understand better than people think how much we yearn to be helpful, especially amongst our friends and family. An example of this came about during the pandemic from someone I considered a COVID-conscious friend. She was someone I think meant well but wasn't really thinking about the results of said help.

Like the East Coast, the Pacific Northwest is a popular hub for creatives. Many of the well-read writers in the world live here, and as such, there are many writing conferences and retreats in the area. I attend one in particular that gives me the opportunity to isolate myself in a cabin and write like the wind. There are a few workshops on writing as well as communal meals and such, which are optional to partake in, but during these pandemic years, I've avoided anything large group, especially if it involves unmasked people. Being in a cabin gives me a way to be part of my community, yet safe as I write.

During the first two years of the pandemic, the retreat was cancelled as were most conventions and conferences. In the third year, the writing retreat returned with limitations. I made it clear in communications to all attendees that my requirements were more involved since I am high risk.

I would remain in my cabin for the entire five day retreat, including meals. If anyone wanted to visit me, they could do so outside on the cabin's porch as long as everyone masked. As far as I knew, everyone understood this, especially those colleagues of mine that I considered friends.

Of late, my wife accompanies me as it's a break from her work and allows her to help with the loading and unloading bits. Shortly after we'd arrived, there was a knock at our cabin door which was open since we were still unpacking the car. We weren't expecting anyone yet, so the knock surprised us.

When I turned towards the door, one of my friends had stepped inside our cabin, *maskless*.

Seeing as we were inside our private cabin and not expecting visitors yet, our masks had been tossed on the table with our keys. I immediately donned my mask and waved my friend back. She stood there, confused at what my motions meant.

"I need you to step outside and put on a mask."

My friend stepped back, pulled her mask out of a pocket, and slipped it on. Then she stepped back inside the cabin. While it was in the 50's outside, that's not cold for this state and this was the upper 50's at that. She was wearing a big coat and had no reason to be cold. If she was cold, tough shit. I was high risk. If anyone understood that, it should have been her as she was high risk herself.

"I need you to be outside and not potentially contaminating our cabin."

She rolled her eyes but stepped outside where we chatted for a few minutes before she left. Afterward, I made a few paper signs in bold marker that I hung up on the cabin's porch to remind people of my needs. The rest of the retreat, no one else struggled to follow my request.

It was after the retreat that a conversation took place online where this friend expressed how COVID careful she was being. Because I wanted her to be more careful, I ate my foot by reminding her of how not-careful she'd been with me at the retreat.

"You wanted people to come visit you, so I did!"

After some back and forth, I realized our conversation was pointless. She had no idea she'd done anything wrong. To her, she'd been *helping*.

She saw a friend who was having a lonely experience during the pandemic and in her attempt to alleviate that loneliness, she came for a visit. She believed she'd done the right thing, completely oblivious to how she'd risked us.

This is a small example of what we're seeing at a larger

scale. Despite my frustration and anger, I know most people mean well. Some are trying to keep people safe, including themselves, but they lack the knowledge to do so correctly. They don't have the full medical history of the friend they're trying to cure, or they don't understand how serious airborne viruses can be. Either way, they aim to help until it's no longer a help but a hindrance.

As I endeavor to stop fighting so hard to help when help's not needed, perhaps you, too, will take a closer look at how you help others in your life, and when all else fails, *ask first*.

WHEN I DISCOVERED the vocabulary necessary to describe me and who I am, it was like a dam broke loose inside. Events and decisions in my life clicked in a way that made complete sense. The day I told my wife that I was nonbinary, specifically agender[1], I wondered how our relationship would change. Some folks aren't well-equipped to deal with change, and others, especially those who are homophobic, worry that a change in their partner's gender somehow makes them gay. But my wife and I grew up together—not just as friends in high school—but throughout our life together.

We married young because we grew up old.

Through a variety of traumas, we found solace in one another as our childhood was stolen from us, so I should have known that she would roll with my announcement the way she'd rolled with so many others—with complete grace and love.

Changing my pronouns or gender did nothing to change

---

1. Agender means being a person who is neither male nor female nor some combination of male and female, or being a person whose gender identity is genderless or neutral.

the love she has for me, and watching me navigate through finding myself has helped her hopefully find her way through her own identity. It was during this time that a loathsome, atrocious excuse for a human was elected president, one who felt that people like us shouldn't have the right to exist.

I watched some of my former teaching colleagues praise him for "telling it like it is," which is code for getting away with being a hateful bigot. You should worry when hate no longer feels it needs to hide.

It was then that I wrote this poem.

During those bleak days, I worried that it was too late. That finding me now meant possibly dying tomorrow, and if that were true, how would I go down?

Would I go out fighting or hiding?

During high school, I wrote my fair share of angsty, teenaged poetry. A college professor told me it was horrible twaddle and it would be better for me to stop writing alto- gether and save the world from my horrible attempts. For many years, I avoided writing poetry because of that asshole, but poetry and I have found each other again. This time, I think our relationship is in a better place.

> *Too many posts consist of one word: THIS.*
> *Or maybe just: So much THIS.*
> *But I have more to say than simply THIS.*
> *I am afraid,*
> *But my fear erodes, leaving anger in its wake.*
> *A raging fire, all consuming,*
> *Reminding me what burns within all those who*
> *   fight.*
> *In another life, I would've been a rebel or a freedom*
> *   fighter.*
> *I would've been brave enough to fight for equality*
> *and equity*
> *and love,*
> *in ways my disabled self can only dream about now.*

But I am not without.
No, I am enough.
I may not have the physical strength of Wonder
    Woman,
But I have the will of a firestorm
And the sting of a writer.
I will rebuild this country one letter at a time,
    starting with U.
If U *voted for those who would destroy the land*
and salt it with black and brown and queer bodies,
and flood it with the screams of women,
U are guilty.
U have been complacent,
We are coming for U.
And we are not forgiving.

IT'S Pride Month (or it was when I wrote this).

And surprise, surprise, I'm angry. I'm fired up and fed up. I didn't know that asking to exist was like asking someone to light themselves on fire.

Today was my physical with my primary care physician— a woman who I *thought* was a good physician, a trustworthy physician, but today I am reminded of why Pride Month exists and of why it began as a riot[2].

Sitting in the room, my doctor erased me. Then she grew angry that I advocated for myself and my wife. She made several critical mistakes that have earned her a place on my "Never Again" spreadsheet of shitty and bigoted doctors, of which the list seems to have grown exponentially since the pandemic.

---

2. You can find out more about the Stonewall Riots at https://en.wikipedi-a.org/wiki/Stonewall_riots

This physician swore an oath to do no harm but much harm was done by her bigotry and callous approach to issues outside her lane.

In order to prove to her bosses that she was a good doctor, she needed all of my specialists to be those affiliated with her practice. She needed access to all of my records so she could ensure that all of my doctors were correct in their diagnoses. From a financial standpoint, I could see why her boss wished me to see only *their* doctors. I could also understand why she felt she needed to view my records so she could better treat me as my primary doctor. But there was no need for her to serve as a general oversight committee with regards to my health.

With the fall of Roe v. Wade, having female anatomy comes with a potential cost. With states wanting to charge women with crimes for exercising their body autonomy in other states, many women have chosen to lock down their reproductive records. Being a member of the queer community, my reproductive health stays firmly between me and my gynecologist. This was a conversation I'd had seven times now with this doctor and her medical assistant, both in person and in writing.

Today, she chose to harp on it. If I didn't comply, she'd "look bad" to her bosses. How she looks to her employers wasn't my problem. That's between them and no one else, which I stated.

Because I am an immunocompromised, complicated patient, I have specialists associated with several different hospitals as I seek out the best doctors I can, no matter where they are, something that's growing more difficult by the day in the Seattle area. If I only saw specialists at her clinic, I wouldn't receive the comprehensive help I needed—the very task she claimed was her focus.

But the kicker today was this line of questioning.

ME: As a part of the queer community—

HER: The what community?
ME: Queer.
blank look
ME: LGBTQ+?
blank look
ME: GAY?!
HER: "But you're married to a man!"[3]

Talk about erasure. Bi and pansexual people so exist in the world, no matter who they're married to, but I'm used to the erasure. What bothered me more was her lack of knowledge surrounding the word *queer*. How do you live in this world and not know what the queer community is?

Molli was not out as trans yet, but seeing how we shared the same doctor, there was no way I was letting her transition with this woman behind the wheel. Fuck that.

I reminded my doctor that I am nonbinary, which she claimed not to understand. When I also mentioned that there are states where people could probably get away with murdering me, she commented, "I doubt that. Not in the United States!"

Try telling that to the parents of Nex Benedict[4].

How can I trust someone with my records who doesn't understand who I am? Better yet, how can I trust someone with my *health* if they don't understand me?

Her next comment was that I should be tested as soon as possible for HIV. Because Gay. You can't be gay without having AIDS, right?

I defended my rights and openly accused her of being a

---

3. This was before my wife transitioned.
4. Nex was a transgender teen who was bullied and beat up by other teens at his school in Oklahoma. He later died, and while the autopsy says it was suicide, many believe it was murder as he was bullied to the point of potentially taking his own life. Those who bullied him have not been charged with any crimes, despite his injuries requiring a hospital stay.

bigot. She was angry that I raised my voice against her for "just trying to do [her] job."

I left angry that in the year 2023, we're still fighting for the right to breathe. Not to mention access safe healthcare.

So here we are.

Happy Pride.

CHAPTER
SIXTEEN
RECIPE OF ME

" *I got my own back."*

MAYA ANGELOU

THE LETTER that I wrote to Bob in a previous chapter made me think about what makes each of us ourselves. If we each wrote a recipe of what forms us and makes us tick, what would we include? How would others change it up to their taste? Would they change anything at all?

These thoughts kept me up that night as I considered who I am. A few minutes before sunrise, I wrote this recipe of me. It's not complete as I'm not done baking, but it is something I felt worth sharing.

Recipe of Raven

Ingredients
2 cups of What Did I Forget Now
2 cups of Excitement
1 bunch of Nerves
½ lb. of Triple Checking Everything I Do

1 Tb of I Found a Mistake (& I Fixed It)
3 lbs. of questioning everything
2 tsp of fury

Take all ingredients and mix it together in a blender of anxiety. Set mix outside in the Seattle rain for an hour. Yum.

CHAPTER
SEVENTEEN
ARMED & DANGEROUS

> *Those who cannot remember the past are condemned to repeat it.*
>
> GEORGE SANTAYANA

CHANGE IS a pain in the ass to put it lightly. Especially when those changes come at the expense of what we believe to be right and true. The phrase often used in situations like this is cognitive dissonance, meaning that there's a mental cost to experiencing contradictory information. There's a price to pay in our attempt to cram it into our brains in some manner that makes sense.

Growing up, church taught me to sing about a god who loved "all the little children of the world," whether they were "red or yellow, black or white."[1] While singing this, I watched as his followers spoke ill of those same people. It made my young brain hurt to think on, and when I asked questions about it, I found myself in trouble for talking back or being argumentative. I wasn't trying to be either, but I couldn't

---

1. From the hymn "Jesus Loves the Little Children" by Clare Herbert Woolston.

make sense of what I was seeing. In other words, how in the world could my family urge me to follow the god of love while being racist, misogynist, homophobic, and otherwise hateful towards anyone different? The two ideals warred in my brain forming cognitive dissonance.

As humans, we're meant to be adaptive creatures, able to learn from our mistakes and rework ourselves as needed for survival. But as children, we look to those around us to serve as role models. We need those adults to help make sense of the world around us. So what does one do when those adults aren't the role models we need?

Sometimes we make our own.

Writing certainly helped with that as creating people I could count on gave me a way to make sense of the world around me. I survived the war, but I still wear the scars across my skin so to speak.

This is one reason I endeavored to be the kind of teacher who pushed back against the status quo. A part of me needed to give developing minds the opportunity I didn't have growing up. That's not to say I wished to indoctrinate my students into my way of thinking—far from it. More of an effort to help them comprehend how others come to the conclusions that they do, and to decipher logos from pathos and ethos[2].

Why does advertising work? Why is change hard? When is it acceptable to walk away from or fully embrace an idea? Who decides what morals and rules we live by and why? Big questions with no easy answers.

As a former English teacher, it was my job to help students understand the process of critical thinking. Reading gives us the thoughts of others and questioning those thoughts are

_____

2. Logos, pathos, and ethos are the three elements of persuasion from Aristotle. Logos refers to the logic, words, and reasons of an argument. Ethos refers to the ethics and believability when speaking or making an argument. Pathos is the emotional content and your ability to connect when trying to motivate someone to change their way of thinking or take a particular form of action.

how we better develop ourselves and our world. As a writer, it's still my job to help others learn and grow in that way. I suspect this is why many politicians find people like me dangerous or a threat because I encourage people to ask difficult questions.

During my second year of teaching, I ended up with a new transfer student named Greg. He and his family were South African and had recently emigrated to the United States. His move coincided with our study of the Civil Rights Movement and the reading of *The Watsons Go to Birmingham — 1963*, a historical fiction novel based on the real life 16th Street Baptist Church bombing in Birmingham, AL.

While my students at the time were seventh graders, they were old enough to understand the harsh realities of prejudice and to see the consequences of hate. When my students entered my room the next day, they were met with a wall of images from the Civil Rights Movement. Yes, there were the typical pictures of Rosa Parks and Martin Luther King, Jr., but also photos of white men and women screaming the N-word at little children of color, bulldogs tearing the skin from black bodies, and lynchings on court house laws. Names like Emmett Till, Ralph Abernathy, Medgar Evers, and Fannie Lou Hamer were added to their knowledge, as were terms like Jim Crow and status quo.

All of the images in my room were taken from books in our school library, our history spread out in bloody color for my students.

Was it gruesome? Absolutely.

Was it necessary? Abso-freakin-lutely.

It's a struggle to face hate, but it's what we must do to overcome it. It's easier to turn away and pretend these events happen in a vacuum, but the reality is, hate is everywhere. None of us are immune to it, and none of us can hide from it, not if we want change.

I was curious what Greg's reaction to our subject matter would be seeing as he grew up in a country that suffered through Apartheid. It's a topic that doesn't get taught much in history classes in the States. Nelson Mandela might get a brief mention in world history classes, but that's about it as history in the States is very ethnocentric, meaning we tend to focus on our country as the best and the most important, whether or not this is actually true.

Greg examined the pictures but said nothing.

My students paled at brutality on display, but it wasn't until we read *The Watsons Go to Birmingham—1963* that those flat photographs became real. The little girls who died in the 16th Street Baptist Church had names and faces. They were somebody's child or sister.

They would never grow up to be someone's mom.

While the fictional characters in the story weren't present at the real life bombing, they could've been. Having a connection with the fictional characters gave my students a way to connect with very real strangers.

Suddenly, the white women throwing rocks at kids became their grandparents. The man lynched for smiling at a white woman could have been their great uncle. The images shifted from static moments in history to a harsh reality, one that we're still seeing today.

Greg remained silent throughout our study of the Civil Rights Movement. He read when asked to read and chose a research topic like the rest of my students. He presented his information—I allowed him to choose Apartheid for obvious reasons—with all the sincerity and seriousness of someone discussing their home country in times of turmoil, but what shocked me was his statement at the presentation's end.

His posture shifted as his face flushed beet red. "Being new to America, I wasn't sure what to expect. Everything's very different here compared to South Africa. I'd heard my parents talk about Apartheid, but I'd never really paid attention to what it meant to separate people based on skin color. It's like World War II—something that happened a long time ago that didn't impact me.

Seeing the pictures hurt, but not as much as the ones from my home country. When I got here, I didn't like black people. South Africa is mostly white so I didn't have any black friends until we moved here. Knowing what people like me have done to black people makes me sick. I'm glad we came to America so I could learn better. So I could be better."

I'm paraphrasing a bit, but you get the gist. I remember him standing at the front of my classroom, horrified to admit his previous hatred aloud. He was embarrassed to speak these words in a class where the majority of students were of color. In two short months, Greg had learned that skin color didn't make a person better or right. He still stepped in it with his classmates now and again as change takes time, but for the most part, Greg was a different young man than the one who'd entered my classroom that September.

Later, he mentioned to me in private that he was a better person because I'd forced him to face the violence of hatred. "They aren't just shadows. They're real people, the ones dying in those pictures."

This is why some people are afraid, especially when educators are teaching actual history. It's easier to white-wash our country's past and pretend we've had the best of intentions, but the reality is, we've messed up. Our belief that we are the best or our way is the *one and only* way to be has led to death and destruction.

I was taught that those who don't learn from history are doomed to repeat it. The irony is that I heard that phrase almost weekly growing up from folks who only remember a revisionist's form of history. Educated people who question are seen as dangerous because we have the power to make real change.

Words can change our minds and our beliefs. They can influence us into being better people and help us empathize with those different from ourselves. If reading a book and talking about history could shift this kid away from racism, imagine what else it could do?

Imagine a world where we could live in harmony and love one another? I'm pretty sure there are a few songs on that topic for a reason.

As we head into another election year, I worry about what's to come. While I'm no longer a teacher of K-12 students, I'm still an educator. Being a writer, people read my words, contemplate them, and maybe endeavor to be a better person. I'm not perfect, but no one is. I have to believe that there's hope for humanity, in spite of all the harsh lessons my life's taught me. I have no intention of repeating history.

If questioning others means I'm a threat, consider me armed and dangerous.

CHAPTER
EIGHTEEN
OWNER OF A LONELY FART

> *In our house, we don't take ourselves too seriously,
> and laughter is the best form of unity, I think, in a
> marriage."*
>
> MICHELLE OBAMA

A QUESTION I often see asked in the long COVID groups
on social media is how do we survive? I think it's a question
that could be asked about anything. How do we survive any
form of trauma? How do we find the joy in life again and
move past that which weighs us down?

I know my wife and I aren't the only ones living in a state
of lockdown, nor are we the only ones whose friends have
flittered on to sunnier hills. In these groups, people are
desperate for answers, not only to their symptoms but to the
loneliness that comes with being silenced and expendable.

For me, my answer has always been humor.

When I first met my wife, her humor is what caught my
attention. Twenty-eight years together and her humor still
grabs ahold of me. I can have a scathing retort to something
online on the tip of my tongue and one drop of humor

dissolves it. My anger at some stranger fades as I fall into a fit of giggles.

Laughter's gotten us through the heaviest of times, and I believe it will continue to carry us through this pandemic, however long that may be. As someone who suffers from anxiety and panic attacks, pulling me out of the worry spiral can be challenging. I have tools that I use to help, but sometimes, I need a good cry, a warm hug, and some laughter.

Many parts of this book come from a darkness that permeates society and threatens to overwhelm us. Some folks think that in giving voice to such grim thoughts, I give it power over me, but I disagree. Hiding it away as if it doesn't exist is how one drowns. By speaking up and out, I break its hold. I claim my power through *my* voice as I drive the narrative that is my life.

Not every day is a good one, but with humor, we survive. We *thrive*.

One particular evening, around the time when our state dropped its mask requirements, my wife and I lay in bed, neither of us able to sleep. One of the problems with anxiety is that your mind loves to whisper all sorts of half-truths and worries which keep you up at night. The lack of rest means you spend the next day not only worrying but too tired to boot. In this case, my brain was convinced that with the masking requirements dropped, COVID would continue to control our ability to leave the house[1].

I leaned over to Molli and asked, "Can you sleep?"

"Nope."

We both glanced at each other and frowned. Neither of us said anything more for a time until one of our cats farted. Usually, cat farts are silent, but in this case, the sound reverberated across the room like a sputtering engine, and we both erupted into childish giggles.

For all that we're both in our 40's at the time of this writ-

---

1. Which ended up being true. :(

ing, farts render both of us eight-year-olds in a moment, especially me. There's nothing worse than being the teacher who can't help but laugh when a kid farts in class. No matter how much I'd try to keep a straight face, I couldn't. It's worse with kitty farts, particularly Riley's, because his carry the stench of a thousand nightmares[2].

One of us would stop laughing only for the other to start up again. We'd be laughing in bed while gagging on the smell. It was during this laugh-fest that I couldn't help but break out into song. "And take it! Take another little piece of my fart now baby[3]!"

You can imagine the laughter that followed—it was side-cramping intense.

Soon, my wife began singing about a "Fart of Gold[4]." I took up the "Total Eclipse of the Fart[5]," followed by "Unbreak My Fart[6]." She interrupted with "Owner of a Lonely Fart[7]," which Riley was likely to be if he kept polluting our bedroom.

Twenty minutes later and we'd arrived at "Fart and Soul[8]," followed then by "Harden My Fart[9]" and "The Fart of the Matter[10]." At this point, all of our cats had fled the bedroom as our giggles were too loud during "sleep time," and this fact made us laugh all the more.

I think we were awake for over an hour singing what we deemed "fart songs." When we'd run out of songs, there'd be a brief gap until someone thought of another one and up went more laughter.

Silly though it was, exhausting ourselves with laughter and fart jokes did what it was supposed to do. For a time, we

---

2. A side effect of all the medication he takes.
3. Sung to the melody of "Piece of My Heart" by Janis Joplin.
4. aka "Heart of Gold" by Neil Young.
5. aka "Total Eclipse of the Heart" by Bonnie Tyler.
6. aka "Unbreak My Heart" by Toni Braxton.
7. aka "Owner of a Lonely Heart" by Yes.
8. aka "Heart and Soul" by Connee Boswell and Hoagy Carmichael.
9. aka "Harden My Heart" by Quarterflash.
10. aka "The Heart of the Matter" by Don Henley.

forgot about the stress of the world and in laughter itself, we exhausted our bodies until they were ready for sleep.

I think it was the best night's sleep I'd had in ages...at least until Riley returned and farted.

CHAPTER
NINETEEN
VOICES CARRY

Everyone you meet is fighting a battle you know nothing about. Be kind. Always."

ROBIN WILLIAMS

WALKING through my past has been an examination of who I am. While my voice needs to be heard, these words have been a closer examination of the events that have shaped me into an advocate for many people and many things.

When this year began, I had settled in to finish an epic fantasy novel long, long overdue[1], but when I sat at my desk, different words came forth like a volcanic eruption, full of fury and pain and healing. Like lava, the fire spread until it became new land, new soil for a new me to exist. This story wasn't a queen trying to save her people, but a memoir of a teacher-turned-writer who was done sitting in the corner in silence.

While I tried to force my brain to return to that fantasy novel, it refused. After all, how could I tell her story—one in which she has to use her past self to become the person

---

1. Thanks, COVID!

needed to save her people—when I haven't done the same? Could I do justice to a story like that if I allowed my past to stay buried?

The easy answer is no.

Voices Carry has been the fastest book I've ever written as I managed the first draft in the span of twenty-two days. At a little over 82,000 words, that's *fast*, at least for me. I haven't seen this speed since before COVID and its brain fog curse, which told me this was something that needed telling. In this, the muse would not be silenced anymore.

When it's late at night and I'm having trouble sleeping, I sometimes steal away to the teacher subreddits on Reddit where I see a world of teachers with experiences similar to mine. On other social media platforms, I find long Covid survivors desperate to connect and writers who've watched their careers change through the pandemic as sales dried up.

Watching others has been a reminder to me: for all that I *feel* alone, I'm nowhere near it. I used to believe that people like Coach Rage were an oddity or a rare occurrence, but they aren't. There are Coach Rages all over this country, in classrooms in Texas and Florida and New York. There are piss-poor doctors everywhere too, driven by greed and bias rather than the Hippocratic Oath[2]. Anti-maskers and anti-vaccers exist in every state and probably every city. COVID isn't going anywhere anytime soon, so figuring out my survival is critical.

The only way I can continue to fight injustice and hate is with my words.

They've always been with me and have always allowed me to speak for those who can't. For a good stretch of time, that was me—silenced and ostracized but no longer. I can't

---

2. This oath is an ethical one taken by physicians dating all the way back to Ancient Greece, and is attributed to the Greek doctor Hippocrates. To summarize, the oath states that the main purpose of a doctor is to do no harm. You can read the full oath here:

https://en.wikipedia.org/wiki/Hippocratic_Oath.

change the decisions of others, but I can change how those decisions affect me.

I set out to be a teacher, to change the world into a better place. In high school, I was part of a writing group whose motto was "Changing the world with the written word," and it's a phrase that's lived in me since I held my first pencil.

By learning better, I can do better. By speaking out, I can be the change I want to see in the world[3]. I can be an example for others in hopes that we can come together and remember that we're all we've got on this little planet. If we can't help each other, then what's the point?

It all comes back to the idea of a village. Of helping others. Of laughter and dreams.

The title for this book was lovingly taken from a song called "Voices Carry" by a group called 'Til Tuesday, which included Aimee Mann before she went solo.

I remember the song from 1985 and the video, which featured a couple having a fight. The man was abusive towards the woman, and often told her to hush because someone might hear. In other words, the neighbors might catch them fighting and realize he's an abusive asshole.

It's something I understood well as a kid because I was often told shut up, usually when I was about to complain about something my father had said or done. Anything that could be perceived as an embarrassment wasn't allowed. Silence ruled our home as much as the hand.

It wasn't until high school that I caught the nuances of both the lyrics and video, but it's a song that's remained a favorite of mine for most of my life[4].

Writing this book has been a maelstrom of emotions and memories. I spent three weeks with no idea what to title it. To be honest, I've never been good with brainstorming book

---

3. It may be a cliche but it's a good one.
4. If you haven't heard this song or anything else by Aimee Mann, you should fix that pronto! If you love cats, you should watch the video for Goose Snow Cone by Aimee as well.

titles[5]. As with most ideas, I was in the shower when the song popped into my head and the title was born.

So I'm allowing my words to go out into the world in hopes that they will encourage others to speak and help others understand they aren't as alone in this as they thought. Maybe that knowledge will help the right people at the right times so we can do better by each other and for each other.

If there's anything the pandemic's taught me, it's that I have a voice.

All I can do now is hope that this time, voices carry.

---

5. You know I love you all, dear readers, when I came up with not only a book title, but chapter titles for this book. You're welcome.

NOTES

CHAPTER 2

i. *Mapping attacks on LGBTQ rights in U.S. state legislatures in 2024 | American Civil Liberties Union.* (2024, March 15). American Civil Liberties Union. https://www.aclu.org/legislative-attacks-on-lgbtq-rights-2024

ii. Alim, H. Samy; Reyes, Angela; Kroskrity, Paul V. (eds.). *The Oxford Handbook of Language and Race.* Oxford University Press. pp. 276-277.
   Romano, Aja (October 9, 2020). "A History of 'Wokeness'". *Vox.* November 21, 2020.

iii. Grinspan, Jon (2009). "'Young Men for War': The Wide Awakes and Lincoln's 1860 Presidential Campaign". *The Journal of American History.* **96** (2): 357–378.
   Wills, Matthew (June 29, 2020). "Abolitionist 'Wide Awakes' Were Woke Before 'Woke'". *JSTOR Daily.* July 2, 2020.

CHAPTER 5

i. Johns, M. M., Lowry, R., Haderxhanaj, L. T., et al. (2020). Trends in violence victimization and suicide risk by sexual identity among high school students — Youth Risk Behavior Survey, United States, 2015–2019. *Morbidity and Mortality Weekly Report, 69,*(Suppl-1):19–27.

ii. *Understanding intimate partner violence in the LGBTQ+ community.* (n.d.). Human Rights Campaign. https://www.hrc.org/resources/understanding-intimate-partner-violence-in-the-lgbtq-community

iii. Zero Abuse Project. (2023, October 5). *Sexuality of Offenders - Zero Abuse Project.* https://www.zeroabuseproject.org/victim-assistance/jwrc/keep-kids-safe/sexuality-of-offenders/

iv. *Facts about homosexuality and child molestation.* (n.d.). https://lgbpsychology.org/html/facts_molestation.html

CHAPTER 6

i. *How Science is Helping Us Understand Gender.* (n.d.). https://education.nationalgeographic.org/resource/how-science-is-helping-us-understand-gender/

CHAPTER 8

i. Data on school shootings from: https://www.cnn.com/us/school-shootings-fast-facts-dg/index.html

CHAPTER 11

i. Montgomery, Amanda. "School of Public Health." *School of Public Health | University of Illinois Chicago*, https://publichealth.uic.edu/community-engagement/collaboratory-for-health-justice/addressing-weight-stigma-and-fatphobia-in-public-health/. Accessed 5 Mar. 2024.

ii. Richard, Patrick, et al. "Disparities in Physician-Patient Communication by Obesity Status." *Sage Journals*, Sage Journals, 28 Nov. 2014, http://journals.sagepub.com/doi/full/10.1177/0046958014557012.

iii. Schvey, Natasha. "Weight Bias in Health Care." *Journal of Ethics | American Medical Association*, American Medical Association, 1 Apr. 2010, www.journalofethics.ama-assn.org/article/weight-bias-health-care/2010-04.

iv. Didier, Kevin, et al. "Autoantibodies Associated With Connective Tissue Diseases: What Meaning for Clinicians?" *National Library of Medicine*, 26 Mar. 2018, http://www.ncbi.nlm.nih.gov/pmc/articles/PMC5879136/.

v. Obuobi, S., MD. (2023, March 6). Yes, Doctors Can Fat-Shame. Here's What to Do about It. *Washington Post*. https://www.washingtonpost.com/wellness/2023/02/01/doctors-fat-shaming-fat-phobia/

CHAPTER 12

i. Shmerling, R. H., MD. (2020, May 26). *When dieting doesn't work*. Harvard Health. https://www.health.harvard.edu/blog/when-dieting-doesnt-work-2020052519889

CHAPTER 13

i. Bates, K. G. (2021, August 5). Romance Writers of America was doing better with race until a recent award choice. *NPR*. https://www.npr.org/2021/08/05/1025195204/romance-writers-of-america-was-doing-better-with-race-until-a-recent-award-choice

ii. *Systemic racism in Romancelandia*. (n.d.). Melanie Greene. https://www.melaniegreene.com/blog/systemic-racism-in-romancelandia

iii. Controversy hits Romance Writers of America this holiday | AP News. (2021, April 21). *AP News*. https://apnews.com/article/04e649d97d72474677ae1c7657f85d05

CHAPTER 14

i. *Healthcare workers*. (2020, February 11). Centers for Disease Control and Prevention. https://www.cdc.gov/coronavirus/2019-ncov/hcp/planning-scenarios.html#table-1

Johansson, M. A., Quandelacy, T. M., Kada, S., Prasad, P., Steele, M., Brooks, J. T., Slayton, R. B., Biggerstaff, M., & Butler, J. C. (2021). SARS-COV-2 transmission from people without COVID-19 symptoms. *JAMA*

Network Open, 4(1), e2035057. https://doi.org/10.1001/jamanet workopen.2020.35057

ii. Topol, E. (2023, July 19). From asymptomatic Covid to long Covid: major advances in genetic underpinnings. *Ground Truths*. https://eric topol.substack.com/p/from-asymptomatic-covid-to-long-covid

iii. Rapid COVID tests miss 90% of asymptomatic cases. (2023). *Nature*, 619(7970), 439. https://doi.org/10.1038/d41586-023-02254-9

iv. *More proof COVID is a multi-system cluster bomb - InSight+*. (n.d.). InSight+. https://insightplus.mja.com.au/2022/46/more-proof-covid-is-a-multi-system-cluster-bomb/

v. SARS-CoV-2 can damage mitochondrion in heart, other organs, study finds. (2023, August 9). *CIDRAP*. https://www.cidrap.umn.edu/covid-19/sars-cov-2-can-damage-mitochondrion-heart-other-organs-study-finds

vi. Komaroff, A. L., MD. (2023, March 1). *Does COVID-19 damage the brain?* Harvard Health. https://www.health.harvard.edu/mind-and-mood/does-covid-19-damage-the-brain

vii. Requarth, T. (2023, January 31). What is COVID actually doing to our immune systems? *Slate Magazine*. https://slate.com/technology/2023/01/immunity-covid-research-airborne-aids-debunk.html

viii. *Nearly one in five American adults who have had COVID-19 still have "Long COVID."* (n.d.). https://www.cdc.gov/nchs/pressroom/nchs_press_re leases/2022/20220622.htm

ix. Parker, M. (2023, October 31). What is a BSL-3 (Biological Safety Levels) Lab? | Charles River. *Charles River*. https://www.criver.com/eureka/what-bsl-3-lab

x. *Omicron BA.5 strain may shorten COVID immunity from 3 months to 28 days, research shows*. (2022, July 13). ABC7 San Francisco. https://abc7news.com/ba5-covid-immunity-omicron-ba4-reinfections-how-long-are-you-immune-from-after-having-it/12047575/

xi. COVID and the heart: it spares no one. (2022, June 9). *Johns Hopkins Bloomberg School of Public Health*. https://publichealth.jhu.edu/2022/covid-and-the-heart-it-spares-no-one

xii. Sharp, C. (2022, September 22). Risk of deadly blood clots 'remains elevated' for nearly a year after Covid infection. *Express.co.uk*. https://www.express.co.uk/life-style/health/1672465/covid-coron avirus-blood-clots-risk.

xiii. Patreon. (n.d.). *We need to talk about covid and pets* | *Violet Blue*. https://www.patreon.com/posts/we-need-to-talk-91185856 (This post has links to further scientific sources.)

xiv. https://www.publichealthontario.ca/-/media/Documents/nCoV/voc/2022/07/evidence-brief-ba4-ba5-risk-assessment-jul-8.pdf

xv. Atkinson, E. (2022, June 28). Covid warning as more times people get reinfected 'more likely it is they get unlucky' and develop long Covid. *The Independent*. https://www.independent.co.uk/news/health/long-covid-warning-reinfection-b2111221.html

xvi. Watson, R. (2023, March 31). *Physics Girl & the Devastating Effects of Long COVID*. Skepchick. https://skepchick.org/2023/03/physics-girl-the-devastating-effects-of-long-covid/

xvii. American Medical Association & American Medical Association. (2023, January 20). What doctors wish patients knew about COVID-19 reinfection. *American Medical Association*. https://www.ama-assn.org/delivering-care/public-health/what-doctors-wish-patients-knew-about-covid-19-reinfection.

xviii. Schreiber, M. (2022, July 1). Coronavirus FAQ: Can I get COVID outdoors? *NPR*. https://www.npr.org/sections/goatsandsoda/2022/07/01/1109444481/coronavirus-faq-can-i-get-covid-outdoors-with-printable-poster-on-how-to-cut-ris

xix. *CDC's Covid tracking changes come as "99 percent plus" of the U.S. is at low levels*. (2023, May 5). NBC News. https://www.nbcnews.com/health/health-news/cdc-stop-tracking-covid-levels-communities-rcna82059

xx. *CDC Museum COVID-19 timeline*. (2023, March 15). Centers for Disease Control and Prevention. https://www.cdc.gov/museum/timeline/covid19.html

xxi. Achenbach, J. (2021, June 16). NIH study suggests coronavirus may have been in U.S. as early as December 2019. *Washington Post*. https://www.washingtonpost.com/health/when-was-coronavirus-first-in-us/2021/06/15/1aaa6b56-cd2d-11eb-8cd2-4e95230cfac2_story.html

ACKNOWLEDGMENTS

Many thanks to the village that raised me. So many parents who weren't mine stepped forward when mine could not, and I remember each of you fondly.

Also, a huge thank you to the underpaid and overworked teachers who still fight the good fight, despite a populous who continually belittles you. I see you.

This acknowledgements page wouldn't exist without all of my friends—my chosen family—who've encouraged me time and time again to tell my story about growing up me. Your support has once again resulted in a surprise book.

Every person who exclaimed, "That doesn't really happen in education, does it?"—I blame you for this book!

Even more thanks to my amazing wife who is the best superhero I know. Being you in a world like this takes serious guts, and I love you for it.

If you're reading this page, a special thanks to you as well. You're part of the village now, so welcome.

ABOUT THE AUTHOR

Multi-international award-winning speculative fiction author and artist Raven Oak (she/they) is best known for *Amaskan's Blood* (2016 Ozma Fantasy Award Winner, Epic Awards Finalist, & Reader's Choice Award Winner), *Amaskan's War* (2018 UK Wishing Award YA Finalist), and *Class-M Exile*. She also has over a dozen short stories published in anthologies and magazines. She's even published on the moon! (No, really!) Raven spent most of her K-12 education doodling stories and 500-page monstrosities that are forever locked away in a filing cabinet.

Besides being a writer and artist, she's a geeky, disabled ENBY who enjoys getting her game on with tabletop games, indulging in cartography and art, or staring at the ocean. She lives in the Seattle area with her wife, and their three kitties who enjoy lounging across the keyboard when writing deadlines approach. Her hair color changes as often as her bio does, and you can find her at *www.ravenoak.net*.

Do you like what you've read? Want to find out when more books and stories by Raven Oak are released? Want to geek out over the world of science fiction, fantasy, and horror with Raven and other readers?

Then *Join the Conspiracy*, the official newsletter and reader group for fans of Raven Oak.

If you prefer email updates, you can sign up for *The Conspiracy* newsletter here: https://conspiracy.ravenoak.net/

If you also like discussions, memes, and fun, you can join *The Conspiracy—For Readers of Intriguing Sci-Fi & Fantasy* on Facebook at: https://www.facebook.com/groups/ravenconspiracy/

ALSO BY RAVEN OAK

The Boahim Universe

Amaskan's Blood

Amaskan's War

Amaskan's Honor*

Ear to Ear*

The Xersian Struggle Universe

The Eldest Silence*

Class-M Exile

Stand-Alone Works

Ol' St. Nick

The Ringers

From the Worlds of Raven Oak: A Coloring Book

Hungry

The Loss of Luna

Peace Be With You Friend

The Bell Ringer & Other Holiday Tales

Dragon Springs & Other Things: A Short Story Collection Book I

Space Ships & Other Trips: A Short Story Collection Book II

Anthologies

"Weightless" (2ND PRINTING) in *Soul Jar* (Forest Avenue Press)

"Not Today" in *99 Fleeting Fantasies* (Pulse Publishing)

"Drip" in *99 Tiny Terrors* (Pulse Publishing)

"Weightless" in *The Great Beyond Anthology* (BDL Press)

"Scout's Honor" in *The Last Cities of Earth* (Sturgeon Press)

"Amaskan" in *Hidden Magic* (Magical Mayhem Press)

"Pretty Poison" in *Wayward Magic* (Magical Mayhem Press)

"Honor After All" in *Forgotten Magic* (Magical Mayhem Press)

"Alive" in *Swords, Sorcery, & Self-Rescuing Damsels* (Clockwork Dragon Press)

"Mirror Me" (1ST EDITION) in *Unveiled Magic* (Creative Alchemy Inc.). (2ND EDITION) in *Mercedes Lackey Fantasy Quarterly Magazine, Issue 0* (Pulse Publishing)

"Ol' St. Nick" and "The Ringers" (1ST EDITION) in *Joy to the Worlds: Mysterious Speculative Fiction for the Holidays* (Grey Sun Press)

"Q-Be" in *Untethered: A Magic iPhone Anthology* (Cantina Publishing)

* Forthcoming

LIKE WHAT YOU'VE READ?

Word of mouth is the number one **best** way to ensure that your favorite authors have continued success—better than any paid advertisement.

If you enjoyed this book, please consider leaving a **review** or starred ranking on bookstore websites and other retail or reviewer sites. Reviews tell the publisher you want to see more from the author, so help an author out today!

Your review is greatly appreciated.